Responding to Problem Behavior in Schools

The Guilford Practical Intervention in the Schools Series

Kenneth W. Merrell, Founding Editor
Sandra M. Chafouleas, Series Editor

www.guilford.com/practical

This series presents the most reader-friendly resources available in key areas of evidence-based practice in school settings. Practitioners will find trustworthy guides on effective behavioral, mental health, and academic interventions, and assessment and measurement approaches. Covering all aspects of planning, implementing, and evaluating high-quality services for students, books in the series are carefully crafted for everyday utility. Features include ready-to-use reproducibles, appealing visual elements, and an oversized format. Recent titles have Web pages where purchasers can download and print the reproducible materials.

Recent Volumes

Responding to Problem Behavior in Schools

The Check-In, Check-Out Intervention

THIRD EDITION

LEANNE S. HAWKEN
DEANNE A. CRONE
KAITLIN BUNDOCK
ROBERT H. HORNER

THE GUILFORD PRESS
New York   London

Copyright © 2021 The Guilford Press
A Division of Guilford Publications, Inc.
370 Seventh Avenue, Suite 1200, New York, NY 10001
www.guilford.com

Printed in the United States of America

This book is printed on acid-free paper.

Last digit is print number: 9   8   7   6   5   4   3

Library of Congress Cataloging-in-Publication Data

Names: Hawken, Leanne S., author. | Crone, Deanne A., author. | Bundock, Kaitlin, author. | Horner, Robert H., author.
Title: Responding to problem behavior in schools : the check-in, check-out intervention / Leanne S. Hawken, Deanne A. Crone, Kaitlin Bundock, Robert H. Horner.
Description: Third edition. | New York : The Guilford Press, 2021. | Series: The Guilford practical intervention in the schools series | Includes bibliographical references and index.
Identifiers: LCCN 2020034102 | ISBN 9781462546060 (hardback)
    ISBN 9781462539512 (paperback)
Subjects: LCSH: Behavior modification—United States. | School psychology—United States. | Problem children—Education—United States.
Classification: LCC LB1060.2 .C76 2021 | DDC 370.15/28—dc23
LC record available at *https://lccn.loc.gov/2020034102*

About the Authors

Leanne S. Hawken, PhD, BCBA, is Director of Content and Curriculum at Parent Playbook and Professor Emeritus in the Department of Special Education at the University of Utah. She has worked in the field of behavior analysis since the 1990s, applying the technology across a range of students and adults. Dr. Hawken has been training, coaching, and conducting research on Check-In, Check-Out (CICO) since the early 2000s. She is coauthor of *Building Positive Behavior Support Systems in Schools, Second Edition,* and the training DVD *Check-In, Check-Out, Second Edition: A Tier 2 Intervention for Students at Risk.*

Deanne A. Crone, PhD, is a Research Associate at the Center on Teaching and Learning at the University of Oregon. She has directed several research and training grants addressing behavior disorders, positive behavior support, and functional behavioral assessment. Dr. Crone has conducted extensive training in functional behavioral assessment and positive behavior support with teachers, paraprofessionals, principals, and directors of special education.

Kaitlin Bundock, PhD, is Assistant Professor of Special Education and Rehabilitation at Utah State University. A former teacher of special education high school mathematics, Dr. Bundock's research and teaching focus on effective instruction and intervention for students struggling in mathematics at the secondary level. Dr. Bundock also focuses on behavioral interventions and supports in secondary schools. She has provided school and district teams with training in the CICO intervention, and has assisted with implementing CICO in elementary and middle schools.

Robert H. Horner, PhD, is Emeritus Professor of Special Education at the University of Oregon. His research has focused on applied behavior analysis, positive behavior support, multi-tiered instructional systems, equity in education, and systems change. Since the 1990s, Dr. Horner has worked with George Sugai to develop and implement schoolwide positive behavioral interventions and supports (PBIS). He is a recipient of the Education Award from the American Association for Mental Retardation, the Public Service in Behavior Analysis Award from the Society for the Advancement of Behavior Analysis, the Fred S. Keller Behavioral Education Award from Division 25 of the American Psychological Association, and the Distinguished Researcher Award from the Special and Inclusive Education Research Special Interest Group of the American Educational Research Association.

Preface

Check-in, check-out is one of the most widely implemented Tier 2 interventions for schools who choose to implement a comprehensive system of positive behavioral interventions and supports (PBIS). We have 20 years of experience in implementing and researching this intervention, which was originally named the "Behavior Education Program, or "BEP," by Fern Ridge Middle School, the school in Elmira, Oregon, that initially developed the intervention. Researchers and practitioners in the field have subsequently renamed the intervention "Check-In, Check-Out" (CICO), and it is referred to as CICO throughout this book. When we published the second edition of this book in 2010, the field was relatively new to implementing Tier 2 interventions within a comprehensive system of PBIS. In the past 10 years, much research has been conducted on the basic version of CICO that was outlined in the first and second editions of the book, and CICO is now considered an evidence-based practice. During this time, educators around the country and around the world have adapted CICO to support more students and have taught us how to more effectively and efficiently implement this intervention. We share some of these insights in the new edition of the book.

Overall, the book has been expanded from 12 to 15 chapters. This new edition includes new chapters on how to apply CICO principles across populations, including high school students and students served in alternative educational settings. It also includes information on how CICO can be expanded to target additional problem behaviors, including internalizing behaviors, academic and organizational skills deficits, attendance issues, and problem behaviors exhibited at recess. This new edition also includes a chapter for trainers and coaches on how to effectively train school teams on CICO, with a step-by-step training guide and supplementary materials that complete the training and that provide follow-up coaching.

Chapter 1 provides an overview of the critical components of CICO and a discussion of which schools should consider implementing this intervention. In addition, this chapter briefly introduces the companion DVD, *Check-In, Check-Out: A Tier 2 Intervention for Students at Risk, Second Edition* (Hawken & Breen, 2017).

Chapter 2 details how CICO fits into a school's overall behavior support system as a Tier 2 targeted intervention. Schools are encouraged to have multiple Tier 2 interventions, so we describe the key features of these interventions and provide examples of different Tier 2 interventions that can be implemented as part of a school's PBIS system. This chapter also provides an updated summary of the research on CICO, including three published literature reviews summarizing the effectiveness of the intervention.

Chapter 3 provides the nuts and bolts of how to implement the "basic" CICO intervention. We highlight the term "basic" in this chapter to emphasize the essential elements of CICO as it was originally designed, so that we can contrast this version of the intervention with "adaptations" and "modifications" to the basic intervention that are presented in other chapters. We highly encourage all schools to start with the basic version of CICO prior to trying out more advanced applications.

Chapter 4 offers a detailed description of how to successfully introduce and implement CICO schoolwide. This chapter includes a description of how to encourage faculty commitment, including when and how the CICO DVD (mentioned previously) should be shown to the staff, and also includes the "CICO Development and Implementation Guide." To design the CICO to fit the needs and culture of your school, behavior support teams should set aside at least a half or full professional development day and answer all the questions in this guide prior to piloting CICO.

Chapter 5 provides not only an in-depth look at the roles and responsibilities of each person in the school who will be involved in CICO implementation (e.g., a CICO coordinator/facilitator, teacher, behavior support team), but also a summary of the training needs for everyone involved, including parents. Some of the figures included in this chapter feature "scripts" of phrases that the CICO coordinator/facilitator can say at check-in and check-out, as well as sample statements that teachers can make when giving feedback to students.

Chapter 6 equips school teams with guidelines on how to effectively develop a Daily Progress Report (DPR) to fit their school culture. Information regarding ranking systems, the number of rating periods, and other essential information that should be considered when designing a DPR is included. The chapter also explains how to develop an effective reinforcement system to use with CICO. Sample reinforcement systems are also provided, along with a tool for assessing reinforcer preference with older students.

Chapter 7 presents information on how to select data systems to guide CICO decision making. Specifically, schools are given examples of data that can be easily tracked pre- and post-CICO implementation. The web-based CICO information system, which is embedded in the School-Wide Information System (SWIS), is outlined in this chapter as one tool for collecting and summarizing data. This system allows schools to track both office discipline referrals and CICO DPR data. The chapter also details how to collect fidelity of implementation data, along with strategies to fade students from the CICO intervention.

Chapter 8 offers strategies for adapting CICO to support more students with different target behaviors and to support younger students. The chapter has been updated and expanded from the previous edition to include information on how to use CICO to target attendance problems, academic and/or organizational issues, and problem behavior exhibited during recess.

Guidance is provided through sample DPRs for how to support students in preschool and in the younger elementary grades (i.e., kindergarten/first grade).

Chapter 9 is new to this edition and provides a model of how to layer interventions onto basic CICO. Much research has been conducted on CICO since the publication of the second edition. This research, as well as our practical application in thousands of schools, has led to new recommendations about how functional assessment fits into the process of CICO implementation. Our goal is to help schools and districts create sustainable systems that can be supported without significant researcher and/or university faculty or graduate student involvement. We propose a model in Chapter 9 that allows the school faculty to more effectively and efficiently implement CICO in school settings.

Chapter 10 has been significantly revised for this edition and covers both family and cultural considerations related to implementing CICO. The chapter begins with a brief definition of culturally responsive practices, then details how school staff should examine their own behavior in relation to interacting with students from different ethnic, cultural, socioeconomic, and religious backgrounds. It also discusses how to partner with families in the CICO implementation process to improve outcomes for students.

Chapter 11 summarizes the adaptations that are necessary to implement CICO in high school settings. The chapter explains how to select students for the intervention, how to conduct the daily features of CICO, and how to combine the social aspect of the CICO intervention with the needed academic supports at the high school level. Adaptations to traditional DPRs are provided, including a discussion of a DPR app that is currently in development. Information is also provided on how to evaluate intervention effectiveness.

Chapter 12 is a new chapter that discusses how to adapt CICO to support students who are experiencing internalizing (e.g., anxious, shy, depressed) behavioral concerns. Recent research has documented the efficacy of CICO for these behaviors. A summary of this research is included, as are the ways of altering basic CICO to support these students without greatly modifying the intervention.

Chapter 13 is also a new chapter that outlines how CICO can be adapted to support students who are educated in alternative education settings, such as residential and day treatment. Much research has been conducted since the second edition was published in 2010 on how to intensify CICO to support students with more significant behavioral needs. This chapter details the necessary modifications, including how a midday check-up has been shown to be effective for students in alternative education settings.

In Chapter 14, we are excited to share information for coaches and trainers about how to teach school teams to effectively implement and provide coaching for the CICO intervention. This chapter includes objectives and a sample agenda with suggested time lines for topic coverage for an initial training. It also outlines best practices for delivering evidence-based professional development.

Chapter 15 answers frequently asked questions related to implementing CICO. This chapter has been updated and expanded on the basis of our work in schools across the country and in light of the many questions that have come up in our workshops and inservice trainings. In helping schools implement CICO, we have learned the telltale signs that indicate that CICO will not be implemented correctly or that implementation will suffer, such as use of CICO as a punishment system rather than as a positive behavior support system. We have presented these warning signs as precorrections to ensure that school personnel can be successful in implementing CICO.

This new edition attempts to respond to questions and challenges experienced by schools across the country and around the world that used the second edition to build a Tier 2 level system of positive behavior support for their students. We hope that the new and revised material in this edition increases the relevance, feasibility, and functionality of CICO for schools that begin or continue implementation of the intervention in coming years.

Please note that to be inclusive of all genders, we use the pronouns "they/them/theirs" throughout the book to refer to individuals, both in the singular and plural forms. Additionally, we confirm that the case examples used in the book are either fictional or are sufficiently disguised (i.e., through the use of pseudonyms or a compilation of multiple cases or scenarios) to preserve individuals' anonymity.

Acknowledgments

We extend appreciation and credit to the faculty and staff of Fern Ridge Middle School who created CICO over 20 years ago, shared their knowledge with us, and allowed the world to benefit from their pioneering efforts. A special thank you to Christine Downs, Mishele Carroll, Andrea Miller, Alex Graves, and Emily Davis, the practitioners who taught us how to most efficiently and effectively implement CICO. A special thanks to Granite School District and the members of the Behavior Response Support Team (BRST), including Aaron Fischer, the BRST project director. Many of the updated forms and training materials came from our collaborative work, including how to adapt CICO for students exhibiting internalizing behavior problems. We would like to acknowledge Kent McIntosh and Steve Goodman for providing feedback and suggestions on revisions to include in this edition. Kimberli Breen needs special recognition, as she has been instrumental in moving the field forward in relation to implementing CICO and was a key contributor both to ideas presented in this edition and the CICO DVD. We thank our other contributing authors, including K. Sandra MacLeod, Sara C. McDaniel, Allison Leigh Bruhn, K. Brigid Flannery, Mimi McGrath Kato, Angus Kittelman, Breda O'Keeffe, Kristen Stokes, Kristin Kladis, Nicole Swoszowski, Robin Parks Ennis, and Kristine Jolivette.

Major thanks to Hannah Wright, whose attention to detail helped us more effectively communicate our message, and to Hannah Glass for serving on the CICO research team. Finally, thank you to all the school staff across the country and around the world who have shared their enthusiasm for CICO and provided many suggestions during our workshops and training sessions.

Contents

CHAPTER 1

Introduction to Check-In, Check-Out

WHAT IS THE PURPOSE OF THIS BOOK?

The purpose of this book is to describe a targeted system of positive behavior support called Check-In, Check-Out (CICO): what it is, how it works, who can benefit from it, how it is implemented in a school, and how it can be adapted to meet the needs of certain groups or individuals. The goal of the book is to provide the reader with the rationale, procedures, and tools to (1) determine if the CICO intervention is appropriate for your school and (2) implement a variation of CICO that fits the needs of your school.

The CICO intervention is intended to be one piece of the larger positive behavioral interventions and supports (PBIS) effort in a school. On a schoolwide level, PBIS is a systematic approach to managing behavior that prioritizes the establishment of a positive school culture to prevent problem behaviors, the efficient and timely implementation of research-based interventions to respond to problem behaviors, the accessibility of a continuum of comprehensive interventions and supports to meet students' needs, and the use of data to guide decision making (Sugai & Horner, 2008). Research conducted on PBIS has found that schools are able to implement PBIS effectively, and that PBIS improves school climate, reduces the occurrence of problem behaviors, and improves students' academic and social outcomes (Sugai & Horner, 2008). Schools that have effective and complete systems of PBIS in place address three levels of behavioral need:

1. *Tier 1: Universal support.* All students must be taught the schoolwide behavioral expectations, and teachers must have proactive classroom behavioral instruction procedures in place.
2. *Tier 2: Targeted support.* Students who are at risk of developing patterns of problem

1

behavior must be able to access an efficient and well-articulated system for reducing problem behavior before it becomes worse over time.

3. *Tier 3: Individualized support.* Students with serious problem behavior must receive intensive, individualized behavior support.

The basic CICO intervention addresses the second level (Tier 2) of behavioral need. (For resources on Tier 1 and Tier 3, refer to the Resources section at the end of Chapter 2.) CICO is designed for students who demonstrate persistent problem behavior, but not dangerous or violent behavior, in classroom settings. They are students who need more practice and feedback to follow schoolwide behavioral expectations and benefit from preventative classroom management practices. They are *not* students with serious, chronic behavior problems who require comprehensive, individualized interventions. *A primary function of CICO is to improve the overall efficiency of the Tier 1 schoolwide procedures, while reducing the number of individualized interventions that are needed.*

A large portion of this book will be dedicated to describing what we call "basic CICO." This is the proactive Tier 2 intervention meant to be implemented with students who are at risk but not currently engaging in problem behavior. This book also details how basic CICO can be adapted to support students with more significant behavioral needs and for different behavioral concerns, such as those students who have internalizing behaviors (e.g., shyness, anxiety, depression; see Chapter 12). Additionally, the book details how CICO can be adapted for special populations, such as students in high school and alternative educational settings (see Chapters 11 and 13).

Access to adequate resources has long been an issue and challenge in schools. At the same time, schools are expected to do more to support students with diverse academic, emotional, and behavioral needs. This book provides teachers, administrators, school psychologists, educational assistants, and other school personnel with the tools to implement an *efficient* and *cost-effective* system of PBIS in schools. The book details the logic, procedures, administrative systems, and forms needed to build a CICO intervention. Tools for ongoing evaluation and improvement of the system are also provided. A list of abbreviations and definitions appears in Appendix A.1 for a quick review of terms, as needed.

WHAT IS CICO?

CICO, is a school-based intervention for providing daily support and monitoring to students who are at risk for developing serious or chronic problem behavior. It should be noted here that CICO is also known as the Behavior Education Program or BEP. Students who fail to respond to schoolwide and classroom preventative approaches and who receive several office discipline referrals (ODRs) per year may benefit from a Tier 2 intervention like CICO. It is based on a daily check-in/check-out system that provides the student with immediate feedback on their behavior (via teacher rating on a Daily Progress Report [DPR]) and increased positive adult attention. Behavioral expectations are clearly defined, and students are given both immediate and delayed reinforcement for meeting those expectations. Collaboration between the school and the families of identified students is encouraged by sending home each day a copy of the DPR to be signed by the parents or caregivers and returned the next school day. We detail ways of adapting parental collaboration if daily signing is not possible for the families in your school. A critical feature of CICO is the use of data to evaluate its effectiveness in changing student behavior. Percentages of points earned on the DPR are recorded on a summary graph for each student. These data are reviewed by the school's behavior support team, at least every 2 weeks, and are used to make decisions about whether to continue, modify, or fade the CICO intervention.

CICO incorporates several core principles of PBIS, including (1) clearly defined expectations, (2) instruction on appropriate social skills, (3) increased positive reinforcement for following expectations, (4) contingent consequences for problem behavior, (5) increased positive contact with an adult in the school, (6) improved opportunities for self-regulation and self-management, and (7) increased home–school collaboration.

The CICO intervention goes beyond its impact on a single student. It provides the school with a proactive, preventative approach for addressing recurrent problem behavior. In addition, the CICO intervention enhances communication among teachers, improves school climate, increases consistency among staff, and helps teachers to feel supported.

HOW EFFICIENT AND COST-EFFECTIVE IS CICO?

The CICO intervention is continuously available and can be implemented within 3–5 days following baseline data collection and identification of a problem. CICO typically requires no more than 5–10 minutes per teacher per day. Although additional coordination time is required, this intervention places low demands on time by all teachers and staff in a school. The entire staff are trained to implement CICO, which is available for students who need additional positive behavior support. Unlike intensive, individualized interventions (i.e., those requiring a functional behavioral assessment [FBA] and an intensive behavior support plan), no lengthy assessment process is conducted prior to the student receiving CICO support. A student who is referred for the CICO intervention can be deemed an appropriate candidate and begin to receive support following 3–5 school days of baseline DPR data collection. Personnel time required to implement the intervention is minimal (see Chapter 4 for resource and time requirements), and many students (20–30) can be supported on the intervention at the same time. Implementation and maintenance costs are low (see Figure 4.5 in Chapter 4 for an example middle school budget).

WHY ARE TIER 2 INTERVENTIONS LIKE CICO NECESSARY?

Most schools do not have the time nor resources to provide comprehensive individualized behavior support for *all* students who need varying levels of extra support. For example, in a school with a population of 500 students, it is estimated that approximately 15–20%, or 75–100 students, will need more support than what schoolwide and classroom prevention efforts provide. Conducting intensive, individualized interventions with all of these students would be unmanageable and would tax school resources beyond capacity. Many students will successfully respond to simple interventions, like CICO, that are less time intensive and more cost-efficient to implement. Thus, utilizing an intervention like CICO will reduce the overall number of students who need individualized support.

Implementing CICO in your school does not negate the need to provide intensive, individualized interventions to some students. There will be students for whom CICO will not be adequate to produce significant reductions in problem behavior. For those students, an FBA should be conducted, and data from the assessment should be used to develop an individualized behavior support plan. (For more information on intensive, individualized positive behavior support, refer to Crone, Hawken, & Horner, 2015.)

WHICH SCHOOLS SHOULD CONSIDER IMPLEMENTING CICO?

Schools that are implementing Tier 1 schoolwide and classroom PBIS (Lewis & Sugai, 1999; Sugai & Horner, 1999) with fidelity and that still have 10 or more students in need of extra support should consider implementing CICO. Tier 1 schoolwide and classroom prevention efforts clarify expectations both for the students and the staff, thus reducing the overall number of students engaging in problem behavior. If schools do not have Tier 1 support in place, it is recommended that they work on that level of support first prior to implementing CICO. Schools that do not have effective Tier 1 supports in place will likely have too many students who will require Tier 2 interventions like CICO. If Tier 1 prevention efforts are used and there are fewer than 10 students who engage in problem behavior, a school may be able to simply implement individualized behavior supports for each of them, rather than invest in CICO.

Although CICO is cost-effective and requires minimal staff time, the sincere commitment of *all* staff members and the support of the building administrator are crucial to the success of the intervention. Administrator support includes the allocation of personnel time and resources to the implementation, coordination, and ongoing evaluation of the intervention. Chapter 4 details the steps necessary to get CICO started in your school, and includes a self-assessment checklist to determine readiness for implementing the intervention.

"IF MY SCHOOL IS ALREADY IMPLEMENTING AN INTERVENTION LIKE CICO FOR AT-RISK STUDENTS, WILL I STILL BENEFIT FROM READING THIS BOOK?"

Yes! This book may help you improve the efficiency of your CICO-type intervention, or help you impose an organizing structure that you may currently lack. If your CICO intervention is being implemented with fidelity (see Chapter 7 on how to assess CICO fidelity) and is effectively supporting students who are at risk, you will learn how to address other problem behaviors, such as attendance issues, academic and/or organizational deficits, and students who have problem behaviors during unstructured times, such as recess. Additionally, in Chapters 8 and 9, we discuss adaptations and elaborations of the CICO intervention that may help you identify effective modifications that can be used when basic CICO is inadequate for a particular student. We provide schools with step-by-step details of how to layer additional interventions onto CICO when the basic intervention is not sufficient.

"ARE THERE ADDITIONAL RESOURCES TO AID IMPLEMENTATION OF CICO IN MY SCHOOL?"

Yes. A primary resource that schools use in tandem with this book is a DVD titled *Check-In, Check-Out: A Tier 2 Intervention for Students at Risk, Second Edition* (Hawken & Breen, 2017), which is available for purchase at *www.guilford.com*. This DVD outlines the essential features of CICO and provides video examples of effective CICO implementation. Chapter 4 describes how and when the CICO DVD could be used as a training resource for your school staff. In addition, interactive e-learning modules to train staff and faculty on CICO are available for subscription at *https://evokeschools.com*. Finally, additional resources are recommended at the end of some chapters throughout this book.

CHAPTER 2

The Context for PBIS in Schools

Schools face a growing challenge in meeting both the instructional and behavioral needs of all students. Students arrive at school with significant and diverse needs and present educators with a unique set of challenges (e.g., English learners, difficulties associated with low socioeconomic status, and significant learning and behavioral needs; Sugai et al., 2000; Tyack, 2001). To be effective in supporting all students, schools need to implement a continuum of PBIS, from less intensive to more intensive, based on the severity of the problem behavior presented (Sugai et al., 2000; Walker et al., 1996). This continuum includes PBIS at three levels: (1) Tier 1, schoolwide and classroom PBIS strategies; (2) Tier 2 interventions for students at risk; and (3) Tier 3 interventions for students engaging in severe problem behavior. The continuum of positive behavior support is detailed in Figure 2.1.

The triangle represents all students in the school and is divided into three levels of intervention. The bottom part of the triangle represents the approximately 80% of students who will benefit from Tier 1 interventions (Colvin, Kame'enui, & Sugai, 1993; Sugai & Horner, 1999, 2008; Sugai et al., 2000; Taylor-Greene et al., 1997). Tier 1 interventions are implemented with all students and in all settings, and include two components: (1) implementing a schoolwide PBIS plan and (2) implementing proactive classroom behavior instructional strategies. A school that implements schoolwide PBIS (1) generates staff agreement on three to five positively stated rules or expectations, (2) directly instructs students on the expectations, (3) provides reinforcement for following expectations, (4) provides minor consequences for rule infractions, and (5) uses data on a regular basis to determine whether the schoolwide behavior plan is working. Schools must have an effective and well-established Tier 1 PBIS plan in place *prior* to implementing CICO. In addition, it is important for teachers to utilize effective classroom behavioral instruction prior to implementing CICO.

Once Tier 1 interventions are in place, we recommend the addition of a Tier 2 intervention system to support students who continue to engage in frequent problem behavior. In the

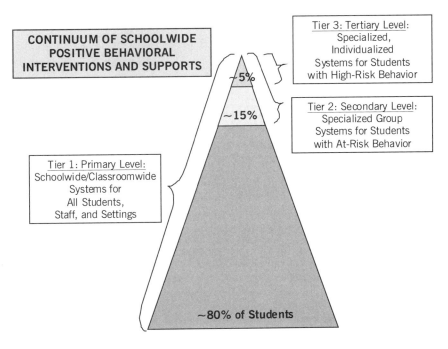

FIGURE 2.1. Three-tiered prevention model for schoolwide positive behavior interventions and support. Adapted from Sugai and Horner (2002). Copyright © 2002 Sage Publications, Inc. Adapted by permission.

triangle, the middle portion represents the approximately 15% of students who will benefit from Tier 2 interventions (Bruhn, Lane, & Hirsch, 2014; Sugai & Horner, 2008; Sugai et al., 2000). These students may require extra practice in following schoolwide expectations due to poor peer relations, low academic achievement, chaotic home environments, or a multitude of other reasons. *Interventions at the Tier 2 level are very efficient "standardized protocol" interventions that can be implemented with a group of students needing similar levels of support* (Hawken, Adolphson, MacLeod, & Schumann, 2009; Hawken & Horner, 2003; March & Horner, 2002). CICO, as described in this book, is one example of such an intervention.

Some students will need more support than CICO can provide. The top part of the triangle represents the approximately 5% of students who engage in the most severe forms of problem behavior (Sugai & Horner, 2008; Sugai et al., 2000) and thus require intensive, individualized interventions. For these students, an FBA is conducted, and this information is used to develop an individualized behavior support plan (see Crone, Hawken, & Horner, 2015).

COMMITMENT TO PREVENTION OF PROBLEM BEHAVIOR

Schools across the country that have implemented effective schoolwide PBIS plans have experienced significant reductions in problem behavior and improvements in the overall climate of their school (Bradshaw, Koth, Thornton, & Leaf, 2009; Bradshaw, Mitchell, & Leaf, 2010; Bradshaw, Waasdorp, & Leaf, 2012; Gage, Whitford, & Katsiyannis, 2018; Kim, McIntosh,

Mercer, & Nese, 2018; Sugai & Horner, 1999). As a next step, schools should focus on students who engage in frequent problem behavior despite effective Tier 1 prevention efforts.

Consider the student who does not have a history of problem behavior. The student begins acting out at school when their parents go through a difficult divorce, and could benefit from extra attention or support at school. In some schools, this student's behavioral change might be overlooked because it is not severe enough to warrant a behavior support team meeting or to involve the support of special education services. In a school with CICO in place, a teacher, parent, or other school staff member could inform the behavior support team that this student needs additional adult monitoring, feedback, and attention. Within 3–5 school days following baseline data collection and securing parental permission, the student could be receiving the support they need. In a school without a CICO intervention, the student's problematic behavior might have to become intense or chronic before it warrants attention and they receive support. *By implementing CICO, schools are committed to preventing problem behavior. In essence, the school is reaching a student before they are in crisis and before the student develops a long history of engaging in problem behavior.*

KEY FEATURES AND EXAMPLES
OF INTERVENTIONS AT THE TIER 2 LEVEL

Although CICO has been shown to be an effective intervention for students with frequent problem behavior (e.g., Drevon, Hixson, Wyse, & Rigney, 2018; Hawken, Bundock, Kladis, O'Keeffe, & Barrett, 2014; Maggin, Zurheide, Pickett, & Baillie, 2015; Mitchell, Adamson, & McKenna, 2017; Wolfe et al., 2016), schools should have available a menu of Tier 2 interventions for responding to the diverse range of student needs. In order to be effective in preventing severe problem behavior, Tier 2 interventions should contain certain features that differentiate them from Tier 1 and Tier 3 levels of behavior support (Hawken et al., 2009). The following key features of Tier 2 interventions have been outlined by the Office of Special Education Programs (OSEP), Technical Assistance Center on Positive Behavioral Interventions and Supports (OSEP, 2017): (1) similar implementation across students (i.e., low effort required from teachers); (2) continuous availability of and quick access to the intervention; (3) all school staff are trained on how to make a referral and, if appropriate, how to implement the intervention; (4) intervention is consistent with schoolwide expectations; (5) intervention is flexible based on functional assessment; and (6) data are used continuously to monitor progress on the intervention. These features are listed in Table 2.1 and discussed in further detail below.

The goal of Tier 2 interventions is to support the approximately 15% of the student population who are at risk for but not currently engaging in severe problem behavior (Anderson & Borgmeier, 2010; Mitchell, Stormont, & Gage, 2011; Sugai & Horner, 2008; Walker et al., 1996). In a school of 500 students, this group could include as many as 75 students who need more support than a Tier 1 schoolwide PBIS plan can provide. For this reason, Tier 2 interventions need to be efficient in terms of the time and resources required, as schools are not adequately equipped to implement individualized interventions with all of the students who are at risk. Tier 2 interventions should involve using a similar set of procedures across a group of students. For example, if social skills training is required for students who have problems with anger management, a similar curriculum should be used across this group of students.

TABLE 2.1. Key Features of Tier 2 Interventions

- Similar implementation across students.
- Continuous availability of and quick access to the intervention.
- All school staff are trained on the intervention.
- Intervention is consistent with schoolwide expectations.
- Intervention is flexible based on functional assessment.
- Data are used continuously to monitor progress on the intervention.

To be effective in preventing problem behavior, students must be able to access Tier 2 interventions quickly. Unlike more intensive and individualized interventions, which may take weeks of assessment prior to developing a comprehensive behavior intervention plan, Tier 2 interventions should be accessed by the student relatively quickly—usually within a week (OSEP, 2017). Students are identified quickly and proactively, either by frequently assessing risk factors, such as the number of ODRs, absences, or tardies or by teacher nomination or referral (Cheney, Blum, & Walker, 2004; Crone, Hawken, & Horner, 2010).

For Tier 2 interventions that are implemented schoolwide, all staff should receive training on their role in the intervention. The intervention should be consistent with schoolwide expectations (OSEP, 2017). For example, if a middle school has the schoolwide rules "Be Safe," "Be Respectful," "Be Responsible," and "Keep Hands and Feet to Self," the Tier 2 intervention should provide practice and feedback on how to meet these behavioral expectations. Often, these interventions are implemented with the support of a school psychologist, counselor, or paraprofessional, so that the burden of the intervention is not solely on the student's teacher (Crone et al., 2010; Hawken, 2006; Lane et al., 2003). Typically, consultation from experts outside of the school is not necessary or is minimized because the intervention procedures are systematic and standardized (OSEP, 2017).

Tier 2 interventions should have systems in place to monitor student progress, make modifications, and gradually decrease supports as a student's behavior improves. One component of this system is a team, which may already exist, such as a multi-tiered systems of support (MTSS) or a behavior support team consisting of teachers, counselors, parents, and students (Christenson, Sinclair, Lehr, & Hurley, 2000; Pool, Carter, & Johnson, 2013). Teams should meet regularly and have systematic procedures for monitoring, troubleshooting, and adding or removing students to or from the intervention (Crone et al., 2010). Team decisions and monitoring of student progress are based on data from a number of different sources depending on the type of intervention. The team may review student progress on the intervention using information such as the percentage of daily points earned, grades, attendance, participation in school activities, and other indicators of student progress (Bruhn et al., 2014; Crone et al., 2010; Pool et al., 2013; Sinclair, Christensen, Evelo, & Hurley, 1998). Although many Tier 2 interventions have the features we have described, not all of them meet all six of the OSEP-recommended features illustrated in Table 2.1.

Implementation features of Tier 2 interventions will vary depending on the needs of individual schools and students. For example, Tier 2 interventions in elementary schools may focus on preventing escalation of disruptive behavior in the classroom, whereas interventions in large urban high schools may focus on a dropout prevention program (Osher, Dwyer, & Jackson, 2004). Examples of Tier 2 interventions for social behavior include small-group social skills training (e.g., Lane et al., 2003; Powers, 2003); mentoring programs, such as Check and Connect (Christenson, Stout, & Pohl, 2012; Powers, Hagans, & Linn, 2017; Sinclair et al., 1998); newcomer clubs (e.g., programs to teach schoolwide rules/expectations to students who are new and transfer into the school midyear); and systems or programs for supporting students who struggle in unstructured settings (e.g., having a structured recess for a group of students engaging in problem behavior on the playground). An additional Tier 2 intervention includes First Step to Success (Walker et al., 1998, 2009), a prevention program for kindergartners with social and behavior problems.

ADVANTAGES OF CICO AS A TIER 2 INTERVENTION

Although each school should have several options for Tier 2 interventions to meet different needs, research supports CICO as easily implemented, effective, and evidence based (Anderson & Borgmeier, 2010; Bruhn et al., 2014; Mitchell et al., 2011; Sugai & Horner, 2008). In addition, CICO is the most widely implemented Tier 2 intervention across the United States (Mitchell et al., 2011; Rodriguez, Loman, & Borgmeier, 2016), and it has been implemented in other countries, including Norway, Australia, Germany, Russia, and Poland (e.g., Crone et al., 2010). There are several advantages to implementing CICO. To begin with, depending on school size and resources, up to 30 students can be supported at one time with one CICO coordinator. The students check in each morning with a CICO coordinator who is a paraprofessional (e.g., teacher's aide). Use of a paraprofessional, rather than a school psychologist or behavioral specialist, has the advantage of reducing the overall costs of delivering the intervention. Some schools decide to have one CICO coordinator who oversees multiple CICO facilitators. The role of the facilitators involves checking students in and out. The role of the coordinator is to check students in and out, but to also oversee the program (e.g., summarize data for decision making, manage referrals). Research has shown that by using multiple CICO facilitators schools can get up to 11% of their student population on the intervention (Hawken et al., 2015).

Many small-group social skills programs can be delivered by trained paraprofessionals, but group sizes typically are limited to five to seven students. Furthermore, when delivering social skills interventions, it is difficult to add new members once the groups have been formed. As a result, the intervention can no longer be continuously available for all students. Other Tier 2 interventions have been shown to be highly effective in reducing problem behavior, such as the First Step to Success intervention (Walker et al., 1998, 2009). However, First Step requires an outside expert to facilitate the intervention and at least 20–40 hours of consultation both with the school staff and parents. In many cases, this intervention would be cost prohibitive for schools to implement.

Another major advantage of CICO is that there is a built-in progress monitoring component. Students receive feedback throughout the day on a DPR, and the percentage of points earned is calculated for each student at the end of each day. The DPR allows teachers and school personnel to easily track daily social behavior and determine if the intervention is working or not for that student. Many Tier 2 interventions do not have built-in progress monitoring mechanisms.

For example, much of the data gathered and published for small-group social skills training are for research purposes, whereas in CICO data are easily collected and readily accessed by school personnel. Tier 2 interventions, such as mentoring, often have no ongoing data collection systems, but rather collect data at the end of a certain period of time, such as after 12–16 weeks, to determine the impact of the intervention. To be most effective in preventing serious problem behavior, Tier 2 interventions need to incorporate ongoing data collection and decision making.

A final advantage is the ease of generalizing the procedures from one student to another. Once teachers have implemented the intervention with one student, they can easily implement the intervention with other students. Teachers rapidly become fluent with implementing the intervention because intervention procedures are the same for everyone. Teachers learn how to embed the intervention into their classroom schedule and routines so that when a new student begins the intervention, they know how to make it work in their classrooms.

IS THERE RESEARCH THAT SUPPORTS THE FEASIBILITY AND EFFECTIVENESS OF CICO?

Yes, research results support both the ability of schools to adopt and implement CICO and its effectiveness in reducing problem behavior. The CICO intervention is based on empirically driven behavioral principles for behavior change. Numerous publications (Chafouleas, Christ, Riley-Tillman, Briesch, & Chanese, 2007; Chafouleas, Riley-Tillman, Sassu, LaFrance, & Patwa, 2007; Davies & McLaughlin, 1989; Dougherty & Dougherty, 1977; Leach & Byrne, 1986; Warberg, George, Brown, Chauran, & Taylor-Greene, 1995) support the basic underlying principles of CICO:

1. Define behavioral expectations.
2. Teach the expectations.
3. Provide frequent feedback and reinforcement.
4. Build a regular cycle of checking in and checking out with adults.
5. Formalize consequences for problem behaviors both at school and at home.
6. Use a percentage of points on DPRs to evaluate intervention effectiveness.

The technology of embedding CICO into a schoolwide system of behavior support was originally demonstrated at Fern Ridge Middle School (FRMS) in Veneta, Oregon. The leadership staff at FRMS were responsible for developing and testing the original critical features of CICO. Since then, CICO has been implemented across the United States as well as around the world.

CICO is the most widely implemented, evidence-based Tier 2 behavior intervention (Bruhn et al., 2014; Mitchell et al., 2011). Since Hawken and Horner (2003) published the first single-case experimental research study on CICO implemented as part of a continuum of behavior support, additional research has been conducted evaluating the effects of the intervention. Due to CICO's widespread implementation, its effects have been summarized across research studies. In a review of CICO studies by Hawken et al. (2014), which included unpublished doctoral dissertations, the researchers concluded that across all studies, CICO was found to be effective for 72% of students who received the intervention. In a review by Maggin et al. (2015), the researchers applied the What Works Clearinghouse (WWC) criteria to evaluate studies on CICO, and found that a sufficient number of single-case studies ($n = 8$) met WWC criteria to include CICO as an evidence-based practice. The authors also found that fidelity of implementation was high across the eight single-case studies, but that no group studies met the criteria for inclusion. An additional literature review by Wolfe et al. (2016) summarized the effects across 15 single-case and one group study and concluded that CICO was an evidence-based practice for attention-maintained problem behavior. A recent, more comprehensive meta-analytic review of CICO indicated that the intervention improved student behavioral outcomes by more than one standard deviation (effect size: $d = 1.10$) compared to baseline or control conditions (Drevon et al., 2018). This is considered a large effect size for an educational intervention (Hattie, 2008).

The majority of studies on CICO indicate that it is most effective with students whose behaviors are maintained by adult or peer attention (McIntosh, Campbell, Carter, & Dickey, 2009; Smith, Evans-McCleon, Urbanski, & Justice, 2015; Wolfe et al., 2016). Some studies indicate that CICO may be effective without modifications for students who engage in problem escape behaviors (Hawken, O'Neill, & MacLeod, 2011; Swoszowski, Jolivette, Fredrick, & Heflin, 2012), while others indicate reduced effects with students with escape-maintained behaviors (Ennis, Jolivette, Swoszowski, & Johnson, 2012; Wolfe et al., 2016).

Research has indicated that for students who do not respond to the basic CICO, the intervention can be combined with a behavior support plan based on an FBA. This addition intensifies and individualizes the intervention to more effectively support the function of the problem behavior and has led to a reduction in problem behavior across multiple studies. (e.g., MacLeod, Hawken, O'Neill, & Bundock, 2016; March & Horner, 2002). Although basic CICO is intended for students who are at risk and can benefit from Tier 2 behavior support, research studies have indicated that with some modifications, it can be implemented effectively in alternative educational settings, such as day treatment and residential facilities (Ennis et al., 2012; Fallon & Feinberg, 2017; Swoszowski et al., 2012). Most important, research has documented that implementing CICO reduces the number of students who require intensive Tier 3 level supports (Hawken, MacLeod, & Rawlings, 2007).

Collectively, the reviews of CICO research have demonstrated the following outcomes:

1. Schools are able to implement CICO successfully.
2. The use of CICO is functionally related to reduced levels of problem behavior, and, for some students, increased levels of academic engagement.
3. CICO is likely to be effective with 60–75% of at-risk students.
4. If a student is not successful on CICO, conducting an FBA and using the FBA information to adapt CICO can be effective in improving behavioral outcomes.

RESOURCES

Building Tier 1 (Schoolwide) Systems of Behavior Support

Handler, M. W., Rey, J., Connell, J., Thier, K., Feinberg, A., & Putnam, R. (2007). Practical considerations in creating schoolwide positive behavior support in public schools. *Psychology in the Schools, 44*(1), 29–39.

Lewis, T. J., & Sugai, G. (1999). Effective behavior support: A systems approach to proactive schoolwide management. *Focus on Exceptional Children, 31*(6), 1–24.

Lewis-Palmer, T., Sugai, G., & Larson, S. (1999). Using data to guide decisions about program implementation and effectiveness. *Effective School Practices, 17*(4), 47–53.

Office of Special Education Programs (OSEP) Technical Assistance Center on Positive Behavioral Interventions and Supports: *www.PBIS.org.*

Sailor, W., Dunlap, G., Sugai, G., & Horner, R. H. (Eds.). (2009). *Handbook of positive behavior support.* New York: Springer.

Simonsen, B., Sugai, G., & Negron, M. (2008). Schoolwide positive behavior supports: Primary systems and practices. *Teaching Exceptional Children, 40*(6), 32–40.

Sugai, G., & Horner, R. H. (2008). What we know and need to know about preventing problem behavior in schools. *Exceptionality 16*(2), 67–77.

Sugai, G., & Horner, R. H. (2009). Responsiveness-to-Intervention and Schoolwide Positive Behavior Supports: Integration of multi-tiered system approaches. *Exceptionality, 17*(4), 223–237.

Taylor-Greene, S., Brown, D., Nelson, L., Longton, J., Gassman, T., Cohen, J., et al. (1997). Schoolwide behavioral support: Starting the year off right. *Journal of Behavioral Education, 7,* 99–112.

Todd, A. W., Horner, R. H., Sugai, G., & Sprague, J. R. (1999). Effective behavior support: Strengthening schoolwide systems through a team-based approach. *Effective School Practices, 17*(4), 23–27.

Building Tier 2 Systems of Behavior Support

Anderson, C. M., & Borgmeier, C. (2010). Tier II interventions within the framework of Schoolwide Positive Behavior Support: Essential features for design, implementation, and maintenance. *Behavior Analysis in Practice, 3*(1), 33–45.

Chafouleas, S., Riley-Tillman, C., Sassu, K., LaFrance, M., & Patwa, S. (2007). Daily behavior report cards: An investigation of the consistency of on-task data across raters and methods. *Journal of Positive Behavior Interventions, 9*(1), 30–37.

Christenson, S. L., Stout, K., & Pohl, A. (2012). *Check & Connect: A comprehensive student engagement intervention: Implementing with fidelity.* Minneapolis: University of Minnesota, Institute on Community Integration.

Filter, K. J., McKenna, M. K., Benedict, E. A., Horner, R. H., Todd, A. W., & Watson, J. (2007). Check-In/Check-Out: A post-hoc evaluation of an efficient, Tier II-level targeted intervention for reducing problem behaviors in schools. *Education and Treatment of Children, 30*(1), 69–84.

Hawken, L. S. (2006). School psychologists as leaders in the implementation of a targeted intervention: The Behavior Education Program (CICO). *School Psychology Quarterly, 21,* 91–111.

Hawken, L. S., Adolphson, S. L., MacLeod, K. S., & Schumann, J. (2009). Secondary-tier interventions and supports. In W. Sailor, G. Dunlap, G. Sugai, & R. Horner (Eds.), *Handbook of positive behavior support* (pp. 395–420). New York: Springer.

Hawken, L. S., MacLeod, K. S., & Rawlings, L. (2007). Effects of the Behavior Education Program (CICO) on problem behavior with elementary school students. *Journal of Positive Behavior Interventions, 9*(2), 94–101.

Interactive E-learning modules detailing how to effectively implement CICO, see *https://evokeschools.com.*

McCurdy, B. L., Kunsch, C., & Reibstein, S. (2007). Secondary prevention in the urban school: Implementing the Behavior Education Program. *Preventing School Failure, 5*(31), 12–19.

Pool, J. L., Carter, D. R., & Johnson, E. S. (2012). Tier 2 team processes and decision-making in a comprehensive three-tiered model. *Intervention in School and Clinic, 48*(4), 232–239.

Rodriguez, B. J., Campbell, A., Falcon, S. F., & Borgmeier, S. (2015). Examination of critical features and lessons learned for implementation of a Tier 2 intervention system for social behavior. *Journal of Educational and Psychological Consultation, 25,* 224–251.

Todd, A. W., Campbell, A. L., Meyer, G. G., & Horner, R. H. (2008). The effects of a targeted intervention to reduce problem behaviors: Elementary school implementation of Check In-Check Out. *Journal of Positive Behavior Interventions, 10*(1), 46–55.

Building Tier 3 Systems of Behavior Support

Benazzi, L., Horner, R. H., & Good, R. H. (2006). Effects of behavior support team composition on the technical adequacy and contextual fit of behavior support plans. *Journal of Special Education, 40*(3), 160–170.

Borgmeier, C., & Horner, R. H. (2006). An evaluation of the predictive validity of confidence ratings in identifying accurate functional behavioral assessment hypothesis statements. *Journal of Positive Behavior Interventions, 8*(2), 100–105.

Crone, D. A., Hawken, L. S., & Horner, R. H. (2015). *Building positive behavior support systems in schools: Functional behavioral assessment* (2nd ed.). New York: Guilford Press.

CHAPTER 3

Basic CICO

Critical Features and Processes

DEFINING FEATURES OF BASIC CICO

Basic CICO has several critical defining features that establish it as an efficient, effective, and sustainable Tier 2 intervention. These features include the following:

1. CICO is an *efficient* system that can provide behavioral support to a moderate-size group of at-risk students (approximately 10–30 students) at the same time. If schools are interested, the number of students supported can be increased. This option will be detailed in Chapter 4.
2. CICO is continuously available within the school, so a student who is identified as needing support can get access to CICO within 3 to 5 days.
3. The backbone of CICO involves a daily "check-in" and "check-out" with a respected adult.
4. CICO is designed to increase the likelihood that each class period begins with a positive interaction with the teacher or supervisor.
5. CICO increases the frequency of contingent feedback from the teacher or supervisor.
6. CICO requires low effort from teachers. That is, teachers should experience significant, positive changes in student behavior even though the individual teacher's CICO workload will be minimal.
7. CICO links behavioral and academic support.
8. CICO is implemented and supported by all administrators, teachers, and staff in the school building.
9. Students choose to participate and cooperate with the CICO intervention. They are not required to do so.
10. CICO employs continuous monitoring of student behavior and active use of data for decision making.

Based on Behavioral Principles

CICO is a school-based intervention for providing daily support to students at risk for developing serious or chronic behavior problems. The CICO intervention is based on three "big ideas" from behavioral research. *First,* at-risk students benefit from (1) clearly defined expectations, (2) frequent feedback, (3) consistency, and (4) positive reinforcement that is contingent on meeting goals. *Second,* problem behavior and poor academic performance are often linked. *Third,* behavior support begins with the development of effective student–adult relationships. Implementation of CICO creates increased collaboration between school and home and increased opportunities for self-management, each of which is also important for behavioral change in students at risk. The administration and staff at your school will apply these three "big ideas" as they develop your CICO intervention.

Why Does CICO Work?

At the heart of CICO are two procedural goals: (1) teach and support each student to perform the social and self-regulation skills that promote school success (self-monitoring, self-instruction, self-evaluation, self-recruitment of feedback and help) and (2) minimize rewards (social and procedural) for problem behavior. The behavior support team can use CICO to accomplish these goals by addressing six core functions. The *first* is early identification of students at risk for school failure due to problem behavior. CICO is most helpful when initiated during the first third of the school year. Research indicates that most students who will benefit from CICO can be identified by mid-October (McIntosh, Frank, & Spaulding, 2010). The *second* CICO function is explicit instruction on core self-regulation skills. The emphasis is placed on going beyond establishing general expectations, and teaching students specific social and learning skills for their current educational settings. The *third* function is to use the principle of "behavioral momentum" (Mace et al., 1988), which emphasizes starting each day and each class with a positive experience and using that success to snowball additional successes. Students are taught to (1) start each school day with a positive connection with adults, (2) greet teachers upon entering class and assess if they are following schoolwide expectations, and (3) recruit adult feedback throughout the day. The *fourth* function is to increase the structural prompts that make it easier for students to know when they should self-monitor and manage their behavior. This is done through a morning check-in, the use of the DPR throughout the day, and checking out with an adult at the end of the day. The *fifth* function of CICO is to increase the frequency and efficiency of feedback, with the explicit goal of increasing the number and specificity of positive statements from adults (at school and home). The *sixth* function of the CICO approach is to use data for problem solving when minor adaptations are needed to make CICO better fit the needs of a student.

When these functions are combined, the result is an efficient and effective system of support in which an at-risk student (1) gains access to CICO before they develop major problem behavior patterns; (2) starts each school day with a positive experience that builds momentum for school engagement; (3) recruits a personal greeting from the teacher when entering the classroom; (4) uses their DPR to monitor the flow of events during the school day; (5) receives feedback on the quality of their behavior and, when developmentally appropriate (e.g., middle

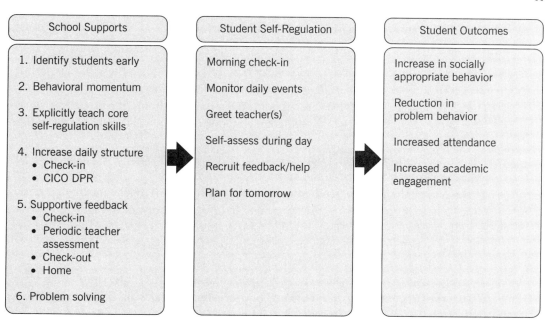

School Supports	Student Self-Regulation	Student Outcomes
1. Identify students early	Morning check-in	Increase in socially appropriate behavior
2. Behavioral momentum	Monitor daily events	Reduction in problem behavior
3. Explicitly teach core self-regulation skills	Greet teacher(s)	Increased attendance
4. Increase daily structure • Check-in • CICO DPR	Self-assess during day	Increased academic engagement
5. Supportive feedback • Check-in • Periodic teacher assessment • Check-out • Home	Recruit feedback/help	
6. Problem solving	Plan for tomorrow	

FIGURE 3.1. Conceptual logic of CICO.

and high school) self-assesses their own behavior; (6) recruits feedback from adults (at school and home); and (7) recruits help when academic or social challenges arise. Figure 3.1 provides a visual integration of these functions, with intended student self-regulation behaviors and student outcomes. The self-regulation aspects of CICO will differ depending on the age of the student involved in the intervention. Younger students (i.e., K–5) will need more support and prompts to engage in self-evaluation over the course of participating in CICO, whereas older students (e.g., high school age) can begin this process upon entry into the intervention.

A Brief Tour of CICO Elements

The elements and procedures for implementing the CICO intervention are described in more depth later in this chapter. It is helpful, however, to have a general overview of the key elements.

1. *Personnel.* The CICO intervention is managed by a CICO coordinator and a behavior support team. All teaching faculty in the school have an opportunity to participate.
2. *Student identification.* A student is identified to begin CICO in one of three ways: (a) either a grade-level or behavior support team screens student variables associated with risk (e.g., an increase in the rate of ODRs or absences); (b) through systematic screening of all students for behavior problems; and/or (c) by teacher, parent, or student nomination. When a student is nominated for participation, both parents and students must agree to participate in the intervention. All students eligible for the CICO intervention must agree to willingly participate.

3. *Process.* CICO involves a daily, biweekly, and quarterly cycle. The daily cycle consists of the following:

- The student arrives at school and checks in with an adult (e.g., the CICO coordinator). At this check-in, the student receives their DPR.
- The student carries the DPR throughout the day and hands it to the teacher or supervisor at the start of the day (for elementary school) or at each class period (for middle or high school).
- The student retrieves the DPR after each class period and receives feedback from the teacher or supervisor related to expected social behaviors.
- At the end of the day the student returns the DPR to the CICO coordinator, determines whether daily point goals were met, and carries a copy of the DPR home.
- Family members receive the DPR, deliver recognition for success, and sign the form. The next morning the student returns the signed DPR to the CICO coordinator.

On a biweekly basis, data are reviewed to determine overall CICO intervention effectiveness and examine the percentage of points earned by each student and adjust support options as needed. The decisions made after assessing student progress are to continue basic CICO, add additional support, or determine if the student is ready to exit the intervention. More information on using data for decision making is provided in Chapter 7. A diagram of the basic CICO cycle is provided in Figure 3.2.

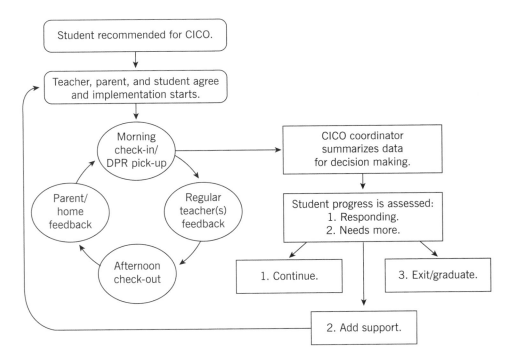

FIGURE 3.2. Diagram of the basic CICO cycle.

Antecedent Features of Basic CICO

Antecedents are events or situations that occur before problem behavior. They can be thought of as the triggers that set off the behavior. In order to prevent problem behavior, the key is to reduce the likelihood that the behavior will occur by adjusting its behavioral triggers. These adjustments may involve steps to increase the likelihood of appropriate behaviors that are not compatible with inappropriate behaviors.

There are certain antecedent features of CICO that increase its overall effectiveness. The CICO intervention creates a structure that eliminates antecedents to *problem behavior* by increasing antecedents for *positive* or *appropriate behavior*. These antecedent features include (1) provision of school supplies as needed at the beginning of the school day, (2) a prompt to have a good day, (3) a prompt to have a good class period, and (4) a reminder about behavioral expectations.

Disorganization is a common characteristic of the students on the CICO intervention. These students often come to school without a pen, paper, their daily planner, or with an uncharged, school-issued device. Coming unprepared for class is an antecedent, or trigger, for getting into trouble as soon as the teacher gives the class a direction. For students on CICO, this entire scenario can be avoided by checking whether they have their needed supplies first thing in the morning and providing them with whatever materials they are missing before sending them to class. Each morning when a student checks in, the CICO coordinator reminds them to have a good day and prompts the student to remember the schoolwide expectations. The CICO coordinator also asks the student what they are working on to improve behavior (e.g., "I need to work on keeping my hands and feet to myself"). This daily prompt can mean the difference between starting the day out poorly or making better choices that start the day off in the right direction. Finally, students on CICO also receive a prompt at the beginning of each class period (for middle and high school students) or at each class transition (for elementary students). This prompt reminds students of the class and schoolwide expectations and helps them keep their behavior on target during class time.

FOR WHOM IS BASIC CICO MOST APPROPRIATE?

Basic CICO is most appropriate for students who are considered "at risk" for developing serious or chronic behavior problems. These students consistently have trouble in "low-level" problem areas. For example, they frequently come to school unprepared, talk out, talk back to the teacher, or cause minor disruptions in the classroom. In other words, their behavior is disruptive, detrimental to instruction, and interferes with their own learning and that of others but is not dangerous or violent. CICO involves frequent positive interactions between students and teachers as well as increased monitoring of student behavior by adults at school and at home. For this reason, basic CICO will be most effective for students who engage in problem behavior in order to obtain adult attention *or* who find adult attention reinforcing. Students who are not reinforced by adult attention, or who even find it aversive, would not be good candidates for basic CICO. For those students, basic CICO may worsen their behavior. Chapter 9 provides information on how CICO can be modified for students who are not responding to basic CICO.

CICO is not adequate for students who engage in serious or violent behaviors or infractions, such as bringing a weapon to school or vandalizing the school. While these students might receive some benefit from CICO, they require more individualized attention and support than can be provided by basic CICO alone.

CICO is not necessary for students who have been sent to the office on rare occasions or whose behavior is driven by a problem in the environmental setting. For example, school cafeterias can be loud, chaotic places. A student who is repeatedly referred to the office for yelling in the cafeteria is not an immediate candidate for additional behavior support. In a loud, chaotic cafeteria, the setting should be assessed and modified first. If the student's problem behavior continues and is highly discrepant from the behavior of peers in the same setting, the student might then benefit from CICO or from individualized behavior support.

Basic CICO is a classroom-based intervention for students who have problem behavior throughout the school day. In essence, it is not appropriate for students who exhibit problem behaviors only at specific times of the day or in certain situations. For example, at the elementary school level, if a student only engages in problem behavior during reading instruction, or, at a secondary level, if a student only engages in problem behavior in one teacher's class and no other classes, another Tier 2 intervention should be considered. Another Tier 2 intervention should also be considered if the student is only engaging in problem behavior in unstructured settings, such as the cafeteria or hallways.

When deciding who is appropriate for the CICO intervention, it is important to remember that the problem behaviors of students eligible for the CICO will look different in elementary school than in middle or high school. A typical CICO student in elementary school might have difficulty taking their turn, refuse to share materials with others, have difficulty remaining seated or completing tasks, or be mildly aggressive toward other students, especially on the playground or in areas with a poorer ratio of adult-to-child supervision. A CICO student in middle school may be more likely to use inappropriate language, to be frequently late to class,

TABLE 3.1. Appropriate and Inappropriate Candidates for CICO

Appropriate candidates for CICO	Inappropriate candidates for CICO
• Engage in problem behavior throughout the day in multiple settings.	• Engage in problem behavior during one class period or only in unstructured settings (e.g., playground, hallways, lunchroom, bus area).
• Engage in mild acting-out behaviors, such as talking out, off task, or out of seat.	• Engage in serious or violent behavior, such as *extreme* noncompliance/defiance, aggression, injury to self or others.
• Problem behavior is not related to trying to escape difficult academic work. Assessments indicate instructional material is at the student's level.	• Problem behavior mainly occurs when student is trying to escape a difficult task or academic subject. Assessments indicate that instructional material is not at the student's level.
• Problem behavior is maintained by adult attention, and/or the student finds adult attention reinforcing.	• Problem behavior is maintained by escape from academic tasks, and/or the student *does not* find adult attention reinforcing.

to be defiant toward adults, or to refuse to do work. *Whether the setting is elementary, middle, or high school, the key is to identify those students who have a consistent pattern of problem behavior that has not yet reached serious or chronic levels.* Table 3.1 provides a summary of the characteristics of good candidates and poor candidates for basic CICO.

HOW IS THE CICO INTERVENTION INTEGRATED INTO A SCHOOL'S OTHER IDENTIFICATION SYSTEMS FOR STUDENTS IN NEED?

Every school provides a range of services to students with diverse needs. For example, every public school provides Section 504 and Special Education services. Many schools provide mentoring programs, extracurricular tutoring, or even mental health services. Each service typically requires a process for identifying students who are eligible for, or in need of, the service. The more services available, the more cumbersome it may be to navigate the multiple identification processes. Adding the CICO intervention can further complicate matters.

School administrators should carefully coordinate the multiple services and interventions offered within their school. Each school should examine the identification processes used for each service, and assess if any of the interventions are inefficient, redundant, or overly bureaucratic. Representatives from each service area (e.g., CICO coordinator, special education teacher, and school nurse) should meet. They should determine how to reduce any inefficiency, redundancy, or red tape created by their multiple services.

The first step is to increase awareness of the services and interventions that are provided by each professional or team. The next step is to create a collaboration or partnership among the various services. Real collaboration among service providers in a school will reduce the likelihood that services provided by one group will be replicated or even contraindicated by another group.

The teams used (or created) to develop and implement CICO will vary from school to school. In some schools, the schoolwide behavior support team designs CICO to fit the culture of their school, but a multidisciplinary team or student support team is in charge of examining data for decision making. In other schools, a multidisciplinary team that oversees both academic and behavior support (e.g., MTSS) embeds CICO implementation and evaluation into the team's existing meetings.

We recommend that schools review their current set of teams and consider if a team already exists that can manage CICO implementation. Some schools find it helpful to list the teams/committees at a school, along with the purpose of the committee and the staff who are involved. The Working Smarter, Not Harder Matrix illustrated in Figure 3.3 can be used as a guideline for accomplishing this task. (A blank matrix is included as a handout in Appendix B.1.)

DECISION PROCESS FOR CICO PLACEMENT

Before a student can be placed on basic CICO, it must be determined that the student is an appropriate candidate for the intervention. In some schools we work in, behavioral concerns are raised at the weekly grade-level team meeting attended by an instructional coach. If the school has clear CICO entry criteria (e.g., two ODRs in a month, low-level problem behavior not due

Committee, project, or initiative	Purpose	Outcome	Target group	Staff involved
Behavior support team	Address students who are engaging in problem behavior.	Provide teachers with interventions.	Students with repetitive behavior problems	School psychologist, principal, representative sample of staff
Schoolwide climate committee	Improve school climate.	Reduce behavior referrals, increase safety, and increase organization and understanding of school routines.	All students and staff	Principal, counselor, teachers, educational assistants
Discipline team	Provide negative consequences for inappropriate behavior.	Individual students receive disciplinary action as necessary.	Students with ODRs	Vice principal, counselor
School equity and social justice committee	Oversee activities to improve issues related to equity and social justice in the school.	Provide teachers with tools to implement caring circles in the classroom and provide the schoolwide climate committee with disaggregated discipline data.	All students	Principal, counselor, grade-level representation of teachers, educational assistants
After-school tutoring programs	Provide opportunity for help with homework and other tutoring needs.	Students receive small-group instruction in academic areas of need.	Students with specific academic needs	School counselor and interested teachers and staff

FIGURE 3.3. Sample Working Smarter, Not Harder Matrix. Matrix template reprinted with permission from George Sugai.

to poor academic performance across the day), the grade-level team with the support of the instructional coach (who is a member of the schoolwide behavior support team) can nominate a student for the CICO intervention. In these cases, we recommend that the school administrator, counselor, or psychologist also quickly review the data to ensure that entry criteria are met. The reason for using a grade-level versus a behavior support team as the entry point to CICO is to provide students who are at risk with quicker access to the intervention. Most behavior support teams meet biweekly and can be "full" with handling other cases when students are identified as at risk. Allowing more of the decision making to be made by the grade-level team with the support of an instructional coach and someone on the administrative team will typically allow for quicker access to the intervention.

In some schools, the behavior support team makes the decision for CICO placement. In these situations, it is recommended that schools create a referral form and standardize the referral process. More detailed information on student selection for CICO is provided in Chapter 7.

Referral Form

For schools that decide to use behavior support teams as the gateway to CICO, a referral or request for assistance form is used to access the behavior support team. An example of such a form is included in Appendix B.2. The referral form should include the student's name, the date, the name of the referring person, the reason for referral (i.e., description of problem[s]), the hypothesized reason for why the problem is occurring (i.e., What does the student gain by misbehaving? What skills is the student missing?), and the strategies tried thus far. There should be a place on the form to summarize relevant academic data (e.g., oral reading fluency scores) and behavior data (e.g., number of absences, tardies, interclass time-outs, phone calls to parents or to guardians/home contacts). All the faculty and staff within a building should be familiar with how to use the form to make a referral to the behavior support team. The referral forms should be easily accessible and, once completed, should be given to the person in charge of the behavior support team.

CICO Placement Decision

As discussed previously, not all students who are referred for CICO will be appropriate candidates for the intervention. School staff should also recognize that some students may have behavior that is so chronic or severe that it cannot be remedied by a simple intervention like CICO. These students will require more intensive, individualized behavior support (Crone et al., 2015).

Once a referral is received, the behavior support team decides if a student should be placed on the CICO intervention. If the student is an appropriate candidate, the grade-level team or behavior support team should secure parental or guardian consent for the intervention. (See Appendix B.3 for a sample copy of a parental permission form.)

Gathering Baseline Data and Signing Contracts

A powerful way to test the effectiveness of the CICO intervention for an individual student is to begin by collecting baseline data for 3 to 5 days. Baseline data can be collected during the time period that the team is waiting for parents to provide consent for participation. Baseline data is gathered by having the teacher rate the student's behavior on the DPR, but not provide verbal feedback to the student. The referring teacher is provided with a packet of three to five DPRs. During the baseline period, the student should not be aware that their behavior is being rated. Students do not check in or check out with the CICO coordinator during this time period.

Baseline data can help establish if a student truly needs the intervention, and can also be used to determine the daily point goals for the student. Moreover, baseline data provide a gauge for assessing a teacher's commitment to implementing the intervention. If the teacher is unwilling or sporadic in completing baseline DPRs, it is unlikely that they will follow through with the feedback, reinforcement, and other critical components of the CICO intervention. For middle and high school settings, teachers for each class period should be given DPRs, and the CICO coordinator should gather and summarize the baseline data.

Once consent for participation is obtained from the parent or guardian, it is recommended that the parents or guardians and the student sign a "contract" delineating each person's role in CICO implementation. In some schools, one document serves as both the parental contract and permission form.

CICO IMPLEMENTATION

In this book, we present a basic CICO process as well as ways to adapt the intervention to meet specific needs. Adaptations and elaborations to basic CICO are described in detail in Chapters 8 and 9. Typically, students are placed on basic CICO if they have attention-motivated problem behavior and/or if they find adult attention reinforcing. In some cases, basic CICO may prove to be ineffective or inadequate for a particular student, and the school staff should consider introducing modifications after a few weeks of implementation. Figure 3.4 presents a flowchart for deciding whether a student should participate in the CICO intervention and when to implement modifications to basic CICO or layer additional behavior support onto basic CICO.

The following section outlines the *basic* CICO process for an elementary and a middle school student. Information about how this basic CICO can be adapted for high school is presented in Chapter 11.

THE BASIC CICO INTERVENTION

There are critical features of the CICO process that must occur on a daily, biweekly, and quarterly basis. The daily features involve both the daily participation of the identified students and the day-to-day management and implementation of the system. On a biweekly basis the data should be summarized, reviewed, and used in making data-based decisions regarding whether the overall CICO intervention is working and its effect on individual students. On a quarterly basis, there should be a system for providing feedback to the teachers, staff, students, and parents on the impact of CICO. Feedback should include a discussion of the impact on individual students as well as on the overall school climate. This next section details the critical features that are necessary at each point in this process.

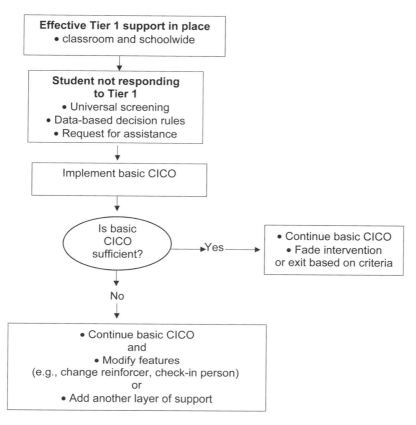

FIGURE 3.4. Flowchart for determining student participation in the CICO intervention.

DAILY FEATURES OF BASIC CICO

Each student on CICO starts and ends each day with a positive contact with an adult in the school and receives frequent monitoring and behavioral feedback throughout the day. In the morning, the students check in with the CICO coordinator. The CICO coordinator makes sure that each student has brought all the necessary materials for the day (e.g., pencil, paper, and assignment notebook) and reminds the student to follow the schoolwide expectations. In elementary schools, it is not as important to check for materials because students typically keep these school supplies in their desks or somewhere else in their classroom. The student picks up a DPR from the CICO coordinator and begins the school day. In each class, or at natural transition points throughout the day in elementary settings, the student checks in with the teacher and hands them the DPR. The teacher uses the DPR to rate the student's behavior within that class period (for middle and high school) or class activity (for elementary school). In this manner, the student receives continual behavioral feedback and prompting throughout the school day. In addition, the student is asked to reflect on their behavior throughout the school day, which begins the process of students learning to self-assess and self-regulate their behavior. It's *critical* for teachers to understand that the student who is on CICO needs feedback not only during the rating periods (e.g., at the end of the period), but also in between to know how they are progressing during the 60–90 minute time block. Continual feedback throughout the period is the active ingredient of the CICO intervention. At the end of the day, the student turns in the DPR to the CICO coordinator. A copy of the DPR is sent home for the student's parents or guardians to review and sign—a simple strategy for including daily home–school collaboration. It should be noted that some schools opt to send DPRs home weekly rather than daily to decrease the burden on parents of daily signing. Some schools prefer to email scanned copies of DPRs to save money on No Carbon Required (NCR) paper and because parents have requested electronic communication directly from the school.

Case Example of CICO in a Middle School Setting

Schools should identify a team to support CICO implementation. Due to personnel shortages, some schools have relied on one individual to coordinate the entire CICO intervention. In our experience, schools that adopt a team model to support CICO are more successful at implementing and maintaining the intervention than schools that depend on one person to build and sustain the program. Similar to the process of working with students requiring special education services, a team approach is effective in assessing progress on CICO, developing recommendations for modifications to the intervention, and planning for transition off CICO. Throughout this chapter, we assume that a team model is adopted for CICO management.

It is easiest to illustrate the CICO intervention by describing the entire process for a sample student. Our sample student is a seventh grader we will call Jeremy. He received seven ODRs the previous school year and two ODRs during the first few weeks of the current school year. Jeremy's referral summary for the previous school year is presented in Figure 3.5. According to his summary, Jeremy has a pattern of disruptive, off-task behavior in the classroom and mildly aggressive behavior toward peers. The majority of his problem behaviors occur in classroom settings. According to his teachers, problem behavior is more prevalent toward the end of the class period.

Based on the pattern of his behavior, the behavior support team decides that Jeremy would be a good candidate for CICO. Three requirements must be met prior to implementation of

Student Name: Jeremy Walker

Behavior	Time	Date	Location	Referral issued by:
Physical aggression	2:00	9/23	Gym	Gym teacher
Inappropriate language	8:30	10/12	Room 214	Homeroom teacher
Disruption/noncompliance	1:15	11/6	Art room	Art teacher
Inappropriate language	12:00	12/15	Room 226	Science teacher
Disruption/noncompliance	10:15	1/17	Music room	Music teacher
Physical aggression	9:00	2/15	Hallway	Assistant principal
Physical aggression	11:00	3/03	Room 124	LA teacher

FIGURE 3.5. Jeremy's referral summary for the previous school year.

the CICO intervention. First, baseline data must be gathered by his teachers, which begins the school day following the behavior support team meeting. Second, the CICO coordinator must obtain permission from Jeremy's parents. Third, the purpose and process of the CICO intervention must be explained to both Jeremy and his parents, and they must agree to actively participate.

The school counselor calls Jeremy's parents, describes the concerns with his behavior, and details how the team determined that CICO would be a good support for him. The counselor also shares the baseline data information with Jeremy's parents. Multiple teachers have communicated with Jeremy's parents prior to this occasion about their concerns with his behavior, so this phone call from the school counselor is not a surprise to them. His parents agree that CICO would be a positive support for Jeremy. They are eager to have him begin and are willing to cooperate and participate. The CICO coordinator and school counselor meet with Jeremy to describe the CICO intervention and secure his willingness to participate in the intervention. Jeremy is hesitant to try CICO, but knows that his behavior is causing him problems in multiple classes and ultimately decides to give it a try. Consent forms are sent home that day, are signed by his parents, and are returned the following day.

Jeremy's baseline data show that he is meeting behavioral expectations 50–60% of the time. It is likely that he would benefit from the additional feedback and reinforcement provided by CICO. Prior to intervention, the roles and responsibilities of each participant—Jeremy, his parents, and the school—are discussed. The CICO coordinator meets with Jeremy to provide him with training on where to check in/check out, how to request feedback from teachers, and other critical components of basic CICO. (For more detailed information on CICO training for students, refer to Chapter 5). Finally, a daily point goal for Jeremy is agreed upon.

The goal for most students on the CICO intervention is to receive 80% of the total points per day. Given that Jeremy averaged 50–60% of daily points during the baseline period (without feedback or reinforcement), 80% of daily points is considered a realistic goal. It is important that the initial point goal is set at a level that the student can reasonably achieve. The student must experience success with CICO at the initiation of the intervention (i.e., within the first week) or their commitment and interest in the program will rapidly dissolve. For some students to be successful on CICO, a lower initial point goal (e.g., 60% of the total points) may be necessary. The point goal can be increased as the student demonstrates success. Baseline data will help you determine which goals are realistic.

At the end of Jeremy's meeting with the CICO coordinator and school counselor, he is given an opportunity to ask and receive answers for any remaining questions. Jeremy begins the CICO intervention the following day.

The school day begins at 8:30 in the morning. Students can complete the CICO check-in between 8:00 and 8:30. At 8:00 A.M., the CICO coordinator opens the doors to the counseling office, and the CICO students begin to arrive. Because the students view CICO as positive support, not punishment, many bring their friends to morning check-in (some friends even ask if they can be put on the CICO intervention!). The students who have been on the CICO intervention for a week or more are familiar with the routine. Morning check-in usually proceeds smoothly and efficiently because the routine is so predictable.

Jeremy arrives on time the first morning and is greeted by the CICO coordinator, who is one of the school's educational assistants (i.e., paraprofessional). She commends Jeremy for remembering where and when to show up. Every day, each student picks up a new DPR. Jeremy takes a DPR. The cards are printed on duplicate paper so that one copy can go home to his parents to sign, while the original copy is kept for school records. An example of Jeremy's DPR is presented in Figure 3.6. (A blank version of this form is included in Appendix B.4, and a second example of a middle school DPR is included in Appendix B.5).

This middle school has a block schedule with "A" days (first, second, third, homeroom, and fourth period) and "B" days (fifth, sixth, seventh, homeroom, and eighth period). For schools that do not have block schedules, all periods should be given a separate column on the DPR. Before leaving the check-in room, Jeremy puts his name and the date on the DPR. Next, the CICO coordinator checks to make sure that Jeremy has all of the materials he will need for the day. Jeremy opens his backpack to show her that he has loose-leaf paper, a pencil, a pen, and his assignment notebook/planner. If students arrive in the morning without all of their necessary materials, the CICO coordinator provides them with a few sheets of paper or pencils and pens, as needed. Students are reminded and encouraged to come to school prepared the next day. After Jeremy has completed check-in, he is sent off with a prompt to have a good day and to follow the expectations listed on his DPR.

Often, the students are given "Thumbs-Up!" tickets for checking in responsibly and being prepared with their materials. Thumbs-Up! tickets are part of a token economy system set up by the school to encourage support of the five schoolwide expectations. All students in the building have the opportunity to earn Thumbs-Up! tickets throughout the day for demonstrating appropriate behavior. Students can trade in their Thumbs-Up! tickets for items (such as pens, pencils, other school supplies, water bottles, T-shirts, sweatshirts) from the school store. Smaller items "cost" fewer tickets, while larger items "cost" more tickets. A sample Thumbs-Up! ticket is illustrated in Figure 3.7. (A blank version can be found in Appendix B.6.)

Once Jeremy leaves check-in, he has a few minutes before school starts. At the beginning of each class period, Jeremy gives the DPR to his teacher. All the teachers in the school have participated in an inservice training on CICO, so each teacher knows how to respond to Jeremy's entry into each period. When a student brings a DPR to a teacher, it serves as an opportunity for the teacher to offer a brief positive comment or prepare the student for the class. Often this is the time when teachers will remind students of behaviors they are working on, for example, "Yesterday you had a difficult time completing your work. Let's just try harder today." At the end of the class period, the teacher rates Jeremy on a scale of 0–2 for how well he did for each behavioral expectation. A "2" means "Yes"; the student met the behavioral goal. A "1" means the student did "So-So," and a "0" means "No," the student did not meet that goal for that class period. Jeremy gives his DPR to each teacher throughout the day.

Teachers are encouraged to explain their choice of ratings to the students and to praise them on days when they meet or come close to meeting their behavioral goals (they receive 2's on most of the goals). Teachers are also encouraged to periodically hand out Thumbs-Up! tickets to students who meet all the behavioral goals in one class period. In this way, the CICO student receives continual feedback and prompting, as well as frequent reinforcement for appropriate behavior. In addition, doing poorly in one class does not ruin the rest of the day for the student. Each class period is a clean slate—a new chance to meet behavioral goals.

At the end of the day, Jeremy returns his DPR to the CICO coordinator. Both check-in and check-out are in the same location, so the routine is predictable. The CICO coordinator keeps

Daily Progress Report—Middle School, Example 1

(A- Day)   B-Day

Name: _Jeremy Walker_   Date: _11/19_

Teachers: Please indicate YES (2), So-So (1), or No (0) regarding the student's achievement for the following goals.

Goals	1/5	2/6	3/7	HR	4/8
Be respectful	~~2~~ 1 0	2 ~~1~~ 0	~~2~~ 1 0	~~2~~ 1 0	2 ~~1~~ 0
Be responsible	~~2~~ 1 0	2 ~~1~~ 0	~~2~~ 1 0	~~2~~ 1 0	~~2~~ 1 0
Keep hands and feet to self	2 ~~1~~ 0	~~2~~ 1 0	2 1 ~~0~~	~~2~~ 1 0	2 ~~1~~ 0
Follow directions	2 ~~1~~ 0	~~2~~ 1 0	2 ~~1~~ 0	~~2~~ 1 0	~~2~~ 1 0
Be there— be ready	~~2~~ 1 0	~~2~~ 1 0	~~2~~ 1 0	~~2~~ 1 0	~~2~~ 1 0
TOTAL POINTS	8	8	7	10	8
TEACHER INITIALS	A.K.	B.D.	R.S.	J.T.	B.L.

CICO Daily Goal   40/ 50   CICO Daily Score   41/ 50

In training _____   CICO Member _X_   _Jeremy Walker_
                                              Student signature

Teacher comments: Please state briefly any specific behaviors or achievements that demonstrate the student's progress. (If additional space is required, please attach a note and indicate so below.)

Period 1/5 _Behavior is improving!_

Period 2/6 _____

Period 3/7 _____

Homeroom _Excellent behavior today!_

Period 4/8 _____

Parent/Caregiver Signature: _Angel Walker_

Parent/Caregiver Comments: _Keep up the good work!_

FIGURE 3.6. An example of Jeremy's middle school DPR.

```
┌─────────────────────────────────────────────────────────────┐
│                      THUMBS-UP! TICKET                        │
│                                                               │
│   Student name:    ___Jeremy Walker_____    │
│   Issued by:       ___Teacher_____    │
│   Date:            ___11/16_____    │
│                                                               │
│                        WAY TO GO!                             │
│                                                               │
└─────────────────────────────────────────────────────────────┘
```

FIGURE 3.7. A sample Thumbs-Up! ticket.

the top copy and sends the second copy home with Jeremy for his parents. Check-out goes quickly, because many students must get on the bus. However, it provides another opportunity for a positive adult contact. It also provides an opportunity to prompt Jeremy again for appropriate behavior. In this school, if students have met their goal for the day, they are allowed to select a small snack (candy, juice, crackers, etc.) to take with them. Other schools have different reinforcement systems. You should design one that works for your school (see Chapter 6 for suggestions on designing reinforcement systems).

Jeremy is expected to give the copy of his DPR to his parents, and they are expected to ask for it. There is a place on the DPR for the parents to make positive comments and to sign it, before it can be returned. Jeremy returns the copy of the DPR to the CICO coordinator the next morning at check-in. This is a very simple way to increase the communication and collaboration between home and school—something that is always critical, but especially so during the middle school years.

One of the CICO coordinator's responsibilities is to enter the daily CICO data into a database. It is critical that the school reserve enough time each week for the CICO coordinator to accomplish this task. The CICO coordinator collects the daily CICO data and enters the *percentage* of points (*not* the total number of points) earned into a database for all of the CICO students. This should be done at least on a weekly, if not on a daily basis, or it is easy to fall behind.

The daily percentage point data can be graphed to illustrate each individual student's progress on CICO. Students are typically held to a goal criterion of 80% of total possible points (note that schools may choose different expectations for goal attainment). For example, if 50 points are possible throughout the day, students have met their goal if they have received 40 or more points. Students who fall below this criterion have not met their goal. If a student goes for several days without meeting their goal, or if the student's performance is highly variable, the staff should consider it as a red flag and should investigate possibly modifying the intervention or increasing support for a particular student.

Figure 3.8 illustrates Jeremy's CICO data for the first week, as well as his baseline data. It appears that Jeremy struggled in the beginning of the week, but by Thursday he had begun to meet his goal of 80% of points. From these data, the behavior support team might conclude that Jeremy is beginning to adjust to the CICO intervention and that he has the potential to benefit from it. The team will continue to monitor and examine his daily data for patterns of behavioral success or struggle.

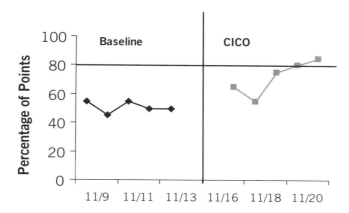

FIGURE 3.8. Jeremy's baseline data and data from the first week of CICO implementation.

Case Example in an Elementary School Setting

For students in elementary school, the CICO intervention is quite similar, but the DPR differs. The DPR reflects the natural transitions of elementary school classrooms (such as the transition between reading and math), versus changes in class periods for middle and high school students. The behavioral goals need to be written in a manner that is understandable for younger students. These students may require visuals (e.g., smiley faces, thumbs-up pictures) to make it clear when goals are met and not met. Two examples of DPRs for the elementary school level are included in Appendices B.7 and B.8.

Younger students may also need more practice and support to learn the routine of the CICO intervention. Students will not always remember to get their DPR in the morning or to check out in the afternoon. The CICO coordinator should provide the necessary support for students who are new to the intervention.

To demonstrate the differences between the CICO intervention at the middle and the elementary school levels, we present a second example, that of Marisa Fernandez, a third-grade student. Marisa attends New Hope Elementary School, which has had a CICO-type intervention in place for 3 years. This is the first year that Marisa has attended this school because she transferred midyear from an elementary school across town.

Marisa's school records are late in arriving, so for the first 3 weeks of her attendance, New Hope has no information about her academic or behavioral performance. However, by the fourth day of school Marisa is already demonstrating frequent, repetitive behavioral problems. She has trouble finishing tasks, she gets into arguments with her female classmates on the playground, and she frequently talks out while the teacher is presenting a lesson. Marisa's teacher, Mr. Lee, makes a request for assistance from the behavior support team.

After reviewing Mr. Lee's request for assistance, the behavior support team agrees that Marisa would be a good CICO candidate. Currently, there are only eight other students on the intervention, so an additional student can be easily accommodated. In addition to reducing her behavioral problems, the CICO intervention will help Marisa become better integrated into the school. She will meet more of the New Hope staff, and she will be taught the behavioral expectations at the school. She will also have positive adult contacts on a daily basis.

Before Marisa can begin CICO, the school counselor must obtain permission from her parents. Also, as in middle school settings, baseline data should be collected. Additionally, the purpose and process of the CICO intervention must be explained to Marisa and her parents. Both of Marisa's parents are Spanish speaking, with limited English language skills. New Hope Elementary has a high percentage of EL (English learner) students as well as staff who are bilingual in Spanish and English. Because Marisa is new to the school and an explanation of CICO will require the use of a translator, the behavior support team decides to hold an in-person meeting to explain the intervention to her parents and Marisa. Mr. Romero, the EL teacher for the primary grades, is asked to attend the meeting between the school counselor, the CICO coordinator, Marisa, and her parents. Mr. Romero is able to act as an interpreter and can address any concerns or questions Marisa's parents have.

Initially, Marisa's parents feel reluctant to have Marisa start the CICO intervention. They are afraid that she is being identified as a "bad student." By working together, the school counselor and Mr. Romero are able to help them understand that CICO will be a positive support rather than a punishment for Marisa. In the end, both parents agree to have Marisa begin the intervention. After learning that there will be opportunities to earn rewards, Marisa is excited to begin. The CICO coordinator initiates the intervention for Marisa on the next school day.

Following the meeting with her parents and prior to beginning the intervention, Mrs. Saborski, the CICO coordinator, who has been hired part-time to manage CICO, gives Marisa a "CICO tour." That is, the afternoon before Marisa begins, Mrs. Saborski walks her through each element of the intervention. She shows Marisa where to go for check-in the next morning, and where she will pick up her DPR. She walks with Marisa to her classroom to practice giving the DPR to the teacher. By the end of the tour, Marisa feels comfortable with the new intervention.

At New Hope Elementary, the school day begins at 8:15 A.M. Students can do the CICO check-in between 7:55 and 8:15. Students are instructed to come to the library for check-in. At 7:55 A.M., Mrs. Saborski opens the doors to the library. Six of the nine CICO students check in with her between 7:55 and 8:15. The remaining three students are in kindergarten or first grade. Mrs. Saborski will go to their classrooms immediately after the 8:15 bell and check in with them individually. She found that it was difficult for the youngest children to remember to come to the library first, and that they would often be late to class when they arrived for the check-in before class. The students in second through fifth grades appear to have no difficulty with checking in.

When Marisa arrives for check-in, she is shy and unsure. Mrs. Saborski asks one of the other CICO students to help Marisa. The other student reminds her where to pick up her new DPR and then stands in line with her. An example of a DPR used in Marisa's elementary school is included in Figure 3.9.

When it is Marisa's turn to check in, Mrs. Saborski praises her for remembering to come to the library. She shows Marisa where the schoolwide expectations are listed on her DPR and has Marisa read the expectations to her. With Mrs. Saborski's help, Marisa writes the date at the top of her DPR. Because most elementary school students have supplies in their classrooms, check-in does not include asking students if they have their materials. Like the other students, Marisa is given a "Chuckie-Buck" for checking in on time (Chuckie, an owl, is the school's mascot). Chuckie-Bucks are part of the schoolwide recognition and reward program at New Hope. Students can put their names on the Chuckie-Bucks and put them in the raffle box at the entrance to the school. Every Friday, the principal draws five names from the raffle box, and each of those

Daily Progress Report

Name: _____   2 = Good Points earned: _____

Date: _____   1 = OK   Goal: _____ Goal reached? Yes No

0 = Needs Improvement

GOALS	Reading	Math	Music	Art	Library	P.E.	Title I
Be Responsible	2 1 0	2 1 0	2 1 0	2 1 0	2 1 0	2 1 0	2 1 0
Be Kind	2 1 0	2 1 0	2 1 0	2 1 0	2 1 0	2 1 0	2 1 0
Work Hard	2 1 0	2 1 0	2 1 0	2 1 0	2 1 0	2 1 0	2 1 0
Total Points							

POSITIVE Teacher notes: _____

POSITIVE Parent notes: _____

Parent/guardian signature: _____

Please sign and have your child return this form on a daily basis.

FIGURE 3.9. Example of a DPR used in Marisa's elementary school.

students receives a special prize. After Marisa has completed her check-in, she is sent to class with a prompt to be on time and to meet the schoolwide behavioral expectations for the day.

Once Marisa leaves, she has a few minutes before school starts. She goes directly to her third-grade classroom and is greeted by her teacher. Mr. Lee knows that Marisa is going to begin the CICO intervention that day. He congratulates her on her good start and shows her how to put her card in the box for DPRs on his desk. Mr. Lee waits for natural breaks in the flow of classroom activity to go over Marisa's DPR with her after each classroom transition. For example, after the students have completed morning activities, they begin their reading block. Marisa begins with silent reading. At this time, Mr. Lee talks with Marisa about the points she earned during morning activities.

The rating scale for elementary school students can be different than for middle school students. In Marisa's case, the teacher circles a "2" if Marisa has met her goal and a "0" if she has not. All teachers at New Hope, including the specialist teachers (e.g., music, art), have participated in an inservice CICO training, so Marisa is able to bring her DPR with her to each activity she attends throughout the day.

As in middle schools, teachers are encouraged to explain their ratings to the students and to give them positive praise or Chuckie-Bucks when a student meets all their goals for the class period or for the school day. Students are encouraged to reflect on their own performance, but are taught that arguing with the teacher when a lower rating is given is considered a "nonexample" of expected behavior on the CICO intervention. If a student disputes a teacher rating, the teacher has been trained not to engage the student in a discussion regarding whether the rating should be changed. The teacher's rating is the final rating. In addition, we have found that using the language "based on your behavior, you earned," versus "based on your behavior,

I am going to give you," puts the ownership of the rating on the student's behavior rather than on the teacher.

At the end of the day, Mrs. Saborski comes to each CICO student's classroom to pick up the DPR and say good-bye. The students do not meet her in the library for check-out because of concern that some students might miss their bus. Mrs. Saborski is able to check out with each student, because there are a limited number of students on the intervention and because the check-out portion of the CICO is very brief. The check-out portion of the CICO is another chance for the students to have some positive time with a caring adult. Mrs. Saborski keeps the top copy of the DPR and makes sure that Marisa puts the second copy of her card in her backpack.

Marisa's parents have been instructed to look for her DPR in her backpack when she arrives home. When Marisa gets home, her parents review the DPR. Her parents are asked to sign the form and tell Marisa to return it the next day. They are also encouraged to write positive comments on it. Their comments can be written in Spanish, their first language. If there is any trouble interpreting the comments, Mr. Romero is able to assist.

After Mrs. Saborski completes check-out for the day, she enters the CICO data into a database. It is important to keep up with this on at least a weekly basis, as it is critical that data are used by the behavior support team to evaluate the effectiveness of the intervention. Also, either the behavior support team or the CICO coordinator should be responsible for reporting progress to the staff and parents about the overall effectiveness of the intervention. Teachers want to know that their efforts are making a difference. There are many creative ways to acknowledge their work at an elementary school, one of which we discuss in greater detail as a quarterly feature in a later section. It is up to the principal and the behavior support team to identify the strategy that works best for their school.

BIWEEKLY FEATURES

The power of the CICO resides in two critical elements of the intervention: first, providing continual, specific feedback and positive behavioral support to a student throughout the day, and, second, using data to make decisions. Once the data have been collected on a daily basis, it is critical to use these data for more than just a written record. It is easiest to utilize the CICO data if one or two people are responsible for entering the information into a database on a regular basis. That is, at the end of each day, or at least at the end of each week, the CICO coordinator, or a behavior support team member, enters the percentage of points earned by each student into a CICO database.

Whatever data system is used to analyze student progress (more information on data systems is provided in Chapter 7), the system should graph the data in real time so that data are readily available for school staff to determine student response to the intervention. One of the biweekly features of CICO is the need for school staff to determine if students (1) are responding and should continue basic CICO, (2) need more behavior support or a modification to basic CICO, or (3) are ready to graduate from the intervention. These decisions are based on the graphed data of each student's percentage of points (see the sample graph presented in Figure 3.8). Many schools we work with embed these decisions in an already existing biweekly team that meets to discuss behavior support. Other models we've seen include the CICO coordinator and a member of the school leadership group (e.g., principal, vice principal) who evaluates student progress using data-based decision rules that were developed during the CICO intervention plan development. For example, a data-based decision rule could require that, if on average students who receive 80% of points or more for 4 weeks are ready to graduate, the CICO coordinator and principal could look at the data biweekly to determine who is ready to graduate. Another data-based decision rule may require that if students have not met their goal on 30% of days, additional support or modification of basic CICO should be considered. Detailed information about how to make data-based decisions with CICO data can be found in Chapter 7.

Quarterly Features

The critical quarterly features of the CICO intervention are providing feedback to the teachers and staff as well as to the students and their families. It is important to provide feedback to these two stakeholder groups for the following reasons: (1) to acknowledge the right of parents, staff, and students to be informed about their school or their child; (2) to maintain interest and involvement; (3) to recognize and encourage accomplishments; and (4) to point out needed areas of improvement (new goals) and achieve collaboration in meeting those goals.

Feedback to Teachers and Staff

Teachers and staff need to know how well the CICO intervention is working. Some questions that can be answered include:

How many students have been served on it?
Is there consistent participation from students?
Is there consistent participation from the teachers and staff?
What has been the impact on individual student behavior?
What has been the impact on the overall school climate?
What has been working well?
What is still presenting obstacles?
How can the teachers and staff contribute to improving the CICO intervention?
Which students deserve recognition?
Which teachers and staff members deserve recognition and appreciation?

The behavior support team can be creative about how to provide this feedback to the staff and families. One school created a bulletin called "The CICO Gazette" that was distributed to the staff on a quarterly basis. The bulletin listed the students on CICO (identified by first name only) with a brief indication of their progress, provided reminders about meetings, and gave helpful hints on basic behavior management.

The bulletin can be distributed to the teachers, staff, and CICO families. It is important to preserve confidentiality, so individual students should not be mentioned by their full names unless they and their parents have given their express written consent. This is true even if the student is to be recognized for improvement. Remember, while it is exciting to be recognized for one's accomplishments, not all students may want to be publicly associated with a Tier 2 behavior intervention.

Another way to provide feedback to the teachers and staff is at staff meetings. The CICO coordinator or other representative of the behavior support team can give a report on the CICO intervention and its impact. Students and families can be provided with individual feedback at parent–teacher conferences. Both methods of providing feedback are convenient because both sets of meetings are already incorporated into the school's operating system. The behavior support team takes advantage of existing meetings to achieve this important purpose.

Some schools prefer to update students and families on a monthly basis by giving students a copy of their graph and sending another copy of the graph home to parents. This is a low-cost method to keep both parents and students involved in the intervention.

TROUBLESHOOTING PROBLEMS WITH IMPLEMENTATION OF BASIC CICO

Thus far, we have provided information on how basic CICO works when it runs smoothly. Students check in on a regular basis, take the DPR to their teachers throughout the day, and check out in the afternoon. Students remember to get their DPRs signed by their parents. This trouble-free scenario is not the case for all students. An important aspect of effectively implementing the CICO intervention involves modifying the intervention when it is not working for specific students or when the student is not participating in the program. Adaptations and elaborations to basic CICO are discussed in Chapters 8–11.

CHAPTER 4

Getting a CICO Intervention Started

Before implementing the CICO intervention, schools need to ensure that they are well organized and are proceeding with implementation systematically. It is critical to lay a strong foundation on which to build a sustainable intervention rather than to rush haphazardly into implementation. School administrators and the behavior support team should confirm that all the critical prerequisites are in place to produce an effective intervention that will be maintained over time. Getting carried away with the desire to "implement change now" when the necessary groundwork has not been laid will likely result in an unsatisfactory outcome; that is, no one knows what to do, how to do it, why they are doing it, or what to expect from it. Once an intervention has been tried and has failed, it can be very challenging to convince teachers and staff to give it a second chance. It is critical to demonstrate effectiveness and efficiency from the beginning of CICO implementation.

"IS MY SCHOOL READY TO IMPLEMENT CICO?"

Begin by assessing whether the school, as a whole, is committed to contributing to the successful implementation of the CICO intervention. The CICO Implementation Readiness Questionnaire (see Figure 4.1 and Appendix C.1) lists the critical features that must be in place for successful CICO implementation. The team of individuals who will be leading the implementation should complete this questionnaire together. An administrator must be included on the team to ensure administrative support for CICO implementation.

The team should be able to answer "Yes" to each question *prior* to CICO implementation. In addition, the team should be able to provide evidence that supports their responses. For example, if the team members answer "Yes" to question 2 regarding staff commitment, then the team should be able to supply concrete evidence of that commitment:

Was the CICO system discussed at a staff meeting?
Were the staff polled regarding their interest and willingness to support CICO?
Did 80% or more of the staff agree to support the intervention?
Can staff members accurately articulate their personal responsibilities in CICO implementation?

In our experience, schools that have implemented a schoolwide approach to PBIS are in a better position to successfully implement the CICO intervention than schools without such Tier 1 prevention for behavior support. Without a schoolwide PBIS system, too much time is spent on managing individual student behavior problems, and the Tier 2 intervention becomes overwhelmed and ineffective. In addition to Tier 1 schoolwide PBIS, schools should have a documented Tier 1 system at the classroom level. That is, teachers should have explicitly taught what the schoolwide expectations look like in the classroom and the typical transitions and routines, such as how to ask for help, turning in homework, and the voice levels expected during work periods.

Is your school ready to implement CICO? Prior to the implementation of CICO, it is recommended that the following features be in place. Please circle the answer that best describes your school at this time.

 Yes No 1. Our school has a schoolwide Tier 1 positive behavioral interventions and supports system in place. In essence, we have decided on three to five rules and have explicitly taught the rules to all students. We provide rewards to students for following the rules and provide mild consequences for rule infractions.

 Yes No 2. Our teachers are implementing Tier 1 classroom management strategies, including explicitly teaching what schoolwide expectations look like in the classroom, teaching classroom routines (e.g., how to ask for help, where to turn in homework, appropriate noise levels based on activities), having a high positive-to-negative ratio of praise to negative feedback, and engaging students with multiple opportunities to respond.

 Yes No 3. We have secured staff commitment for the implementation of CICO. The majority of the staff agree that this intervention is needed to support students at risk for serious problem behavior, and they are willing to actively participate in the intervention.

 Yes No 4. There is administrative support for the implementation of the CICO intervention. The administrative staff are committed to implementing and maintaining CICO in our school. Administrators have allocated the necessary financial and staff resources to support implementation of the program.

Yes No 5. There have been no major recent changes in the school system that could hinder successful implementation of the CICO intervention. Major changes include developments, such as teacher strikes, high teacher or administrative turnover, or a major increase or decrease in funding.

Yes No 6. We have made implementation of the CICO intervention one of the school's top three priorities for this school year.

FIGURE 4.1. Sample completed CICO Implementation Readiness Questionnaire.

Along with staff agreement, administrative commitment is crucial. Administrators must be willing to participate in the development and operation of the CICO intervention. They should be willing and able to allocate the necessary personnel and financial resources to adequately support implementation. Administrators should monitor the effectiveness of the intervention and encourage the behavior support team to make improvements as necessary.

Our experience in schools has taught us that implementing new interventions or attempting to change school systems is unlikely to result in success if the school itself is in the midst of significant change (e.g., teachers are threatening to strike, there is a high turnover of administrative or teaching staff). When implemented consistently, CICO is a powerful system for supporting students who are at risk for more serious forms of problem behavior (e.g., Fairbanks, Sugai, Guardino, & Lathrop, 2007; Hawken, 2006; Hawken & Horner, 2003; March & Horner, 2002). If the intervention is implemented incorrectly or attempts are made to change a system that is unstable, implementation of CICO is more likely to be unsuccessful.

Commitment to too many projects at the same time is another threat to the successful implementation of the CICO intervention. For example, a school may choose to implement CICO, adopt a new reading curriculum, and initiate an onsite mental health clinic in the same year. With so many large projects beginning at once, the energy and effort necessary to build and sustain an effective CICO intervention may become too diluted to be effective. Thus, we recommend that implementation of CICO be one of the school's top three priorities and that it only occur when the school is not initiating multiple new, major projects in the same year.

"HOW DO WE BUILD SCHOOLWIDE COMMITMENT TO THE CICO INTERVENTION?"

Establishing schoolwide commitment to the CICO intervention is critical to ensuring its success. The CICO intervention is implemented across all school settings, so the majority (at least 80%) of school staff must agree to participate in the intervention. If you are a school psychologist, counselor, behavior specialist, or other person who is trying to facilitate CICO implementation, begin by meeting with the principal and other administrators to introduce CICO and determine their level of interest.

Once administrator support has been secured, information about CICO should be brought to the school-based team responsible for responding to students with academic and behavioral difficulties. If there is commitment at the team level, this team should present CICO to the whole faculty during a regularly scheduled faculty meeting. During this faculty meeting, it is essential that the administrator or a team member provide a convincing explanation for why CICO is needed by this school at this time. We recommend that the administrator share ODR data with the staff as one means of demonstrating the need for a Tier 2 intervention. Additionally, staff surveys may indicate that a majority of the staff identified Tier 2 interventions as a critical need in the school, and these data could also be shared.

When attempting to cultivate schoolwide commitment to the CICO intervention, we have found it very helpful to show the DVD *Check-In, Check-Out: A Tier 2 Intervention for Students at Risk, Second Edition* (Hawken & Breen, 2017, available at *www.guilford.com*). This DVD illustrates the critical components of the CICO intervention in a 27-minute video.

After the team has shown the CICO DVD or has thoroughly explained the CICO intervention in a different manner, the team should provide a detailed account of the responsibilities of each teacher who participates in the CICO intervention. Once staff members have received information about CICO and the expectations for their involvement, we recommend that the whole staff vote on whether or not they are willing to participate in the intervention. See Appendix C.2 for a CICO intervention voting form.

After the staff have voted, a team member should tally the votes and determine if at least 80% of the staff have agreed to participate. If not, the administrator and other team members must engage in additional consensus building. If only a small percentage of the staff are willing to support CICO, the intervention will fail. The staff must wholeheartedly agree that there is a need for CICO at their school, and they must be willing to actively participate.

THE CICO DEVELOPMENT AND IMPLEMENTATION GUIDE

After establishing that the school is ready to implement the CICO intervention, the behavior support team should meet, for at least a half day or an entire school day (typically during a professional development day), to create CICO for the school. The CICO Development and Implementation Guide (see Appendix C.3) provides the structure for developing and individualizing CICO to fit within the culture of the school. The team should work together to develop procedures and systems in answer to each question on the guide. Procedures and systems should be in place prior to beginning the CICO intervention with any one student.

Personnel Considerations

Adequate personnel time should be assigned to implement, manage, and maintain the intervention. Some schools choose to hire an educational assistant (i.e., paraprofessional) part-time to lead CICO or assign CICO to an educational assistant as part of their overall responsibilities. Responsibility for CICO intervention must be part of a person's job description, not an added responsibility without time allocated to do the job effectively. The CICO coordinator must have no other work commitments in the half hour before school begins and after school ends. The CICO coordinator should be highly regarded by the students and interact positively and warmly with them. It is important to designate a supervisor for the CICO coordinator, such as a counselor or school psychologist who has experience in behavior intervention. The CICO coordinator typically requires ongoing training to work with students on CICO, and the supervisor should provide this training. More information about training needs is provided in Chapter 5.

In order to support more students, some schools have decided to hire a CICO coordinator who oversees the intervention and select other school staff to serve as CICO facilitators. The role of the CICO facilitator is to check in and out 5 to 10 students daily. The facilitator is not responsible for aggregating the data, and may not be involved in administering longer-term rewards, but rather is the "cheerleader" for the students with whom they work. In this scenario, the CICO coordinator oversees the facilitators, gathers data from them, and summarizes the data for decision making. The CICO coordinator may also be responsible for checking in and

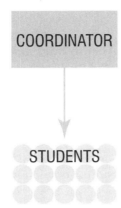

FIGURE 4.2. CICO model with one coordinator for multiple students throughout school.

out a certain number of students each day along with the CICO facilitators. Figure 4.2 shows the model of one CICO coordinator who is responsible for multiple students throughout the school building, and Figure 4.3 shows an example of one CICO coordinator and multiple CICO facilitators.

The behavior support team should identify one or two substitutes to conduct check-in and check-out if the CICO coordinator is unavailable on a given day. It is disappointing for students to arrive at school expecting to see the CICO coordinator and to find that the coordinator is out sick for the day. Substitutes for the CICO coordinator may be the coordinator's supervisor, a special education teacher, a vice principal, or another educational assistant. This person should also have a flexible work schedule before and after school.

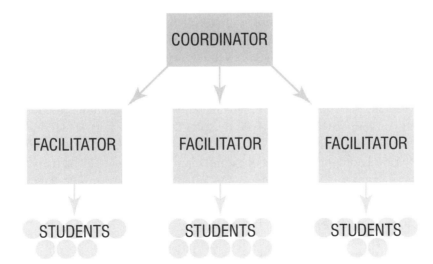

FIGURE 4.3. CICO model with one coordinator and multiple CICO facilitators.

Location

The behavior support team should identify a location for check-in and check-out that is in a central, easily accessible area. At the same time, the setting should be semiprivate. Middle and high school students often prefer to avoid drawing attention to their involvement in an intervention. Conversely, elementary-age students often become excited about the intervention when they realize that students on CICO receive extra attention from the CICO coordinator. The check-in/check-out location must fit with the logistics of your school. It can be located in the counselor's office, library, vice principal's office, or any other room that works well for the school. If schools are using the model with one CICO coordinator and multiple CICO facilitators, there may be multiple locations for checking in and out. This is particularly important in large schools, such as high schools, where the location of the check-in is closer to the student's grade level that is being served versus one that is centrally located.

Developing a user-friendly DPR is important for successful implementation of CICO. The DPR is a tool for teachers to provide quick feedback on the student's behavior throughout the day. DPRs should not require teachers to write long narratives about the student's behavior, but rather provide simple, numerical ratings of behavior. We strongly recommend that schools include their schoolwide expectations on the DPR to provide additional practice and feedback for these students who need it most. More detailed information about designing DPRs is provided in Chapter 6.

Reinforcement System

A critical component of the CICO intervention is to regularly provide reinforcement for appropriate behavior. Reinforcement for students who display chronic behavior problems is controversial for some school personnel. Many staff members have asked, "Why should students who are engaging in problem behavior be targeted to receive extra acknowledgment and reinforcement?" Since students who qualify for CICO support have not made progress with the schoolwide Tier 1 prevention efforts, universally implemented strategies are not effective or adequate for them. Therefore, these students need additional reinforcement and feedback to get their behavior on the right track. Experience tells us that if we do not intervene early with problem behavior, the behavior will worsen over time.

In developing a reinforcement system for the CICO intervention, it is important to emphasize the social aspects of the intervention. This includes increasing adult attention and can also involve utilizing reinforcers that increase positive peer attention. In order to reduce the expense of reinforcers, we recommend using reinforcers that do not incur a financial cost (e.g., spending time with a preferred adult or friend, or engaging in an easily accessible activity, such as additional computer or gym time). More information about developing an effective reinforcement system is provided in Chapter 6.

Referral System

In Chapter 3, we described the students who are appropriate candidates for the CICO intervention. The behavior support team should develop a school-specific referral system prior to

CICO implementation. The team should identify the decision criteria for assigning students to the intervention. A parental permission form should be created if the school determines that a signed permission is required for entry into the intervention. Finally, the team should identify the decision criteria for determining if students who received CICO support during the previous school year should be placed on the CICO intervention at the beginning of the following school year. Most schools prefer to allow students time to become acquainted with their new teachers and classroom(s) before beginning CICO. At times, a change in classroom or teacher results in a significant difference in students' behavior, and they no longer need the support of CICO. The goal is not to wait for the student to fail (i.e., not provide CICO support until they engage in problem behavior), but rather to first allow the new teacher (or teachers) an opportunity to get to know the student and offer behavior support within the classroom.

System to Manage Data and Fade Intervention

During the professional development day or half day, the behavior support team must also decide how to summarize and graph the daily data. In Chapter 7, we describe computer program options for summarizing data. Once the data are evaluated on a regular basis, the team will need to decide when it is appropriate to fade students off the intervention. Sometimes, the end of the school year serves as a natural fade period for the students, and they do not receive CICO support the following school year. Additionally, given that only a limited number of students can be supported on CICO at one time, it is important to systematically fade students off the intervention once they have been successful and demonstrated that they no longer need the support. Detailed information on fading students off the CICO intervention is provided in Chapter 7.

System to Address Training Needs

The final questions from the CICO Development and Implementation Guide are related to staff, student, and parent training needs. Each person who participates or contributes to the intervention must deeply understand and agree to their responsibilities. A comprehensive plan for addressing training needs is presented in Chapter 5.

A completed sample version of the CICO Development and Implementation Guide is presented in Figure 4.4.

BUDGET

The budget for initial and sustained implementation of the CICO intervention will vary, depending on the size of the school, the number of students involved, and the amount of employee hours needed for check-in/check-out, data entry, team meeting coordination, and other CICO coordinator tasks. Our goal is not to stipulate a specific dollar amount needed to implement the CICO intervention, but to suggest typical budget categories and offer at least one operating model budget. The key message is that adequate resources must be allocated to support and maintain successful implementation of the CICO.

1. Determine personnel needs and logistics.
   - Who will be the CICO coordinator? Will there be one CICO coordinator OR one CICO coordinator with multiple CICO facilitators?
   Ms. Gomez—ELL paraprofessional

   - Who will supervise the CICO coordinator?
   Mrs. Carroll—school psychologist

   - Who will check students in and out when the coordinator is absent? (Name **at least two** people who can substitute for the coordinator.)
   Mr. Singh—special ed. teacher, Mrs. Hannon—counselor

   - Where will check-in and check-out occur?
   Small room outside Mrs. Carroll's office

   - What is the maximum number of students that can be served on CICO at one time?
   We will start with three to five, see how it goes, problem-solve issues/concerns, then slowly add up to 20 students.

   - What is the name of CICO at your school, and what will the Daily Progress Report (DPR) be called?
   ROAR = Reinforcement of Appropriate Responses
   DPR = Wild Card

2. Develop a DPR.
   - What will the behavioral expectations be?
   Keep your hands, feet, and other objects to self (KYHFOOTY), be on task, follow directions first time + added work completion to schoolwide rules.
       Consistent with schoolwide expectations?
       There will be two DPRs—upper grade and lower grade.
   - Are the expectations positively stated?
   Yes.

   - Is the DPR teacher friendly? How often are teachers asked to rate the student's behavior?
   Yes, lower grade = 4 rating periods, upper grade = 7 grading periods.

   - Is the DPR age-appropriate, and does it include a range of scores?
   Yes, 0, 1, 2 scale.

   - Are the data easy to summarize?
   Yes.

3. Develop a reinforcement system for students on the CICO intervention.
   - What will the students' daily point goal be?
   Bare minimum score = 70%; students who receive higher scores will receive more points on their credit card.

(continued)

FIGURE 4.4. Sample completed CICO Development and Implementation Guide.

- What reinforcers will students receive for checking in (e.g., praise and lottery ticket)?

Praise and lottery ticket for end-of-week drawing. Public posting of drawing winner and small mystery-motivator prize for student who won the drawing. Student can draw either a banana or coconut off a tree for the mystery-motivator prize.

- What reinforcers will students receive for checking out **AND** meeting their daily point goal?

Praise, daily spinner for meeting the goal and for longer-term rewards— $\geq 70\%$ = 1 point on credit card, $\geq 80\%$ = 2 points on credit card, $\geq 90\%$ = 3 points on credit card, 100 % = 4 points to be spent at school store.

- How will you ensure students do not become bored with the reinforcers?

School store items to be changed frequently and change items on the spinner.

- What are the consequences for students who receive major and minor referrals?

Students cannot exchange points for items if they receive a referral nor receive the daily spinner.

4. Develop a referral system.

- How will students be referred to CICO? What are the criteria for placing students on CICO?

Referred by teacher or after receiving three minor behavior referrals. Data from behavior logs (in-class consequences) will be examined to also determine eligibility.

- What does the parental consent form look like for students participating in CICO?

Will revise example provided in the training.

- What is the process for screening students who transfer into the school?

Behavior support team will review behavior data from the other school. Will determine if CICO is needed. In most cases the student will start without CICO support to acclimate to the school.

- What is the process for determining whether students will begin the next school year on CICO?

Most students will start the new year without CICO support to get used to new teachers/classrooms. In a few cases, a teacher may advocate that it's necessary for the student to be successful and the student will be placed on CICO after the first week of school.

5. Develop a system for managing the daily data.

- Which computer program will be used to summarize data?

The Check-In, Check-Out SWIS data system [see Chapter 7].

- Which team in the school will examine the daily CICO data, and how frequently will the data be examined? (Note: Data should be examined at least twice monthly.)

Multidisciplinary team will carve out 20–30 minutes every other week for CICO data evaluation.

- Who is responsible for summarizing and bringing the data to team meetings?

Ms. Gomez will summarize the data and attend the CICO portion of the behavior support team meetings.

- How frequently will data be shared with the whole staff?

Once per quarter.

- How frequently will data be shared with parents?

A graph will be sent home to parents monthly. Parents will also receive a longer-term graph during parent–teacher conferences.

(continued)

FIGURE 4.4. *(continued)*

6. Plan to fade students off the intervention.
   - What are the criteria for fading students off the CICO intervention?
   Tentatively, we will evaluate all students every quarter. On average, if a student receives 80% or more across 6 weeks, fading will be considered. Teachers will be consulted prior to fading.

   - How will CICO be faded, and who will be in charge of helping students fade off CICO?
   Students will self-monitor their progress and reduce the number of check-ins and check-outs. Over time, students will check in at the beginning of the week and check out at the end of the week. Ms. Gomez will be in charge of teaching students how to self-monitor and other aspects of fading.

   - How will graduation from the CICO intervention be celebrated?
   Lunchtime party with a small cake, parents, teacher(s), and support staff. Students will receive diploma signed by the behavior support team.

   - What incentives and supports will be put in place for students who graduate from the program?
   Quarterly "alumni" parties for students who graduate and do not receive ODRs.

7. Plan for staff training.
   - Who will train staff on the CICO intervention?
   Behavior support team using protocol outlined in the CICO book.

   - Who will provide teachers with individual coaching if the CICO intervention is not being implemented as planned?
   Mrs. Catrell—principal

   - Who will provide yearly booster sessions about the purpose of CICO and key features in implementing the intervention?
   Behavior support team

8. Plan for student and parent training.
   - Who will meet with students to train them on the intervention?
   Ms. Gomez will meet with the students following baseline collection to train them. Role playing will be used, along with giving the student a tour of how/where to check in and check out and how to get teacher feedback.

   - How will parents be trained on the intervention?
   Mrs. Carroll, the school psychologist, will either meet with parents or provide information over the phone about how to participate. She will also be in charge of getting parental permission. As Ms. Gomez becomes more comfortable with implementing CICO, she may also be involved in training parents.

FIGURE 4.4. *(continued)*

Budget categories and estimated annual costs per category for one middle school with approximately 30 students receiving CICO during a school year are provided in Figure 4.5.

FINAL CONSIDERATIONS PRIOR TO CICO IMPLEMENTATION

A crucial component of an effective system of behavior support is that the key stakeholders are aware of it and are willing to use it. If teachers do not know that this source of support exists, they will not make referrals, and consequently very few students will be placed on CICO. In addition, if teachers and staff have not been adequately trained on CICO, they will not know how to respond when a student brings a DPR for their feedback. It only takes a few inconsistent

Budget category	Category description	Example amount
Personnel		
	CICO coordinator (9–13 hours per week)	Per district pay scale
Materials		
	CICO forms on NCR paper	$250
	School supplies	$200
Incentives		
	Small rewards	$500

FIGURE 4.5. Example budget and estimated annual costs for a middle school with approximately 30 students receiving CICO.

or negative responses from an adult for a student to lose interest in cooperating with CICO. Lack of communication among the teachers and staff in the building could put an end to the CICO intervention before it has a fair chance to work. Obtaining teacher and staff commitment prior to CICO implementation is essential.

Equally important, students must understand what the CICO intervention is and how it works. This is true not only for the students on CICO, but also for all the students in the school. When all the students know about CICO, they can support their friends who are on the intervention, because it has become part of the school culture. When only a few students know about it, the intervention may be viewed with skepticism or ridicule. It may be viewed as one of those programs offered for the "bad kids." Students tend to avoid interventions that set them apart or give them a label.

The CICO intervention must become a positive part of the school culture. How can this be accomplished?

1. *Begin by giving CICO a high profile within the school.* Explain the CICO intervention to the teachers and staff at the first staff development meeting of the year. Continue to provide this same professional development in subsequent years. Returning teachers and staff will benefit from the reminder. New teachers will be immediately incorporated into the system. Also, explain the CICO intervention to the student body at the beginning of each school year.

2. *Always stress the positive aspects of the CICO intervention.* Talk about CICO frequently in staff meetings and provide reminders of how to give supportive, corrective feedback versus being harsh and critical during the rating periods. Discuss with your staff the importance of providing positive feedback regularly and building relationships with students as keys to academic success. Point out that CICO provides scheduled intervals of interactions for teachers and students, which provides more opportunities to create a bond between student and teacher.

3. *Ensure that the CICO is viewed as a positive support, not a punishment.* Publicly recognize students for their accomplishments on CICO (with their permission). Use CICO as a way for students to earn privileges. Publicly recognize teachers who contribute to CICO. Publicly recognize and thank behavior support team members for their hard work on CICO.

4. *Provide regular feedback.* It is important to provide regular feedback to the students, staff, and families. We all are more likely to believe in an intervention when we can see the real impact of the program. Regular, specific feedback to each group of key stakeholders in the CICO intervention is essential.

CHAPTER 5

Roles, Responsibilities, and Training Needs Related to Implementing CICO

Deanne A. Crone, Leanne S. Hawken, and K. Sandra MacLeod

Prior to implementing the CICO intervention, schools must understand the roles and responsibilities of everyone involved in the intervention and delineate how CICO training will be conducted. This group includes the CICO coordinator, behavior support team members, administrators, teaching staff, parents/guardians, and students. To a great extent, the success of the CICO intervention hinges on the effectiveness of the CICO coordinator. Therefore, the CICO coordinator must receive adequate training on implementing and managing the intervention. Staff members should receive training on the features of the CICO intervention and on how to implement it within their classroom or school setting. Students and parents should receive training on their responsibilities and on how to successfully participate in the intervention. Finally, the behavior support team members will require training on how to use data for decision making.

The purpose of this chapter is to describe the distinct roles and responsibilities of each person or group of persons involved in the CICO intervention, as well as to delineate the critical elements to be included during the corresponding training sessions.

CICO COORDINATOR

Roles and Responsibilities

The primary responsibilities of the CICO coordinator are to (1) lead the morning check-in; (2) lead the afternoon check-out; (3) enter DPR data into a database or graphing program at

---

K. Sandra MacLeod, PhD, BCBA-D, is a licensed behavior analyst in the Pacific Northwest. She is the owner and clinical director of Mosaic Learning Systems, a private practice supporting families, schools, physicians, and agencies in improving outcomes for individuals with autism, health concerns, intellectual and other disabilities.

least once per week; (4) maintain records in a centrally located, confidential place; (5) create CICO graphs of overall CICO intervention effectiveness and individual student progress for team meetings; (6) prioritize students for discussion at team meetings; (7) gather supplemental information for meetings; (8) if possible, attend behavior team meetings; and (9) complete any tasks assigned at the meetings.

An educational assistant can take on the responsibilities of the CICO coordinator. Most schools employ one or several full-time educational assistants, whose job responsibilities tend to be more flexible than those of a teacher or administrator. Coordinating the CICO intervention should take about 9–13 hours each week, depending on the size of the school and the number of students supported on the intervention. The tasks of the CICO coordinator and the necessary time allotted for each one are illustrated in Table 5.1. A biweekly behavior support team meeting is assumed, but schools may use other schedules for CICO data evaluation.

Leading Morning Check-In and Afternoon Check-Out

Morning check-in is CICO students' first point of contact with the school for the day. On a daily basis, morning check-in provides the students with an ideal opportunity to start the day well. Afternoon check-out is CICO students' last point of contact with the school, and is an opportunity to send students home with a positive attitude and a reason to look forward to the next school day. *The person who does check-in and check-out must be someone whom the students respect, enjoy seeing, and trust.* This person should be enthusiastic, positive, and friendly.

TABLE 5.1. CICO Coordinator's Time Allocation

Task	Frequency	Duration	Total time/week
Lead morning check-in	5 times per week	30–45 minutes	150–225 minutes
Lead afternoon check-out	5 times per week	20–30 minutes	100–150 minutes
Enter CICO data onto spreadsheet or database	1 time per week	30 minutes	30 minutes
Create CICO graphs for team meetings	1 time per week	30 minutes	30 minutes
Maintain records	5 times per week	15 minutes	75 minutes
Prioritize CICO students	1 time per week	20 minutes	20 minutes
Process CICO referrals	As needed	10–20 minutes	10–20 minutes
Gather supplemental information	As needed	30–90 minutes	30–90 minutes
Attend behavior support team meetings (if possible)	1 time biweekly	30–45 minutes	30–45 minutes
Complete tasks from behavior support team meetings	As needed	60–120 minutes	60–120 minutes
		TOTAL TIME	9–13 hours

When students look forward to seeing a person, they are much more likely to cooperate by checking in and checking out on a regular basis than if they find the CICO coordinator to be dismissive, harsh, or punishing. It is also important that the CICO coordinator be able to multitask and manage moderate-sized groups of students. We have seen CICO coordinators who become frazzled when working with more than five students or who struggle because they do not enjoy the quick pace of the check-in/check-out process.

The logistics of leading the check-in and check-out may seem complicated or overwhelming at first. All that is needed, however, is to establish a simple, accessible, predictable routine. Once the CICO coordinator has established and taught the routine to each CICO student, daily check-in and check-out will become almost automatic.

Morning check-in should not last more than 30 minutes and should end before the first bell rings for school to begin. Students should not use participation in CICO as an excuse for being late to their first class! We have found that some of the younger elementary school students need to have their DPRs delivered directly to their classrooms because it is difficult for them to remember to check in in the morning. Also, after the morning check-in time, the CICO coordinator must determine if students who have not checked in are indeed absent or have simply forgotten to check in. If the student forgot to check in, the CICO coordinator should deliver the DPR and then plan to reteach the process of checking in. Afternoon check-out should be even briefer, approximately 15–20 minutes because many students only have a few minutes between the dismissal bell and the time that their bus leaves the school building. The CICO coordinator should collaborate with the bus monitors to ensure that no students are left behind while doing CICO check-out. Some schools have had to adapt the check-out process to be conducted during the last 20 minutes of the school day rather than after school for scheduling purposes.

Morning check-in consists of the following activities:

1. Greet each student individually.
2. Collect the DPR signed by parents/guardians from the previous day (if schools choose to have parents/guardians engage in daily signing).
3. In middle and high school settings, check to see if the student has loose-leaf paper, pens, pencils, planners/agendas, and other necessary items for the day (provide extras to the student if necessary).
4. Make sure that the student takes a new DPR, signs it, and dates it.
5. Prompt the student to have a good day and to meet their CICO goals.
6. Give the student a rewards ticket (if available within the school's reinforcement system) for checking in successfully.

The CICO coordinator should keep a checklist of both the check-in and check-out process. In middle and high school settings, this checklist included places for the CICO coordinator to mark whether the student was prepared for the day (e.g., had a pencil, paper, and daily planner) and to note whether the DPR signed by the parent/guardian was brought back and a place to write the percentage of points the student earned at the end of the day. In elementary school settings, we have found that most students keep supplies in their classroom desk, so checking for supplies is not a necessary part of check-in. Sample check-in and check-out checklists for elementary and secondary settings are included in Appendices D.1 and D.2.

Entering DPR Data and Maintaining Records

The DPRs and the corresponding data are helpful only to the extent that they are used. Completed and signed DPRs that are allowed to pile up week after week only fill up file drawer space. However, DPRs entered into a database on a daily or weekly basis can be used to monitor student progress, make data-based intervention decisions, and evaluate outcomes. A simple database created in Excel is included on the The Guilford Press website for download (see the box at the end of the table of contents). Additional information regarding options for a CICO data management system is presented in Chapter 7. Entering data on a weekly basis should take less than 60 minutes to complete (depending on the number of students supported on CICO).

Keeping well-organized files is a must. After the students' percentage point data have been recorded on the check-in, check-out sheet, each DPR should be filed separately into each student's file folder. Any other information relevant to CICO (e.g., CICO graphs, consent forms from parents/guardians, or teacher interviews) should be kept in individual students' files as well. The files should be orderly so that it is easy to locate information. Maintaining the files should require 15 minutes or less per day.

Information regarding a student's behavior and treatment for that behavior is confidential. While the student's files should be accessible for the behavior support team members involved in working with the student, care should be taken to maintain the student's confidentiality. The files should be kept in a locked filing cabinet when not in use. A student's file should never be left lying out on a table or desk where other students or unrelated staff might have access to it.

Creating CICO Graphs for Behavior Team Meetings

Prior to the behavior support team meeting, the coordinator should create (1) a graph that summarizes the average percentage of points across students who receive the intervention and (2) an individual graph for each student receiving the intervention. Rather than printing these graphs, we recommend that behavior teams show data projected on a screen during the meeting for all members to view. These graphs can be created and shared ahead of time so that team members can examine them prior to the meeting if desired. Individual behavior team members can also have access to graphs electronically during the team meeting.

The coordinator can choose to graph only the data from the previous 2 weeks or to include students' data from a longer period. Whichever method is chosen, the data should be presented in the same manner for each student. Illustrating short-term data for some students and long-term data for other students may create confusion and errors in data interpretation by the behavior support team. The greater part of behavior support team meetings will revolve around the "priority students."

Prioritizing Students and Gathering Supplemental Information for Behavior Team Meetings

Prior to the behavior support team meeting, the CICO coordinator should review the data graphs for each of CICO students. Many of them will be doing well on the intervention, consistently meeting their goals from day to day. Other students may be performing poorly or may experience a sudden decline in performance. Some of the same students may be receiving detention or suspensions or have poor attendance. The CICO coordinator will have access to this information as well. It is important to understand what is troubling these students and to determine if they need additional supports.

The CICO coordinator should prioritize two to four students for discussion at each behavior support team meeting. In addition to displaying CICO graphs for each priority student, the coordinator can generate a copy of the student's detention/ODR record, attendance record, or progress reports. This supplemental information can aid the behavior support team in making data-based intervention decisions. The CICO coordinator may also choose to prioritize a student in order to follow up on a previous decision or discussion.

When the intervention is not working for a particular student, the CICO coordinator can ask the teacher why the student is consistently not meeting goals or discuss with the teacher why the student is not attending check-out. Members of the behavior support team may also be involved in gathering this information.

Attending Behavior Support Team Meetings

If possible, the CICO coordinator should attend the behavior support team meetings whenever CICO data are discussed. Reviewing CICO data is typically only one part of a behavior support team meeting, and therefore the CICO coordinator does not need to attend the entire meeting. In some schools, CICO data are discussed every other week, and the CICO coordinator attends the first 20 minutes of the behavior support team meeting. The coordinator generates graphs for the team to review and brings the critical information to the meeting so that the team can discuss each student and decide on a plan of action. The entire team then shares in the tasks or responsibilities generated at the team meetings. In some of the schools we work in, the educational assistants who serve as the CICO coordinator are unable to attend the behavior support team meetings because either they are working with other students at that time or cannot attend an after-school meeting due to hourly employee constraints. In this situation, data can be shared with the school psychologist or counselor who oversees the CICO intervention prior to the meeting, and who can serve as a substitute for the CICO coordinator.

Completing Tasks Assigned at the Behavior Support Team Meetings

Multiple tasks may be generated from the team meeting. If a new student is added to the CICO intervention, one of the team members will need to contact the parents/guardians for permission to participate and to set up an orientation meeting. If a priority student is not succeeding on CICO, the team may decide to provide the student with additional behavioral support. For example, the team may propose a schedule change, curriculum assessment, or instruction on a behavioral skill. Once a plan of action has been decided on, someone needs to implement the plan. The team members will share responsibility for coordinating the implementation of additional behavioral supports. Some of the responsibility for these tasks will fall to the CICO coordinator.

Training

CICO coordinators are typically paraprofessionals (e.g., educational assistants), supervised by a school psychologist or school counselor. Training for the CICO coordinator is delivered by the specialist or administrator who is leading the CICO effort at the school and who deeply understands the CICO intervention and process. Typically, this trainer is a school psychologist, counselor, special education teacher, or vice principal. The CICO coordinator should receive an initial training session on how to coordinate and manage the multiple components of the intervention. Ongoing training should occur as necessary. Figure 5.1 delineates the content that should be addressed during the CICO coordinator training.

Because the CICO coordinator will train students on the check-in/check-out process, they should be familiar with the student training scripts provided in Figure 5.2. Prior to working directly with students, the CICO coordinator can role-play the student training process with their supervisor. The supervisor should observe the CICO coordinator for the first two or three sessions of student training and provide constructive feedback.

The CICO coordinator should also play a role in assessing students' preferences for reinforcers. A key feature of the CICO intervention is the provision of reinforcement to students for meeting their goals. If a student consistently misses the benchmark for their daily point goal, one of the first questions asked is whether the reinforcement component of the intervention has been implemented as planned. In a follow-up question, the CICO coordinator can assess whether the student considers the reinforcers to be rewarding and desirable. If not, the reinforcers should be changed to reflect the student's interests and preferences. The CICO coordinator should understand the basic theoretical principles of reinforcement and punishment and understand that students will become tired of the reinforcers if they are not varied or changed regularly. More information on choosing effective reinforcers is provided in Chapter 6.

We have noticed that CICO coordinators often repeat the same greeting to students during check-in and check-out. Just as students will grow weary of receiving the same reinforcers (e.g., every day they receive a sticker or a pencil for meeting their daily point goal), they will grow tired of repetitive interactions with the CICO coordinator. Figure 5.3 lists a variety of greetings to use during check-in and check-out.

We are frequently asked how the CICO coordinator manages to check in and check out 20–30 students per day. The CICO coordinator must be skilled in managing groups of students and in managing individual students who may be engaging in problem behavior. Part of the initial training should include teaching the CICO coordinator effective routines for check-in and check-out. For example, it may help to limit the number of students allowed to stand at the CICO coordinator's table at one time and to ask other students to stay behind a line that is taped on the floor. The CICO coordinator may be able to check in and check out more than two students at a time if they are older. The CICO coordinator could sit at a kidney-shaped table, while three or four students show that they have their materials for the day, gather their DPRs, write their names on them, and turn in their DPRs from the previous day. Students who require more individualized attention can be supported after the check-in process is complete. The key to making check-in and check-out work for multiple students is developing and teaching effective routines to make the process manageable and predictable.

In addition to being trained in check-in and check-out routines, CICO coordinators should learn basic behavior management techniques and how to diffuse confrontations between stu-

- Overall PBIS structure of the school
  - Schoolwide rules, how and when taught
  - Other Tier 2 interventions
- Importance of student and CICO coordinator relationship
  - Positive relationship cornerstone to the effectiveness of CICO
  - Goal = 5:1 positive-to-negative ratio of interactions
- Confidentiality and roles of coordinator versus counselor/school psychologist
  - Where should student files be kept? Ensuring all staff do not have access to files, etc.
  - Which staff members should know which students are on CICO?
  - CICO coordinator is not a counselor—importance of being supportive and referring to teacher, principal, or school psychologist if problem is severe.
- Check-in procedures
  - When and where check-in occurs
  - How to greet students—varying positive things to say at check-in
  - Managing multiple students. Provide information on what to do if students do not check in.

An Example of CICO Check-In Procedures

Students check in with the CICO coordinator either before school or at the beginning of school. When students check in, make sure to greet them happily. Ask them how they are doing and praise them for checking in. Ask if they have their DPR signed from the previous day. Praise them if they return it signed. Have students write their name, date, and goal on their new DPR and give it to them to take to class. For students who need help, write this information for them. Remind them when to check out and encourage them to do their personal best in class.

If students don't check in after 10–15 minutes, take their DPRs to them to see if they are absent. If they are at school, ask them why they didn't check in, give them their DPR, and encourage them to do a good job. Check in later if the student is not at school to see if they arrived late.

- Structure of the DPR
  - How to summarize scores
  - Required components (e.g., rating and teacher signature) versus optional components (e.g., additional positive comments)
- Check-out procedures
  - When and where check-out occurs
  - Structure of the reinforcement system
  - Procedure for sending DPRs home with students for parent/guardian signature
  - What to do if student does not check out

An Example of CICO Check-Out Procedures

Take a moment with each student to go over how their day went based on their DPR. It's important to focus on the positive, and help them feel they can succeed in the future. Then calculate their daily percentages to see if they made their goal. If they do, they spin a spinner for a small prize. For a long-term reinforcement idea, after students meet their daily goals for 10 consecutive days, they can pick a prize from a reinforcement menu. (See Chapter 6 for more reinforcement ideas.) The students then take the top copy home to get signed, and the bottom copy stays at school.

- Data entry and graph development
  - What data to enter and how to enter the data
  - How often are data to be entered?
  - How often are data to be graphed?
- Attending team meetings
  - Bring graphs
  - Help prioritize students to talk about and students who need additional reinforcement

(continued)

FIGURE 5.1. CICO coordinator training.

- Training students on CICO
  - How to teach social skills/role-play with students
- Training parents on CICO
  - Calling parents on the phone

Other Topics Covered during CICO Coordinator Training

- Basic principles of applied behavior analysis/behavior intervention
  - Setting Events, Antecedents, Behavior, Consequences
  - Main functions of problem behavior—why students act out
    - Escape, attention, obtaining tangible items/activities, or self-stimulatory
  - Basic principles of reinforcement
    - How to identify reinforcers for students
- Managing confrontations

CICO Coordinator Troubleshooting CICO

Tardy to school
- Find out why student is late.
- Give a lottery ticket or for younger students a sticker for days on time and reward for a certain number of days on time (does not have to be consecutive).
- Set up self-monitoring program by having student record days on time and receive reward for a certain number of days on time (does not have to be consecutive).
- Praise the student every time they are on time for school.

Absences
- Check with home—find out why student is missing school.
- Is student staying home to avoid academic activity? If yes, student needs help in improving the academic skill.
- Inform parent about attendance laws.
- Help the student find an enjoyable school activity.
- Set an attendance goal with student and have a reward for a certain number of days at school (does not have to be consecutive).
- Talk to the student one-on-one about why it's important to come to school.
- Praise the student each time they are at school.

Student not checking in
- Students get a lottery ticket or for younger students a sticker for each check-in—earns small reward for _____ (school to set criterion) days of check-in (not consecutive).
- Check in with a buddy.
- Have a raffle ticket for check-in.
- Surprise drawing—on random days, have a special drawing for students who check in and check out.
- Put a "sticky note" on their desk as a reminder to check in or give them a note for their backpack.
- Praise the student for remembering to check in.

Student not checking out
- Ask the student why they are not checking out—make sure they have the time to check out, etc.
- Check out with buddy (both earn rewards).
- Give raffle tickets for check-out.
- Fun, quick, activity every now and then on a day student checks out.
- Praise the student for remembering to check out.
- Special reward for checking out—special home note.
- Surprise drawing—see above.
- Have a "sticky note" reminder to check out on their desk.

(continued)

FIGURE 5.1. *(continued)*

Complaining/pouting
- Always take note of and reinforce appropriate behavior with specific praise statements, such as "Thanks for taking responsibility for that!"
- Set up a time when the student can talk to you about what they think is unfair (should be during student's free time, i.e., recess).
- Practice (i.e., role-play) accepting feedback on the DPR.
- Make sure the student knows that their behavior *earns* what they receive on the DPR.
- At check-in, precorrect for appropriate behavior when receiving feedback on the DPR.
- Problem-solve (with older students) about a situation that keeps happening.

Stealing/changing scores
- Set up a program in which a student can earn extra stickers for appropriate behavior.
- Take away points for stealing (tickets, reinforcers, etc.).
- Explain that students will not earn points or make their goal when they steal or are dishonest.

Lost Daily Progress Report
- Tell students they can get a new report right away.
- If this happens often, find out if student is having consistent "bad days."
- Is the student enjoying participating in the CICO program?
- Give the student a small basket or a folder that the student and teacher can find easily.

FIGURE 5.1. *(continued)*

dents. They should be taught when and how to seek help from other school personnel if student behavior is severe or extreme. Along with the entire school staff, CICO coordinators should have some knowledge of the functions of problem behavior. That is, they should understand the primary reasons why students act out, which include obtaining peer or adult attention, escaping an aversive activity, academic subject, or social situation, or having access to a tangible object (e.g., favorite toy) they desire. If CICO coordinators understand the basic functions of problem behavior, they can also better help the behavior support team modify the CICO intervention if it is ineffective for an individual student.

BEHAVIOR SUPPORT TEAM

Roles and Responsibilities

The primary responsibilities of the behavior support team members are to (1) attend biweekly meetings, (2) contribute to decisions regarding overall CICO effectiveness and assess individual student progress on CICO, (3) conduct orientation meetings with students and families, (4) gather supplemental information on individual students, (5) participate in student/staff development workshops and feedback sessions on CICO, and (6) complete any tasks assigned at CICO meetings.

The behavior support team should incorporate a certain critical mix of individuals, including an administrator and a representative sample of the school's personnel. It is also helpful to have several individuals on the team who are knowledgeable about behavioral issues and who have had experience working with students at risk for severe problem behavior. Some schools choose to include each of their special education teachers on the behavior support team. The actual size of the team will vary from school to school. We suggest limiting the size

Teaching Students How to Participate in CICO

The purpose of this lesson plan is to teach students who are new to CICO the expectations of the program and how to accept feedback. You'll be giving students many opportunities to see, hear, and perform the expectation correctly and a few examples of what not to do. (Plan on about 15 minutes for this activity and have a copy of the DPR to show the student.)

First step: Introduce the student to the program and give a brief explanation of what you are going to talk about. Say something like "Today we're going to learn about the check-in, check-out intervention. This will help you be more successful in school and we're going to practice today so that you'll know how to be really good at doing this and you can earn all your points."

Second step: Show the student the DPR and, starting at the top, go through each component of the report. Describe the meaning of each score for each expectation. You can say something like this: "This is the Daily Progress Report. Look at what is on it: it has the school expectations and some numbers. The numbers are (say numbers) and here are what the numbers mean. For the rule 'Follow Directions,' '2' means that you followed directions, etc., a '1' means that you had some trouble, and a '0' means that you didn't follow directions."

Ask the student to demonstrate the expectations for a rule (e.g., "Staying on task"). Use lots of praise for demonstrating the expectation and circle the 2 on the DPR example. Practice another expectation if necessary.

Third step: Show how the points are added up to give a score for the day and what the student's goal will be. Use more detail in this section for the older students. Tell them they need to pick up their DPR every day before school or after checking in with the teacher, and they will need to return their DPR to you at the end of the day (give time).

Teaching Students How to Accept Feedback on Their DPR

Feedback at Check-Out

To practice receiving feedback about a poor DPR at check-out, you can teach students how to react to pretend examples of how to act and how not to act.

Steps:
- Fill out a DPR for yourself and tell the student that you are going to pretend that this is yours.
- Give yourself 0's and some 1's so you don't make your goal. Show the student the report and talk about what it means. (Did not stay on task, follow directions, etc. I want to make my goal. . . .)
- Let the student know you are going to act in different ways when you see this report.
- Ask the student to see if they can tell a difference between what we should do and what we should not do when we get a not very good DPR. They can show you by giving you a "thumbs-up" for the right way to act or a "thumbs-down" for the wrong way to act after each situation. ("Is this the way you should act?")

Act out these scenarios:
- Act very upset—cry, or say something like "That's stupid!" ("Thumbs-up or thumbs-down?")
- Say "I'm upset I didn't make my goal, but I'll try harder tomorrow." ("Thumbs-up or thumbs-down?")
- Act out being angry and yelling that it isn't fair, and that the teacher made a mistake, etc. ("Thumbs-up or thumbs-down?")
- Say something about how you wish you could have made your goal, but can still make your week if you try harder to follow directions, etc. ("Thumbs-up or thumbs-down?")

Role play of examples:
- You be the student and demonstrate getting an unsatisfactory DPR and handling it correctly. Ask the student to be the person giving feedback on the DPR. (Ask the student if they have kept hands, feet, and other objects to themselves.)
- Ask the student to demonstrate correctly handling a poor DPR. (Use the "thumbs-up" and lots of praise and encouragement.)

Do not allow the student to practice nonexamples of correct behavior.

FIGURE 5.2. Student training scripts.

Things to say at check-in

- Wow! You brought back your DPR signed!
- You're here on time again—great!
- Looks like you're all set to go.
- It's great to see you this morning.
- Looks like you're ready for a good day.
- You're off to a good start.
- You look so nice this morning.
- You look happy to be here this morning.
- I like the way you said "good morning."
- Thanks for coming to check in.
- Sounds like you had a good weekend.
- We missed you yesterday [if student was absent]; nice to see you today.

Things to say at check-out

- You had a great [awesome, terrific, etc.] day!
- You're right on target.
- Your mom/dad is going to be so proud of you.
- You're really working hard!
- You are such a good student.
- You made your goal—wow!
- Looks like today didn't go so well—I know you can do it tomorrow.
- I know it was a tough day—thanks for coming to check out.
- We all have bad days once in a while—I know you can do better tomorrow.
- You look a little frustrated—what happened? [If a student looks upset take a few minutes to "just listen."]

FIGURE 5.3. Tips for providing feedback during check-in and during check-out.

of the team to a maximum of eight members in order to facilitate the ease of decision making and planning.

The team will need to decide how to best use their time at each meeting. We suggest creating a standard agenda that can be used at each meeting (see Figure 5.4 for a sample agenda). At each meeting, the team should discuss the two to four "priority students," starting with a review of the students' CICO graphs and supplemental information.

For each of these students, the behavior support team should make one of four decisions: (1) remove the student from CICO, (2) continue to monitor the student's progress on CICO, (3) provide additional (minor) behavioral supports or modifications for the student, or (4) conduct a comprehensive function-based assessment and develop an intensive intervention.

After the priority students have been evaluated, the members discuss any new referrals and determine if the newly referred student is an appropriate candidate for the CICO intervention. Note that as discussed previously, some schools prefer to make CICO placement decisions at the grade level rather than the schoolwide behavior support team level. For these schools the behavior support team will not be processing new referrals. For schools who do choose to use the behavior support team process for CICO placement, once new referrals have been discussed, the team members can turn their attention to deciding which students should receive recognition for consistently meeting their goals over the past 2 weeks or for demonstrating a significant improvement on the CICO intervention. These students can be rewarded by having the principal share the graph with them and congratulate them on consistently meeting goals. Some schools combine this recognition with a $1.00 coupon to the school store or a similar

Date: _____   Note taker: _____   Facilitator: _____

Team members present: _____

List of priority students:

1. Determine the overall effectiveness rate of the schoolwide CICO intervention. (Examine average percentage of points across students.)
    a. Are 70% of students responding to CICO? If not, look at systems features of the intervention.
2. Discuss priority students.
3. Discuss new referrals.
4. Identify students who receive a $1.00 school store coupon.
5. Discuss other CICO issues or students.

FIGURE 5.4. Sample behavior support team meeting agenda for CICO.

reward. Finally, if any time remains, behavior support team members can discuss any other issues relevant to the CICO intervention or other CICO students.

Finally, behavior team members must understand how to adapt or modify CICO if it is not working. Chapter 8 provides information on how to make minor adaptations to CICO to target specific behaviors. Chapter 9 provides information on how to modify CICO when it is not working by adding more intensive supports. This information should be presented to the behavior support team prior to implementing CICO. For CICO modifications to be effective, it is recommended that someone on the behavior support team be an expert in functional behavioral assessment (FBA). Many of the adaptations to CICO are based on the function of problem behavior, so having a person on the team who has experience with FBA support will provide the team with the leadership that is needed to develop a more effective, modified CICO (see Chapter 9 for more detailed information).

Training

The team responsible for managing the CICO intervention (whether it is the behavior support team, the individual student service team, etc.) should receive training on their role in managing and supervising CICO implementation and on using data for decision making. For example, behavior teams will need to know how to use data to assess the effectiveness of CICO. ODR data, CICO graphs, attendance records, and academic performance data can all be useful sources of information.

Behavior support teams should meet at least biweekly to examine student progress on CICO. Team members will determine whether each student is making adequate progress and the intervention should be continued, whether modifications are needed, whether an additional layer of behavior support is required, or whether a student is ready for the intervention to be faded. We have found it helpful to provide teams with case examples of DPRs and other data and ask them to practice making data-based decisions prior to implementing an actual CICO intervention. One of the primary mistakes made by behavior support teams is ignoring the importance of a student's academic data. Examining academic data in addition to behavior data can help schools more accurately identify students who may be in need of support (Kalberg, Lane, & Menzies, 2010). School teams should establish a process of examining behavior data (such as percentage of points on DPRs) alongside academic data (such as formative assessments like curriculum-based measurement [CBM]; Shinn, 1989, examples of which include the Acadience Learning Assessments [formally known as the Dynamic Indicators of Basic Early Literacy Skills, or DIBELS]; Acadience Learning, Inc., 2019: Good & Kaminski, 2002). Other relevant academic data includes work completion rates, credits earned, and quarterly grades. More information on using data for decision making is presented in Chapter 7.

ADMINISTRATOR

Roles and Responsibilities

The administrator is a key player in developing and implementing CICO. The administrator must agree to allocate resources to the intervention prior to implementation and is critical in helping solicit commitment from the faculty for the intervention. It is often easier for the staff to commit to participation if the administrator believes in the prevention philosophy of the CICO intervention and has a good rapport with the faculty. If the administrator has a reputation of introducing new programs and interventions to the school every year and has not supported implementation of these interventions, the faculty will treat CICO as the new "intervention for the year" and will be skeptical about whether it will be sustained. In contrast, if the administrator has effectively committed to systems change efforts, such as implementing a Tier 1 school-wide discipline plan, the faculty likely have experienced success with prevention. It is important for the administrator to communicate that CICO is not an "intervention of the year," but rather a system that will be implemented in every future school year to support students at risk.

Once the administrator has generated faculty support and has committed resources to CICO, they remain involved in helping the team match CICO intervention with the school culture. *The administrator should attend the half- or full-day professional development provided for CICO development and implementation.* Some schools have tried to develop CICO without administrator involvement, but many decisions, such as allocation of space, meeting times, and staff training cannot be made without the administrator present. If the administrator is unable to be present during the half or full day of professional development, the training should be rescheduled to ensure that CICO is designed appropriately.

After CICO development and implementation, the administrator should attend behavior support team meetings at least biweekly. By staying involved, the administrator remains aware of student progress, or lack thereof, and may be assigned administrator-specific responsibilities.

The final, and crucial, role that the administrator must serve is that of the implementation leader in the school building. The administrator's job is to provide feedback to teachers who are not implementing CICO correctly. Some teachers may be too harsh and consistently give students low scores on the DPR. Other teachers may write negative comments on the DPR. Some teachers may not provide feedback on a regular basis to the student. Because the CICO coordinator is typically an educational assistant, it is inappropriate to expect this person to give corrective feedback to teachers. In addition to providing corrective feedback, the administrator should also provide reinforcement and positive comments to teachers who are doing a good job at implementing CICO. We have found it helpful to provide administrators with an overview of the critical features of CICO and a list of their roles/responsibilities, which are detailed in Figure 5.5.

What is CICO?
- CICO is an intervention implemented with students who are at risk for, but not currently engaging in, serious problem behavior.
- It should be one of the many Tier 2 behavior interventions in your school to support students at risk.

Is my school ready to implement CICO?
- Please refer to CICO readiness checklist to determine if your school is in a good position to implement this intervention with fidelity.

What are the resources needed to implement the intervention?
- 10–15 hours per week paraprofessional time for check-in, check-out, and data management.
- Half- to full-day CICO development time for behavior support team.
- Allocate 20 minutes at least twice per month for reviewing CICO data in team meetings.
- Money required for reinforcers, NCR paper, follow-up training, etc.

What is my role as an administrator?
- Be involved with the team that develops CICO to fit the culture of your school.
- Serve on the team that analyzes CICO data for decision making.
- *CRITICAL*: Provide feedback/coaching to teachers who are not implementing CICO with fidelity or are being too harsh/negative.
- Give CICO a high profile in the school.
  - Reinforce teachers for good implementation.
  - Reinforce students for doing well on the intervention.
  - Be involved in updates to staff on how the intervention is working.

FIGURE 5.5. CICO overview for administrators.

TEACHING STAFF

Roles and Responsibilities

Prior to voting on whether or not to support CICO, teachers should be informed about their classroom-based CICO responsibilities. Teachers are expected to greet the student positively at the beginning of the school day (for elementary school) or each class period (for middle and high school). For elementary-age students, the teacher is responsible for providing increased feedback throughout the day and rating student behavior on the DPR at predetermined times as well. It is impractical to expect the student to remember to regularly request feedback from the teacher. *It is the teacher's responsibility to remember to provide feedback at the end of each period or transition and to provide an explanation for the rating that the student earned.* Older students (e.g., middle and high school) can help teachers remember to provide feedback, but ultimately the responsibility lies with the teacher who is implementing the intervention. Schools that are using electronic DPRs and apps may have older students rate their own behavior, in addition to the teacher-rating behavior, to help teach self-evaluation and self-regulation skills. Sample feedback statements are listed in Figure 5.6. Each feedback period is a teaching opportunity. Teachers use these opportunities to provide positive examples of appropriate behavior (e.g., "Raising your hand was an example of being respectful") and negative examples of inappropriate behavior (e.g., "Grabbing a pencil from Juanita was not an example of keeping your hands and feet to yourself"). When giving feedback, teachers should also prompt for

The following are suggestions for giving corrective feedback to the student on their DPR. Remember to focus and pay attention to the behavior you want to see more of, but let the student know why they received the score you gave them. Stay positive and upbeat and try to avoid being critical or sarcastic.

For best possible scores:
Wow, you got all [almost all] 2's today! You kept your hands and feet to yourself, and you followed directions. I liked the way you asked nicely for your book from Ashley. Way to go!

For good scores:
_____ [student name], you are doing so well! Look at that score! I saw that you kept your hands to yourself while you were working on that poster. You're going to make your goal! I saw you trying very hard today to stick to the rules and make your goal. Even though you got some 1's today because you were talking instead of doing your work, you did really well on keeping your hands, feet, and other objects to yourself.

For low scores:
Looks like you were having some trouble today. I know you can follow all the rules and finish your work but I didn't see you doing that today. Throwing your book is not keeping objects to yourself and it's important not to use unkind words. What do you think you'll work on tomorrow? You've had some really good days, so even though you missed your goal today, because of being out of your seat and not completing your work, I know you can do much better.

FIGURE 5.6. Sample handout: Things to Say to Keep Students Motivated.

appropriate behavior (e.g., "Tomorrow let's work on. . . .") and reinforce the student for following expectations or making improvements in behavior.

Teachers are also expected to make referrals to the behavior support team (or grade-level team depending on the referral process created in the school) if they believe a student could benefit from CICO or another intervention. Teachers should be informed of the preventative nature of Tier 2 interventions like CICO. They should be encouraged to make a referral when students are just beginning to act out rather than waiting until the problem behavior has escalated. Once a student has been referred and been determined appropriate for CICO, the teacher will need to collect 3–5 days of baseline data before the student begins the intervention. In terms of the day-to-day management of CICO, teachers are asked to provide feedback to the behavior support team on how the intervention is working. This feedback can include information about how the student is responding, a request for additional training on the intervention, or providing the behavior support team with information that may explain performance on CICO.

Training

Initial Teacher Training

After staff members have voted and agreed to implement the CICO intervention, they will need training on how to implement the intervention with individual students in their classroom. They will also need to know basic information about how to make a referral and how students will be faded from the intervention over time. Figure 5.7 outlines both the training content and the materials needed for this all-staff training. This information should be presented at the begin-

Training content
- Characteristics of students who are good candidates for CICO
- How to complete the DPR
- How to provide motivating feedback
- Basic information about fading students off CICO
- How students are rewarded on the intervention
- Frequently asked questions regarding CICO implementation

Materials needed
- DPR (on PowerPoint slide)
- Referral form (on PowerPoint slide)
- Consent form (on PowerPoint slide)
- Things to Say to Keep Students Motivated (handout)
- Frequently Asked Questions (handout)

FIGURE 5.7. CICO staff training.

ning of the school year after the staff have committed to the intervention. It can be used again if additional training sessions become necessary. Each new school year brings many new staff members, so this training should be available on an annual basis.

Training the entire staff on the CICO intervention typically occurs during a regularly scheduled staff meeting. We have found that if training materials are well organized and if the staff have already received background information on CICO, the training can occur during 15–20 minutes of a regularly scheduled staff meeting. As part of the training, the entire school's staff will need to be informed about which students are good candidates for CICO and how to make a referral. Information regarding which students are appropriate or inappropriate candidates, such as that provided in Table 3.1, is useful to include during the training. In addition, staff members should be shown a copy of the school's parent consent form, as they will likely be involved in helping to get consent for the intervention.

All staff members should also receive training on how to complete the DPR. This training should include examples of how to provide motivating feedback to students. Some schools provide role-play opportunities so that teachers can practice providing feedback and can demonstrate positive and negative examples of what feedback should sound like. It is important for the staff to know that the feedback sessions should be quick, corrective (as needed), positive, and encouraging. Examples of motivating feedback were included in Figure 5.6.

The principle that CICO is a time-limited intervention should also be emphasized in staff training, and the process of fading students should be explained. After a student has demonstrated persistent improvement, the student should be faded off the intervention. Your school may choose to set a specific amount of time that each student participates in CICO before the data are examined and fading off the intervention is considered. Many schools that are not overwhelmed by a high number of students needing CICO choose to use the end of the school year as a natural fade. The process of how students exit and graduate from CICO should be explained to the entire school staff during the initial training. They should understand that when students meet their goals, they will earn rewards or reinforcers. The initial training does not have to provide detailed reinforcement procedures, but rather should explain how and when students will be reinforced.

During the initial training, the staff can be provided with a handout about the frequently asked questions for CICO implementation. This document can be placed in the school's student handbook or in the teachers' positive behavior support binder. A sample handout addressing frequently asked questions is included in Figure 5.8.

Ongoing Teaching Training, Coaching, and Feedback

Several months may pass between the initial all-staff training and a teacher referral. As a result, teachers may benefit from a refresher that reviews the components of the intervention, how to greet students, where students should place their DPRs, and how to embed DPR ratings into their classroom routine and provides additional practice on how to provide feedback.

The CICO is a schoolwide, Tier 2 intervention for students who are starting to engage in frequent problem behavior. The intervention will serve up to 30 students at a time. The goal of CICO is to respond early to students who are acting out and to provide them with more frequent feedback on their behavior to prevent future problem behavior. Below are answers to some frequently asked questions about CICO.

Which students would do well on CICO?

Students who are starting to act out frequently but who are not currently engaging in dangerous (e.g., extreme aggression, property destruction) or severely disruptive (e.g., extreme noncompliance/defiance) behavior would be good candidates for the intervention. Students who engage in problem behavior across the day are good candidates for the intervention as opposed to students who have trouble only in one or two settings.

How do teachers participate in the CICO?

Teachers participate by providing both verbal and written feedback to students at predetermined times (see DPR). The feedback should be quick, positive, and help remind the student what they need to work on if the goal was not met. A sample feedback statement is "You did a nice job completing your work so you receive a '2' for work completion. I had to remind you not to flick Savannah's ponytail, so you got a '1' for keeping hands, feet, and other objects to yourself."

Who will be responsible for checking students in and out?

The CICO coordinator _____ [include name] will be in charge of checking students in and out. The coordinator will also keep track of the daily points earned and chart the progress for each student.

How do teachers make a referral?

A referral is made to the behavior support team of the school. In collaboration with the teacher, the team will determine whether CICO is appropriate or whether another intervention would be more appropriate. The team will respond and provide feedback to the teacher within _____ [number] school days.

How long do students remain on the intervention?

At the end of every trimester, the behavior support team will look at each student's data to determine if they are ready to be faded off CICO. Since there are a limited number of students (up to 30) who can receive the intervention, it will be important to fade students off as they become more independent in managing their own behavior.

FIGURE 5.8. Sample handout: Frequently Asked Questions.

The collection of baseline data should be emphasized in the refresher sessions. Depending on your school, it is recommended that 3–5 days of baseline data be taken to help with goal setting. Baseline data can also give the teacher practice in implementing some of the components of the intervention, such as rating the student's behavior on the DPR. The purpose of collecting baseline data is primarily to establish the current behavioral performance of the student. Therefore, it is important that the intervention is not actually implemented during this stage (i.e., students should not yet check in or out, and teachers should not talk with students about their scores on the DPR).

Ongoing training and feedback afford teachers the opportunity to ask questions that remain about implementing CICO and to address any concerns about the intervention. Awareness of teacher concerns will allow the behavior support team to address them prior to collaborating with individual teachers to implement CICO. Some schools provide teachers with an additional handout at this point. The handout provides specific information about the CICO implementation process. This handout should be used after a teacher referral has been accepted, and while the referring teacher is preparing to implement the CICO intervention. A sample handout for supplemental teacher training information is provided in Figure 5.9.

Some teachers will continue to need ongoing support and feedback to successfully implement CICO. Sometimes a member of the behavior support team needs to remind teachers that they must provide feedback at predetermined times rather that at the end of the day. At other times, additional training and feedback are needed when teachers use the DPR to be punitive with students. Behavior support teams should consider retraining and providing feedback when a teacher consistently provides the lowest rankings, writes negative comments on the DPR (e.g., "Student was a jerk this period" or "Never on task!"), or regularly fails to complete the DPR. During these situations, it is critical for the *administrator* to provide the feedback and coaching to the teacher, as this is a work performance issue.

Booster Training

Once or twice a year it is helpful to provide your staff with booster training on how to implement CICO and to resolve any schoolwide issues related to CICO implementation. These trainings can typically be done during 5–10 minutes of a regularly scheduled school staff meeting. We have found that sharing the data with the staff on how CICO is working is a great way to start these booster training sessions. Letting your staff know how many students have been served, the amount of progress that has been made, and any other anecdotal information supporting CICO helps start these trainings off on a positive note. They may need to be reminded about the characteristics of students who are appropriate for CICO, how to make a referral, and any other issues that should be addressed during booster sessions.

Occasionally, a teacher who has experienced success with CICO will want to use the intervention with every student engaging in problem behavior. During the booster training sessions, it is important to remind everyone that CICO is only one type of Tier 2 intervention and is not appropriate for *all* students and to allow the staff to review the other types of Tier 2 interventions that are available in their school. Booster sessions provide an additional opportunity for staff members to ask questions about how to implement CICO and to resolve any implementation issues.

At the beginning of class:
- The student brings their DPR to each class, and gives it to you (the teacher) to rate their behavior at predetermined times.
- If the student doesn't give you the DPR right away (this may happen when they are just starting on the intervention), you may have to ask them for it.
- Be sure to be cheerful and positive with the student.
- Start out by setting the expectation for appropriate behavior. For example, you might say, "Thanks for giving me your Daily Progress Report—looks like you're all set to go! Remember to work on being responsible, safe, and kind." Or, if yesterday was a good class for the student, you may say, "You're having a great week—keep it up! Keep trying to be an active learner who keeps hands and feet to self."
- Avoid negatives: Avoid saying things like "You're way behind—you're not going to make it" or "I don't want to see you doing anything like you did yesterday. . . . " Such comments will focus the student's attention on what not to do and you want to emphasize the appropriate, expected behavior. Let the student know you will be watching for them to follow expectations and engage in appropriate behavior.

How to score the DPR:
- The DPR is quick and easy to score. The numbers on the DPR represent how well the student met behavioral expectations.
- The teacher will circle the highest number on the DPR if the student meets the expectation. For example, if the expectation was "Keep your hands, feet, and other objects to yourself," and the student was able to sit and move about the room without annoying other students, the teacher will circle the highest numbered rating.
- Circle the middle rating if the student had brief incidents of inappropriate behavior and had been warned twice (individually), but then repeated an incident of the behavior. For example, a student grabs another student's eraser without asking, causing a minor disruption *after you have already warned the student twice to keep their hands to themselves. Corrective feedback to the student may be (in a calm voice) "Allison, taking Eric's eraser is not keeping your hands to yourself as I asked you to do," and Allison receives a lower number on her DPR for the time period.*
- Circle the lowest number when the student did not meet the expectation. Students receiving this score have *repeated instances* (e.g., three) of not following directions, being off-task repeatedly, or doing something more serious such as fighting.

At the end of the time period:
- This is the time to rate the student on their behavior and provide instruction and feedback on how to improve or on positive behavior that should continue.
- Use phrases such as "Given your behavior . . . you earned . . ." versus "I am going to give you," as this puts the ownership of the behavior on the student.
- Spend just a minute or so with the student—it should not be a lengthy process.
- Whether their behavior has been good or poor, it is best to be specific about your feedback and again stay positive and cheerful.

For "best possible scores" (appropriate behavior):
- Be enthusiastic! Tell the student what they did to receive the rating and encourage them to continue. For example: "Wow! I am so proud of the way you followed directions, stayed on task, and were kind to your classmates. Looks like you'll make your goal!"

For "not so good" and "poor" ratings:
- These also need explanation. Keep the discussion upbeat and positive, but give specific feedback on what the student did or did not do during the class to meet expectations.
- Try not to criticize, use threats, or get into long explanations. Your rating is the final rating. For example: "Looks like you had a rough time listening and following directions today, but I know you can do it, I look forward to seeing you succeed tomorrow."

At the end of the day:
- The students take their DPRs with them when they leave class and they return them to the CICO coordinator at the end of the day. The coordinator gives a copy to the student to take home for parent/guardian's signature.

FIGURE 5.9. Sample handout: Additional CICO Training Information for Teachers.

STUDENTS

Roles and Responsibilities

Participating students must understand the purpose of the CICO intervention and receive training on how to engage in the intervention. If the student remains unclear about the expectations for involvement, additional training should occur. Students are responsible for checking in every morning and checking out every afternoon with the CICO coordinator. Students pick up a new DPR every morning at check-in. Although teachers are responsible for providing students with feedback, students should hand the DPR to their teacher at the beginning of the school day (for elementary school) or at the beginning of each class period (for middle and high school). Students are also responsible for collecting the DPR from the teacher at the end of the day or class period. On occasion, students may also need to remind their teachers to provide feedback. This procedure will differ if schools are using the electronic DPRs or an app to rate student behavior. Even with electronic DPRs, you will still want to teach students to greet the teacher at each class period

Students are responsible for obtaining a new DPR from the CICO coordinator if they lose one during the school day. They must return the completed DPR to the CICO coordinator at check-out. Students are also responsible for taking home the DPR copy for parent/guardian feedback and bringing the signed copy back the next day. As stated previously, some schools implement the home component on a weekly rather than on a daily basis, so students would be required to bring DPRs home at the end of the week and bring them back to school at the beginning of the following week.

The primary responsibility for students on CICO is to take ownership of their behavior. It is easy to receive positive feedback from teachers, but students on CICO must also accept, and learn from, corrective feedback. Many students with problem behavior want to blame others for their behavioral challenges. An important objective of CICO is that students learn to self-manage their own behavior. Self-management begins with accepting responsibility for one's behavior. Another important feature of CICO is that students begin to learn to self-evaluate their own behavior. For older students, schools may select to have students rate their behavior starting at the beginning of the intervention. This is typically more appropriate in high school settings; more information on self-assessment with high school students is provided in Chapter 11.

If a teacher is giving unnecessarily harsh or punishing feedback, it is the student's responsibility to communicate this information to the CICO coordinator. The student's concern should be discussed at the behavior support team meeting. If the information is accurate, the administrator may need to step in to provide feedback to the teacher.

Training

Before students begin the CICO intervention, it is critical to ascertain that they understand how to participate in all steps of intervention. First, students are given an explanation for why they were selected for the intervention, and then the purpose of the intervention is described. Students should understand that CICO is a positive support system and that the goal is to support them to be more successful in schools. CICO should *not* be introduced as a punishment for a student engaging in problem behavior.

Students should be informed that CICO is a time-limited intervention and that, with practice, they will learn to manage their own behavior. CICO helps students learn which behaviors are positive examples of following expectations and which behaviors are negative examples. As soon as students are fluent in meeting behavioral expectations, CICO support will be gradually faded. Students should be told that the goal is to graduate from the intervention once they're able to manage their behavior. It should be explained in a way that students are striving for graduation. In addition, students should be informed about opportunities for them to have leadership roles once the intervention is discontinued. For example, they can serve as mentors to other students on the intervention once they have graduated. Providing this information gives CICO students something to look forward to and communicates that there are expectations beyond this intervention for engaging in appropriate behavior.

The training of students on the CICO intervention is typically conducted by the CICO coordinator or by the supervising counselor or school psychologist. The initial training takes 15–20 minutes, depending on the level of understanding of the student. Younger students may need more feedback and coaching on how to participate in CICO. A summary of the topics that should be covered during the initial student training is included in Figure 5.10.

The logistics of participating in the CICO intervention are a major emphasis of the student training. Students need to know where and when to check in and where and when to check out. Many of the students who are appropriate candidates for CICO find it challenging to accept corrective feedback from teachers. Furthermore, some of the younger students have a difficult time when they do not meet their daily point goals. For example, a young student might drop to the floor and have a tantrum if they do not earn enough points to receive a reinforcer for the day. The CICO coordinator should demonstrate how to appropriately respond to corrective feedback. Figure 5.2 provided information on one way to teach this skill to elementary school students.

- Purpose of the CICO intervention
  - Positive support system
  - Time-limited
  - Goal is to self-manage behavior
- Where and what time to check in
- Behavioral expectations and daily point goals
- Entering class and handing the DPR to teacher
- Getting feedback from teachers on the DPR
  - Role-play positive and negative examples of following expectations
- Where and when to check out
- Reinforcement system
  - What happens when daily point goals are met?
  - How to handle disappointment if goal is not met
- How to accept corrective feedback
- Plan for fading
  - Discuss CICO graduation and alumni parties

FIGURE 5.10. Topics for initial training of students on CICO.

PARENTS/GUARDIANS

Roles and Responsibilities

Parents/guardians are responsible for signing the consent form to agree that their child may participate in the CICO intervention. This consent form outlines the basic information about the intervention. The form also provides details regarding the parents' role in implementing the CICO intervention.

Parents/guardians are responsible for reviewing the DPR daily (if schools elect to have daily signing), for providing feedback to their child, and for signing the DPR. The student returns the DPR to the CICO coordinator on the following school day. If their child comes home without a DPR, the parents should first ask the child where it is. If the DPR cannot be found two or more times in one week, the parents should call the school and determine the reason. Sometimes, students will hide or "lose" the DPR if they had a rough day and did not meet their point goal. Parents should encourage their child to talk with them about both good days and difficult days. It is important for parents to try to help their children problem solve ways to improve their behavior.

In some cases, parents/guardians are not home in the evenings to sign the DPR and provide feedback. In these cases, the school staff should work with the parents to determine the best way to receive feedback from home. A grandparent, day care provider, or responsible older sibling could provide feedback in place of a parent. Alternatively, if there is no one at home available to sign and provide feedback daily, a "surrogate parent" can be designated at school to provide the student with additional feedback and reinforcement. This surrogate parent might be a school counselor, office staff person, volunteer, or educational assistant. Additionally, as stated previously schools may elect to have parents review DPRs on a weekly rather than on a daily basis, and this schedule may be more possible for the parent to provide feedback.

Although it is not a required part of the intervention, we have seen students make greater behavioral progress when parents provide additional reinforcement at home for meeting their daily point goal. Examples include 15 minutes of additional time to play video games, watch TV, or stay up later. However, parents should not remove privileges if their child does not meet the daily goal. Students who are at risk for problem behavior already receive frequent negative consequences throughout the day. The focus of CICO intervention, however, is to provide more positive experiences and feedback for the student.

Finally, parents/guardians are responsible for communicating regularly with the school regarding their child's progress or any issues that may affect progress on the intervention. For example, if the student is having difficulty at home, has had lots of disruption in their home life, or perhaps has had a change in medication that affects their behavior, this important information needs to be communicated to the school.

Oftentimes, a decline in progress on CICO corresponds with challenges the student is experiencing at home. Regular communication between the parents and the school helps the behavior support team decide if the student should remain on CICO until the issues at home become less disruptive or if a different intervention/support is warranted.

Training

Parents should receive training on the purpose of CICO, on the expectations for their child, and on the expectations for themselves. In most of our schools, this training is conducted over the

- Purpose of the CICO intervention
  - Positive support system
  - Time-limited
  - Primary goal is to learn to self-manage behavior
- Expectations for their child's daily participation in CICO
  - Check-in, teacher feedback, check-out, reinforcement system, home component
- Reviewing and signing the DPR
  - Focus on positive
  - Examples and nonexamples of feedback
- Providing additional reinforcement at home for meeting daily point goals
  - No negative consequences for failing to meet daily point goals
- Plan for fading
  - Discuss CICO graduation and alumni parties
- Troubleshooting and frequently asked questions
  - What to do if the student fails to bring the DPR home
  - Is my child being singled out as a "bad child"?
  - Address any other questions or concerns

FIGURE 5.11. Topics for training of parents/guardians on CICO.

phone rather than in person. The purpose of communicating this information over the phone is to not delay access to the intervention. If it takes 2–3 weeks to set up a meeting with the parent of a child who is at risk, the time spent can greatly delay the preventative features of CICO. A list of important topics to cover during CICO training for parents is provided in Figure 5.11.

When working with parents, the CICO coordinator or other school personnel involved in training should emphasize the positive and time-limited nature of the intervention. Parents should learn that the primary objective of CICO is to teach the student to successfully manage their own behavior. Parents need to know what is expected of their child throughout the day. They should be told to sign the DPR every day (or weekly) when the child comes home and to make sure that their child returns the DPR to school the next day.

Parents should be encouraged to write positive or neutral comments on the DPR before returning it to school. The CICO coordinator or other trainer must emphasize that parents should not punish the child on days when the point goal is missed. If punishment occurs, the student will soon start to avoid bringing DPRs home. Instead, encourage parents to generate a list of activities that can be earned at home for meeting daily point goals. Students can earn extra TV time, visits with friends, time reading with parents, extra computer time, or a special game with their parents if they meet their daily point goals. At the end of CICO parent training, parents should be encouraged to ask questions about any of the information covered in the training.

CHAPTER 6

Designing CICO to Fit Your School

The CICO intervention consists of certain critical features that must always be in place. These features include the use of a DPR, a uniform implementation process for all participating students, regular behavioral feedback to students or self-evaluation with older students, and a frequent use of effective reinforcement. After ensuring that these critical features have been established, each behavior support team has some flexibility to design CICO to accommodate their student population and school. The flexible features of CICO include (1) designing DPRs, (2) naming the intervention to match the culture of the school, and (3) creating an effective reinforcement system. This chapter provides examples of how different schools have personalized their own CICO intervention.

DESIGNING A DPR

Determining Expectations

One of the behavior support team's first tasks is to design the school's DPR. In collaboration with the staff, the team decides which behavioral expectations will be listed on the DPR. Behavioral expectations should be positively worded. That is, expectations should describe the behavior that students are expected to perform, rather than the behavior that they are expected to avoid. For example, positively stated expectations include "Follow directions the first time" or "Keep hands, feet, and objects to yourself." In contrast, negatively worded expectations include "No hitting," "No talking back," or "No disrespectful language."

We highly recommend that the behavior support team choose to use the school's Tier 1 (schoolwide) behavior expectations for the DPR expectations. Students who benefit from CICO support need more practice and feedback on the schoolwide expectations. Some school personnel disagree with this recommendation and assert that each student needs individualized goals. However, *the use of individualized student goals considerably decreases the efficiency of CICO.*

The CICO coordinator manages check-in and check-out for up to 30 students. If each student has individual goals, the amount of time required to complete check-in and check-out increases dramatically. In addition, one reason that teachers can rapidly build fluency in implementing CICO is that the DPR is the same for all students. Once a teacher has supported one student on CICO, they are easily able to implement CICO with a second or third student. Individualized goals reduce the intervention's generalizability to new students. Finally, individualized goals increase the cost of implementing the intervention in terms of staff time. If individualized goals are chosen, the staff need to meet to develop them and the CICO coordinator needs to modify the standardized DPR for each student. Additionally, different sets of DPRs need to be printed, which is less efficient than copying one version. This time can be easily saved by having a standardized DPR for all students who are on the basic CICO intervention.

We recommend using individualized goals only when a student consistently fails to make progress on the intervention. The use of individualized goals is then considered a CICO modification. A discussion of how and when to use CICO modifications is presented in Chapter 9.

As a compromise between using individualized goals or using schoolwide behavior expectations, some schools list their schoolwide expectations, but allow space on the DPR for one individual goal for each student. If schools choose to use one individualized goal per student, we strongly recommend that the *student* write down the goal each morning, rather than require the CICO *coordinator* to complete this extra step. This saves time for the coordinator, while increasing responsibility for the student.

Figure 6.1 illustrates a middle school DPR that includes space for an individualized goal. The schoolwide expectations are listed across the top of the DPR: "Be Respectful," "Be Responsible," and "Be Safe." Under the student's name is a place for the student to write an individualized goal. Next to the schoolwide expectations is a column marked "My Goal," which is used to rate the student's behavior in regard to that individualized goal. Individualized goals should be short, easy to remember, and positively stated. There should be no more than five total expectations listed on the DPR. Requiring a feedback rating for more than five expectations is too cumbersome for teachers to easily embed into their classroom routine.

Another option is for schools to have students write individualized goals under the schoolwide expectations, because Tier 1 expectations are written broadly enough to include most behaviors students should be working on. We prefer this option, because it allows the staff to tie all teaching of expectations to the schoolwide expectations that have already been taught. To do this, the DPR could be designed to have space below each schoolwide expectation to allow room for students to write individualized goals. For instance, in Figure 6.1, the individualized goal "Keep Hands and Feet to Myself" is an example of being safe, and the student could write this goal under "Be Safe" listed as one of the Tier 1 expectations on the DPR.

Some schools choose to further define schoolwide expectations by including examples on the DPR of how to follow those expectations (e.g., if the schoolwide expectation is "Be Respectful," the DPR definition could read "Use kind words and actions."). An example of this type of DPR is shown in Figure 6.2. The schoolwide expectations "Be Safe," "Be Respectful," and "Be Your Personal Best" are further defined in the column subheadings. We have found that if schools are thorough and systematic in teaching the entire student population how to follow Tier 1 schoolwide expectations (including demonstrations of positive and negative behavioral examples) and these expectations are also taught in the classroom by teachers, then adding additional details on the DPR is generally not necessary.

Name: _Chase Johnson_   Date: _10/12/20_

My Goal: _Keep Hands and Feet to Myself_

Parent Signature: _Sylvia Johnson_

0 = No 1 = Good 2 = Excellent	Be Respectful	Be Responsible	Be Safe	My Goal: Keep Hands and Feet to Myself	Teacher Initials	WOW!!! Comments
Period 1	② 1 0	② 1 0	② 1 0	② 1 0	AC	Way to Go!
Period 2	2 ① 0	② 1 0	② 1 0	2 ① 0	BK	Let's work on this together.
Period 3	② 1 0	② 1 0	② 1 0	2 ① 0	LS	
Period 4	2 1 ⓪	2 1 ⓪	2 ① 0	2 ① 0	CT	You can do better tomorrow!
Period 5	② 1 0	② 1 0	② 1 0	2 ① 0	TL	
Period 6	2 ① 0	② 1 0	② 1 0	② 1 0	SM	
Period 7	② 1 0	② 1 0	② 1 0	② 1 0	GN	Good Day!
Total	10	12	13	10	Total:	Total Percent: 80%

FIGURE 6.1. Example of a middle school DPR with an individualized goal.

DPR Rating System

The DPR developed for your school should be teacher friendly. In order to keep CICO efficient, and thus manageable, DPRs should utilize numerical ratings of behavior, rather than require time-consuming narrative explanations. The DPR illustrated in Figure 6.1 includes a section for teacher comments. *It is not required that teachers complete these sections.* Instead, teachers are encouraged to provide written positive feedback when possible. In Figure 6.1, the column is labeled "WOW!!! Comments," prompting teachers to write positive, rather than negative, remarks.

Students should receive lower ratings on their DPRs if they are engaging in inappropriate behavior, but writing negative comments should not be allowed. By virtue of their behavior status, these students often receive frequent negative corrective feedback throughout the day. We recommend that the term "comments" not be used alone on the DPR. Instead, a word or phrase that encourages teachers to provide additional positive feedback should be inserted. Terms such as "WOW," "Successes," or "Celebrations" are good examples that prompt teachers to provide positive feedback.

Each DPR should include a range of scores. Some schools prefer to use a "2, 1, 0" ranking system, whereas other schools prefer to use "3, 2, 1 system," We recommend a 3-point (rather than 4- or 5-point) system, as this makes it easier to obtain consistent rankings for all teachers.

A key defining the corresponding meaning of each numerical rating should be included on the DPR. For example, in Figure 6.1 the DPR includes the following key: "0 = No" (the student did not meet the behavior expectation), "1 = Good" (the student did a good job meeting the expectation), and "2 = Excellent" (the student did a great job meeting the expectation).

Prior to implementation of CICO, the entire staff should clarify and agree on the difference between each rating. Doing so will increase interrater reliability across teachers. In other words, if a student exhibits similar behavior in Classroom A and in Classroom B, then they should receive the same rating for that behavior from each teacher. If one teacher uses a much stricter standard for judging the student's behavior and the student consistently receives a "0" in the first classroom and a "2" in the second classroom for the same behavior, the student will become confused regarding what is appropriate and what is inappropriate. Teachers should be giving students consistent feedback about their behavior by providing consistently similar behavior ratings.

Schools might choose to adopt the following guidelines to increase interteacher rating consistency. If a student needs one reminder or correction during the period, they can still receive a "2." If the student needs two reminders or corrections, they receive a "1"; three or more reminders equals a "0" rating. This simple approach may or may not work for your school. Problem behavior is locally and contextually defined, so your school staff should agree on how to define each score on the ranking system.

Date: 11/3/20   Student: Erika Young

0 = No	1 = Good	2 = Excellent

	Be Safe	**Be Respectful**	**Be Your Personal Best**		
	Keep hands, feet, and objects to self	Use kind words and actions	Follow directions	Work in class	Teacher initials
9:00–A.M. Recess	② 1 0	② 1 0	② 1 0	2 ① 0	DS
A.M. Recess– Lunch	② 1 0	② 1 0	2 ① 0	② 1 0	DS
Lunch–P.M. Recess	② 1 0	2 ① 0	② 1 0	② 1 0	DS
P.M. Recess–3:40	② 1 0	② 1 0	② 1 0	② 1 0	DS
Total Points = 29 Points Possible = 32	Today 91 %		Goal 80 %		

Parent Signature: I. Young

WOW: I'm proud of you.

FIGURE 6.2. Example of an elementary school DPR with expectations defined.

Some schools list the definitions of each rating on the DPR. Figure 6.3 provides an example of a school that has a 4-point rating system, with the rating system key included on the DPR. We recommend that you attempt to keep the ratings key short enough so that the DPR fits on a half page to reduce the amount of expenditures for printing and copying costs, especially if schools choose to use NCR paper to facilitate easy duplication. In addition, the 4-point rating system included on this DPR corresponds with the school's standards-based grading system. The school has detailed standards that students must master for academics as well as social behavior, and the rubric for scoring students is included in their CICO intervention.

The behavior support team must decide how many rating periods to include on the DPR. *At a minimum, include four rating periods.* Fewer than four precludes the student from having a difficult period/class, and still meeting their daily point goal. For middle and high school settings, the periods of the day are used as rating periods. If a school has six periods in a day, there will be six opportunities for the student to receive feedback on their behavior.

In elementary school settings, we recommend that the rating periods correspond to the natural transitions in the school day. For example, as illustrated in Figure 6.2, a natural transition occurs before morning recess and before lunch. Optimally, the marking periods should not last longer than 75 minutes. Students on CICO, especially those who are younger, respond better when they receive feedback after short intervals of time. However, if 75 minutes does not correspond with a natural transition, it is preferable to wait for a time when the teacher can easily incorporate student feedback into their classroom routine. We cannot emphasize enough that verbal feedback to the student who is considered at risk (i.e., requires Tier 2 support) needs to occur throughout the period, not just toward the end when the teacher needs to record the

Shark Code
Sunset Elementary School

		YES	NO
Checked in		YES	NO
Checked out		YES	NO
Parent Signature		YES	NO

Goal: 50%   55%   60%   65%   70%   75%   80%

Student: _____   Date: _____   M Tu W Th F   Goal: _____

Expectations	Arrival to Recess				Recess to Lunch				Lunch to Recess				Recess to Dismissal				Total
	Tough time	So-so	Good	Awe-some	Tough time	So-so	Good	Awe-some	Tough time	So-so	Good	Awe-some	Tough time	So-so	Good	Awe-some	
Safe	1	2	3	4	1	2	3	4	1	2	3	4	1	2	3	4	
Honest & Accountable	1	2	3	4	1	2	3	4	1	2	3	4	1	2	3	4	
Respectful & Kind	1	2	3	4	1	2	3	4	1	2	3	4	1	2	3	4	
Keep Practicing																	

Successes:

4 = Awesome: Met expectations with positive behavior; worked independently without any corrections/reminders.
3 = Good: Met expectations with only 1 reminder/correction.
2 = So-so: Needed 2–3 reminders/corrections.
1 = Tough time: Needed 4 or more reminders/corrections.

Parent/Guardian Signature: _____

Note: Parent comments can be included on the back of this form.

FIGURE 6.3. Example of a DPR with a 4-point ranking system and ranking system defined.

DPR rating. The goal is to catch students "being good"/following expectations and let them know in the moment if they are not meeting expectations. The rating at the end of the period is a summary of all those pieces of feedback that were provided during the 75-minute block.

Some school teams have considered creating different DPRs to correspond with each different grade level. In response, we emphasize that increasing the number of DPR formats decreases the efficiency of the intervention. Elementary school teachers have argued that younger students (e.g., in kindergarten and first grade) have different academic expectations and scheduling than older students (e.g., in fourth, fifth, and sixth grades). One school responded to this dilemma by creating two DPR formats, one for the lower grades and one for the upper grades.

Examples of the lower- and upper-grade DPRs are provided in Figures 6.4 and 6.5. In these examples, Vista Elementary School added an expectation of "Work Completion" to the three schoolwide expectations because the school's behavior support team felt that including it was important. Since the school had only three schoolwide rules, adding an fourth expectation did not make the rating system unmanageable for teachers. Prior to implementing this addition, they received feedback and approval from the entire school staff.

Nonclassroom Settings

Should nonclassroom settings be included on the DPR? Nonclassroom settings include places such as the lunchroom/cafeteria, the playground, hallways, the bus area, and the bathrooms. The focus of the CICO intervention is on classroom behavior. Students who have problems only

Vista Elementary ROAR Program
WILD CARD

Name: _____ Date: _____

GOAL	9:05– A.M. Recess	A.M. Recess– Lunch	Lunch– P.M. Recess	P.M. Recess– 3:45
Follow directions the first time	2 1 0	2 1 0	2 1 0	2 1 0
Be on task	2 1 0	2 1 0	2 1 0	2 1 0
Keep hands, feet, and other objects to yourself	2 1 0	2 1 0	2 1 0	2 1 0
Work Completion	2 1 0	2 1 0	2 1 0	2 1 0

KEY
0 = No
1 = Somewhat
2 = YES!!

Successes: _____

Goal for Today: _____ %

Total for Today: _____ %

Teacher Signature _____ Parent Signature _____

FIGURE 6.4. Example of a lower-elementary grade DPR.

VISTA Elementary ROAR Program
WILD CARD

Name: _____   Date: _____

GOAL	Reading	Language Arts	Spelling	Math	Science	Social Studies	Health
Follow directions the first time	2 1 0	2 1 0	2 1 0	2 1 0	2 1 0	2 1 0	2 1 0
Be on task	2 1 0	2 1 0	2 1 0	2 1 0	2 1 0	2 1 0	2 1 0
Keep hands, feet, and other objects to yourself	2 1 0	2 1 0	2 1 0	2 1 0	2 1 0	2 1 0	2 1 0
Work Completion	2 1 0	2 1 0	2 1 0	2 1 0	2 1 0	2 1 0	2 1 0

Teacher Initials _____   _____   _____   _____   _____   _____   _____

KEY
0 = No
1 = Somewhat
2 = YES!!

Successes: _____   Assignments: _____

Goal for Today: _____ %

Total for Today: _____ %

Parent Signature _____

FIGURE 6.5. Example of an upper-elementary grade DPR.

in unstructured nonclassroom settings should not be placed on CICO intervention, but rather should have an intervention that focuses on the setting where they are engaging in problem behavior. In most schools, there is not enough supervision on the playground or in the cafeteria for up to 30 students to receive feedback at the same time. A playground supervisor could not effectively track the individual behavior of more than three to five students at a time. *We recommend that the DPR should not include nonclassroom settings.*

For a few students who have problem behavior in classroom settings, as well as during recess, we have had success in using a "recess contract" in combination with the DPR. The recess contract looks similar to the DPR (i.e., the same behavioral expectations), but is kept separate from the DPR. It is rated by the person who is supervising the playground or other unstructured area. There should be only one or two students for each recess who receive this type of feedback. Schools that utilize a recess contract typically employ a separate reinforcement system for it. Alternatively, with a little extra work on the part of the CICO coordinator, recess contract points could be embedded into the CICO overall daily point goal. For more information on CICO for recess, see Chapter 8.

Other Considerations

Behavior support teams often choose to include spaces below the columns on the DPR where teachers can initial their ratings (illustrated in Figure 6.5). We also recommend providing a place for the parent/caregiver signature as well as space for parents to provide additional positive feedback to their child.

In designing the DPR, consider whether or not to include a section for the student's percentage point goal. To increase efficiency, many schools use the same goal for all students (i.e., 80% or higher). However, in order to experience initial success on CICO, some students will need to start at a lower percentage point goal. In Figure 6.3, there is a section for the students to select individualized goals by circling a goal between 50 and 80% of points. In addition to having a section for the percentage point goal, there should be a section to write what the student's total points were for the day. Doing so will allow the parents to easily determine if their child has met their goal and will also ease the task of data entry for the CICO coordinator.

Some elementary schools have struggled with how to include nondaily activities on the DPR. For example, elementary school students often attend physical education (PE), music, library, and art classes and computer lab once each week. Many schools have combined these activities into one marking section. Rather than listing these rotations separately, they will list "PE/Music/CompLab" as one of the times in the day that the students can receive feedback. Another issue to consider is early dismissal days. In order to provide adequate teacher preparation time, some schools have early dismissal once a week. In that case, it is important to include a section on the DPR that lists the total points possible for these early dismissal days. For instance, an elementary school might have a total of 40 points possible on every day of the week except Friday. On early-dismissal Fridays, students could earn a total of 30 points. If students arrive late or need to leave early, the rating periods that were missed should be crossed out so that the CICO coordinator knows to not calculate those periods in the total score. *In other words, the percentage of points should accurately reflect the total number of points possible on any given day.*

Summary

The following is a summary of recommendations for creating a DPR to fit your school:

- Include schoolwide expectations on the DPR.
- Expectations must be positively stated.
- No more than five expectations should be listed on the DPR.
- The use of DPR must be teacher friendly and require teachers to circle ratings rather than provide narrative feedback.
- Include a narrow range of scores (e.g., "3, 2, 1").
- Include a ratings key on the DPR.
- Include a column for "successes" rather than just "comments."
- The DPR should fit on a half sheet of an 8½″ × 11″ piece of paper to reduce copying costs.
- Nonclassroom settings should *not* be included on the DPR.
- Include spaces below columns for teachers to initial the rating and a line for parent/guardian signatures and parent comments.
- Determine if the percentage point goal will be listed.
- Include an area for total points earned.

NAMING THE CICO INTERVENTION AND THE DPR

We encourage schools to rename CICO and the DPR to fit the culture of their school. Many schools like to rename CICO to match the mascot of their school. This choice can be left to the behavior support team. We recommend requesting input from the entire staff when renaming CICO and the DPR. Table 6.1 lists examples of alternative names for CICO and the DPR, some of which are based on different school mascots.

Why is renaming the program so important? It helps the staff of the school feel more personally connected to the intervention. Rather than adopting an intervention that was designed and implemented in another school, CICO becomes an intervention that has been redesigned to fit your school's demographics and characteristics. When renaming the intervention, it is important to focus on the positive nature of CICO; as we have discussed, CICO should be a positive behavior support intervention and not a punishment system. Parents and students are more likely to engage in the intervention if its name indicates support rather than punishment. For example, renaming CICO "Supporting Our Antisocial and Rowdy Students," or SOARS, would

TABLE 6.1. Examples of Different Names for CICO and the DPR

Mascot	Name of the intervention	Name of the DPR
	Check-In, Check-Out (CICO)	Daily Progress Report
Eagles	Students On A Road 2 Success (SOARS) Program	SOARS Card
Skyhawks	Helping A Winning Kid (HAWK) Program	HAWK Report
	Hello, Update, and Goodbye (HUG) Program	HUG Card
Lions	Reinforcement of Appropriate Response (ROAR) Program	Wild Card
	Check and Connect Program	Check and Connect Card
Wildcats	Positive Action With Support (PAWS) Program	PAWS Card
Buffalos	Building Up Fantastic Futures *or* Be Up for Future Success (BUFF) Program	BUFF Card
Tigers	Trying All I can to Learn (TAIL) Program	Tiger Tail Card
Rams	Rams Achieve More (RAM) Program	RAM Card
Zebras	Heading with Energy in the Right Direction (HERD) Program	Earn Your Stripes Card
Eagles	Excel And Gain Life Educational Skills (EAGLES) Program	EAGLES Card
Sharks	Safe, Honest, Accountable, Responsible, and Kind (SHARK) Program	Shark Code

likely turn off parents, students, and teachers. In contrast, using the same acronym, CICO could be renamed "Students On A Road 2 Success."

When renaming CICO, we recommend that you do not use the terms "behavior support plan" or "behavior contract." To begin with, CICO is not an *individualized* behavior support plan, and it is critical that teachers not confuse this program with Tier 3 levels of behavior support. Students who need Tier 3 support often require comprehensive FBAs and individualized behavior support plans. In our experience, many teachers have tried behavior contracts in their classrooms. When they request assistance from the behavior support team, they are looking for an intervention beyond what has already been implemented to support the student. If the team mentions implementing a "behavior contract," the teacher might reply, "I've already tried that."

Choose a name that is easy to remember and teach. If you rename CICO using an acronym such as "HAWK—Helping A Winning Kid," make sure that teachers, parents, and students know what the acronym means.

DEVELOPING AN EFFECTIVE REINFORCEMENT SYSTEM FOR CICO

Rationale

Students who qualify for CICO have been unsuccessful in meeting schoolwide behavioral expectations at the Tier 1 level of behavior support. These students typically need additional feedback and reinforcement in order to learn appropriate ways to meet schoolwide behavioral expectations. One goal of CICO is to help the student build positive relationships with adults in the school. A second goal is to help the student become independent in managing their own behavior. To achieve independence, students should be gradually faded from the structured reinforcement system of CICO to the informal reinforcement of the schoolwide behavior system.

The most powerful reinforcer in the CICO intervention should be the CICO coordinator. The CICO coordinator should be someone whom the students like, trust, and look forward to seeing on a daily basis. Some reinforcement systems that are developed by schools for use with CICO include tangible items such as small toys or snacks. These tangible rewards should always be paired with social praise and acknowledgment from the CICO coordinator.

Assessing Reinforcer Preference

When the behavior support team develops CICO to fit the culture of their school, some preliminary development of the reinforcement system should also be addressed. For example, the team typically determines the percentage of points that students must earn in order to receive a reinforcer. It may also consider the different types of reinforcers that students can earn. It is important, particularly for middle or high school students, to choose rewards that are perceived as truly reinforcing by the students themselves.

A *positive reinforcer* is defined as an event or stimulus that follows some behavior and increases the likelihood that the behavior will occur again in the future (Alberto & Troutman,

2017). In other words, whether or not a reward is reinforcing is determined by its impact on the student's behavior, not by whether or not we expect it to have high value to the student. For example, we might consider extra time on the computer to be an effective (and relatively cheap) reinforcer for middle school students. However, if earning extra computer time is not desired by the student, and if it does not cause the student to continue to follow behavioral expectations, then it will not be a suitable reinforcer. Indeed, for a student who struggles with keyboarding skills, extra computer time could actually be perceived as a punishment. The team determines whether or not a reward is reinforcing by examining its impact on the student's behavior. If, after receiving a reward for meeting their goal, the student continues to meet their goal or demonstrates an improvement in their behavior, the team can assume that they have chosen an effective reinforcer for that student.

Staff members often choose "rewards" for students, but in the end discover that these rewards are not very reinforcing. That is, the rewards do not have the intended impact on the students' future behavior. As an example, one school provided school supplies (pencils, erasers, etc.) as rewards for students who met their daily point goal. Many of the students complained that they already had enough supplies and would be more interested in earning a snack or extra recess time. Once the school allowed the students to choose rewards for which they were willing to work (i.e., activities or items that were actually reinforcing), students' progress on CICO improved.

One way to assess reinforcer preference is for students to complete a reinforcer checklist (refer to a sample checklist in Figure 6.6 and a blank version in Appendix E.1). The reinforcer checklist is typically used to assess students' interest in earning different types of long-term reinforcers rather than daily reinforcers. It should be noted that this is just one example of different reinforcers that students may be interested in earning. We recommend that the behavior support team collaborate with the school staff to generate a list of inexpensive or free reinforcers that are available in their school setting. Every school has teachers who have certain talents that they may be willing to share, or has special activities that are already a part of the schoolwide reward system that can be used with CICO. For example, in one school we worked with a teacher who was a former semiprofessional soccer player. Students on CICO could earn a one-on-one soccer lesson from this teacher for meeting their goals for a certain number of days. In another school, the janitor was willing to provide guitar lessons as a reinforcer for students receiving CICO support.

When possible, we recommend trying to identify reinforcers that involve spending time with others, particularly socially competent peers. Students who qualify for CICO often have difficulty with peer relations, and therefore will benefit from more positive interactions with peers through structured reinforcement activities. For example, some schools have allowed the student to choose four other students to participate with them in extra gym time earned for meeting daily point goals.

Reinforcers for Checking In and Checking Out

The primary reinforcer for students checking in and out should be the personal connection with CICO coordinator. However, we have noticed that sometimes when students have a rough day and do not meet their daily point goals, they are less likely to check out at the end of the day. To increase the incentive for checking out, some schools have instituted a "lottery system."

Reinforcer Checklist
(To be completed by the student)

Please circle YES or NO if the item or activity is something you would like to earn.

Activity Reinforcers

Video game	YES	(NO)	Basketball	YES	(NO)
Swimming	YES	(NO)	Magazine	(YES)	NO
Watching video/DVD	YES	(NO)	Drawing	(YES)	NO
Walking	YES	(NO)	Field trips	(YES)	NO
Comic books	(YES)	NO	Puzzles	(YES)	NO
Play-Doh	(YES)	NO	Board game	YES	(NO)
Craft activities	(YES)	NO	Card game	YES	(NO)

Please list any other favorite activities you would like to earn.

Computer Games

Material Reinforcers

Stickers	(YES)	NO	Erasers	YES	(NO)
Special pencils	(YES)	NO	Bubbles	YES	(NO)
Lotions	YES	(NO)	Play-Doh	(YES)	NO
Colored pencils/crayons	(YES)	NO	Rings	YES	(NO)
Free tardy pass	YES	(NO)	Puzzles	(YES)	NO
Bookmarks	YES	(NO)	Trading cards	(YES)	NO
Action figures	YES	(NO)	Small toys	(YES)	NO
Free assignment pass	(YES)	NO	Necklaces	YES	(NO)

Please list any other favorite items you would like to earn.

Edible Reinforcers

Small one-bite candies	(YES)	NO	Cereal	YES	(NO)
Larger candy	(YES)	NO	Fruit	YES	(NO)
Vending machine drink	YES	(NO)	Pretzels	(YES)	NO
Juice/punch	YES	(NO)	Potato chips	(YES)	NO
Vegetables and dip	YES	(NO)	Corn chips	YES	(NO)
Crackers	YES	(NO)	Cookies	(YES)	NO
Donuts	(YES)	NO	Bagels	YES	(NO)
Candy bars	(YES)	NO	Cheese	YES	(NO)

Please list any other favorite name brands or snacks you would like to earn.

Gum

(continued)

FIGURE 6.6. Example of a reinforcer checklist.

Social Reinforcers

Pat on the back	(YES)	NO	Verbal praise	(YES)	NO
Extra P.E./gym time	YES	(NO)	Free time	(YES)	NO
Games with teacher	(YES)	NO	Field trips	(YES)	NO
Games with friends	(YES)	NO	Special seat	YES	(NO)
Lunch with friends	(YES)	NO	High five	YES	(NO)
Visit with friends	(YES)	NO	Awards	YES	(NO)

Please list any other favorites you would like to earn.

_____

_____

_____

_____

FIGURE 6.6. *(continued)*

Students receive a lottery ticket for checking in on time in the morning and receive a second lottery ticket for checking out at the end of the day. A sample copy of a school's lottery ticket is presented in Figure 6.7.

At the end of the week, a drawing is held for students on CICO. The more times students check in and check out, the more chances they have to win. The prizes for the drawings are small (e.g., a coupon to the school store or snack bar), but students typically enjoy this extra opportunity to earn reinforcers. To make the drawing more exciting, some schools employ a "mystery motivator" format and allow the student to select from one of three potential prizes that are placed in sealed envelopes. To provide further reinforcement and encouragement, the weekly prizewinners' names are posted for other students on CICO to see. This public posting should not be accessible to all students in the school because publicizing the names could create tensions with other students who want to be on the intervention.

Some of our schools think that it is unnecessary to have a lottery system because the students really enjoy participating in the program. The lottery system is a component that can be added if a school is experiencing problems with students consistently checking in and checking out. Your school may want to start without a lottery system and add it only if it becomes necessary.

FIGURE 6.7. Sample lottery ticket from Vista Elementary.

Reinforcers for Meeting Daily Point Goals

For CICO to be effective, students should receive reinforcement for meeting their daily point goals. One of the biggest mistakes schools make when first implementing CICO is misunderstanding the importance of frequent reinforcement during the first 2 weeks of the intervention. If a student does not meet their goal within the first 2 weeks on CICO, the goal is set too high, and the student's interest in CICO and willingness to actively participate will rapidly wane.

Collecting baseline data is critical to setting achievable daily point goals. For the sake of efficiency, we recommend using the same daily point goal for all students. Occasionally, however, students will need a lower point goal to achieve initial success. Baseline data will help identify these students.

One way to motivate students to achieve consistent success on CICO is to give them rewards for meeting their point goals for a specified number of days. Behavior support teams will often set a consecutive criterion (e.g., student must earn 80% of points on 5 *consecutive* school days), rather than a cumulative criterion (e.g., after a *total* of 5 school days of earning 80% of points, the student can earn the reinforcer). We recommend using a cumulative criterion. Students on CICO will have difficult days, and therefore a cumulative goal is more achievable and reinforcing than a consecutive goal.

Daily/Short-Term Reinforcers

Some type of small, daily reinforcement is often effective in maintaining students' consistent engagement in the intervention. Although we recommend avoiding the use of edible reinforcers, many schools have found that a piece of candy or a small snack is highly valued by students at the end of the day. We encourage schools to choose healthy snacks if food is to be used as a reinforcer. Although the use of daily reinforcers for meeting point goals is helpful, it is not required. The behavior support team should consider the cost of daily reinforcers and the financial resources budgeted for the CICO intervention.

One creative approach to daily reinforcers is the "Spin the Wheel" game, which gives students a random chance of receiving one out of a variety of rewards. This approach to daily reinforcement is more effective in elementary schools than in middle or high schools. Figure 6.8 provides an example of a spinning wheel that was implemented in Vista Elementary School.

FIGURE 6.8. Spinner system for daily CICO rewards.

On the spinning wheel pictured in Figure 6.8, the wider sections of the wheel (and thus the higher chances of winning) include social rewards such as a "high five" or a secret handshake. It is preferable for students to work for social reinforcement over tangible reinforcers. The narrower sections of the wheel (thus, the lower chances of winning) include a piece of candy, a gumball, or a sticker. Two schoolwide rewards have been included on the wheel. One is a "Lion's Pride 5" ticket, which is a token used for schoolwide rewards. The other is a "Lion's Loot" dollar, which goes back to the student's classroom to be put into a classroom bank. At this school, the "dollar" is associated with a schoolwide social skills intervention. The student on CICO has the chance to earn dollars for the entire class to engage in an activity.

Some secondary schools we have worked with have elected to track points on Class Dojo (Class Dojo, Inc., n.d.), rather than having students carry a DPR from class to class. Class Dojo is a classroom app that allows teachers to track student behavior (both positive and negative), and also enables teachers to communicate with parents by sharing pictures of what is happening during the school day. Points that are tracked on Class Dojo for students on CICO can then be either spent individually by the student in some sort of school store, or some schools have allowed CICO student points to be added to an overall classroom goal for a party or other activity/privilege. Allowing students on CICO to earn points for homeroom classes or a group of classes (e.g., if schools are broken into pods or grade levels) is a positive way to get peer attention for appropriate behavior displayed throughout the school day.

Figure 6.9 illustrates another example of a daily reward provided in a middle school setting. Students who check out at the end of the day and meet their daily point goals can play on a Lego wall for 5 minutes before dismissal. If students do not meet their goals, they receive a schoolwide ticket for checking out and are sent back to class. This type of reward is one that needs to have buy-in by everyone on the staff and work within the school schedule. But, for this school, this daily reward possibility has been a fun and low-cost addition to their CICO intervention.

FIGURE 6.9. Sample Lego wall reward.

Long-Term Reinforcers

Many schools offer opportunities for students on CICO to earn long-term reinforcers. Long-term reinforcers typically require students to meet their daily point goal across several days or even several weeks. These rewards are typically identified on the reinforcer checklist as items that individual students are interested in earning.

To manage a long-term reinforcer system, some schools use a "credit card" strategy to tally points. Other schools use a "savings card" or "point card" strategy. Regardless of its name, the aim is to give the student a choice between using points to receive smaller reinforcers or saving points to earn larger, long-term reinforcers. The CICO credit card system allows students to earn more points for better performance on their DPR. Here is an example of how one school outlined points that students can earn:

- > 70% on DPR = 1 point on credit card
- > 80% on DPR = 2 points on credit card
- > 90% on DPR = 3 points on credit card
- 100% on DPR = 4 points on credit card

Figure 6.10 illustrates an example of a CICO credit card developed by Vista Elementary School that has been used successfully in both elementary and secondary school settings.

The CICO coordinator (older students can self-manage this process) marks the number of points earned by the student by highlighting or placing a checkmark in each box. We recommend against using a special stamp or hole punch for the task because recording points this way for up to 30 students per day would be fairly time consuming.

1	2	3	4	5	6	7	8	9	10
X	X	X	X	X	X	X	X	X	X
X	X	X	X	X	X	X	X	X	20
									30
									40
									50
									60
									70
									80
									90
									100

FIGURE 6.10. Sample credit card.

The credit card system requires that the school develop a menu of reinforcers with different point values. Once a student earns enough points for the reinforcer they desire, the points are exchanged with the CICO coordinator. The credit card is marked to show that the student has spent those points.

The credit card can be used until the student fills up a card with 100 points. Then a new credit card is given to the student. In Figure 6.10, the student has earned a total of 20 points over the course of several days and has decided to exchange 10 points for 5 minutes of extra computer time to play games during lunch.

Who Provides the Reinforcement?

Typically, the CICO coordinator manages the CICO reinforcement system. If a student earns additional computer time, the CICO coordinator provides the time or collaborates with one of the student's teachers to allocate the time. Members of the behavior support team are also often involved in delivering reinforcement. School counselors and school psychologists typically have more flexibility in their day than teachers to provide time-based reinforcers, such as extra gym or computer time or even an extra recess.

When designing CICO to fit your school culture, the issue of how to manage the reinforcement system must be addressed. CICO will be less effective if students do not receive reinforcement soon after they have earned it. Imagine if a student has earned basketball time, but the school counselor in unable to play basketball with the student until 3 weeks after the reinforcer is earned. Extended delays in delivery of reinforcement will result in student frustration and reduced commitment to the intervention.

Reinforcement for Teachers

Reinforcement for active and successful participation in the CICO intervention should not be limited to participating students. Teachers should receive reinforcement as well. Effective teacher participation is the backbone of an effective CICO intervention. Teachers must provide ratings of student behavior on a regular basis and ensure that the student understands how to meet the behavioral expectations.

Teachers complete the DPR on a daily basis but may not know how the student is progressing overall. One way to reinforce teacher participation is to share their student's DPR data graph with them. Additional strategies can be used to reward teachers for implementing CICO with fidelity. Some schools encourage CICO students to nominate their teachers for a "Supportive Teacher CICO Award." Once a month, a different teacher is acknowledged on the basis of student nomination. Other schools examine the positive teacher comments written on the DPR and recognize a teacher for being a positive participant in CICO intervention. Whatever approach is chosen, it is important to recognize teachers' efforts and support in helping students achieve success on CICO.

Reinforcer Budget

The behavior support team will likely have to grapple with the costs of reinforcers against the backdrop of budgetary constraints. Since school budgets are often tight, CICO should be implemented in a cost-effective manner. The greatest financial outlay is the expense of funding a CICO coordinator for approximately 10–15 hours a week. The costs of reinforcers should be a minor portion of CICO budget. The following list provides recommendations for keeping expenses low, while still implementing an effective reinforcement system.

- Solicit donations from the community. All donations to a school are tax deductible, and the school can publicly acknowledge the business or community agency as a supporter of the school.
- Choose rewards that involve the use of time rather than the purchase of tangible items. Some of our favorite examples include (1) time with a preferred adult; (2) time with a (socially competent) peer; (3) time to read a favorite comic book or novel; or (4) extra gym, recess, art, computer, or library time.
- Students will work to earn opportunities for leadership or other positions of status. They include (1) being first in line for lunch, (2) leading the class in a lesson, (3) helping in the library, (4) assisting with computers, (5) broadcasting morning announcements, and (6) leading social skill lessons with the support of counselor.
- Students will work to avoid activities that the student perceives as aversive. With teacher permission, the following can be used as reinforcers: (1) one free homework, (2) one free assignment, (3) skipping problems on an assignment, or (4) being excused from homeroom to do a preferred activity.
- When purchasing games or toys, choose items that are reusable, such as board games, remote-controlled cars, iPads, Wii, or Nintendo. All of these items involve an initial investment up front, but can be used over and over again.

Summary

The following is a summary of recommendations for developing reinforcement systems for CICO:

- Assess student preference for long-term reinforcers.
- Use baseline data to assess if the standard daily point goal is appropriate for the student.
- Consider implementing an incentive system for checking in and checking out.
- Determine if there will be both short-term and long-term reinforcers.
- Identify a system to manage long-term rewards, such as the credit card system.
- Determine who will deliver the reinforcers. Avoid lengthy delays in reinforcer delivery, as delays result in frustration and reduced student commitment.
- Develop a system to provide reinforcement to teachers who actively support CICO.

CHAPTER 7

Selecting Fidelity and Outcome Data Systems to Guide CICO Decision Making

Robert H. Horner, K. Brigid Flannery, Angus Kittelman, Mimi McGrath Kato, and Leanne S. Hawken

CICO is an efficient and effective intervention only if the team managing the CICO process has access to appropriate data in an appropriate format and at the appropriate time(s) for effective decision making. The purpose of this chapter is to review both the array of decisions made by teams managing CICO and the types of data affecting those decisions. The goal is to provide administrators and team members with clear guidelines for selecting data systems and the decision tools needed for effective and efficient CICO implementation.

As with all elements of PBIS (Horner & Sugai, 2015), the collection, summary, and use of data are "core features" of CICO. Data should provide a team with the information needed to make decisions. When a school or district selects data systems to support CICO, it is helpful to consider the decisions that should be influenced by those data. Table 7.1 provides a summary of the evaluation questions typically asked by teams implementing CICO, the decisions associ-

K. Brigid Flannery, PhD, is Associate Professor/Senior Research Professor at the University of Oregon. Her current work focuses on increasing successful school outcomes for students at risk and students with disabilities.

Angus Kittelman, PhD, is a postdoctoral scholar within Educational and Community Supports, a research unit at the University of Oregon. His research focuses on MTSS, implementation science, and vocational rehabilitation.

Mimi McGrath Kato, MS, is a senior researcher in the College of Education at the University of Oregon. All of her grant work over the past 15 years has focused on improving outcomes for at-risk youth in secondary schools.

TABLE 7.1. CICO Decisions, Evaluation Questions, and Data Sources

Evaluation question	Decision/action	Data source
Is CICO being implemented as intended (with high fidelity)?	Implement CICO with fidelity, and define an action plan to correct any fidelity deficiencies.	Fidelity of Implementation Measure (FIM) Tiered Fidelity Inventory (TFI) (Tier 2)
Do students selected for CICO meet selection criteria?	Select students for CICO who (1) are receiving Tier 1 PBIS (including classroom management) supports; (2) have two or more ODRs; and/or (3) are nominated by a teacher, student, administrator, or family member.	Office discipline referrals (ODRs) Universal screening tools (as appropriate) Teacher/administrator/family/student nomination
Are there students on CICO who need adaptations or supplemental supports?	Identify students on CICO who need more assistance. *Note:* If most students are not meeting the CICO criteria, the challenge in most cases will be in implementing basic CICO features, not individual student adaptations.	Proportion of students on CICO who are meeting criterion Proportion of CICO points per student over the last 4 weeks of school
Are the problems encountered by students on CICO who continue to struggle defined with a level of precision that allows for the design of adapted or supplemental supports?	Problem precision: For each student on CICO who continues to struggle, define their behavioral challenge with a level of precision needed for effective problem solving. *Note:* Outcomes include precision problem statement and competing behavioral pathway.	Proportion of CICO points per student per class period over the last 4 weeks of school Brief functional behavioral assessment (FBA) Student-guided FBA
Are adaptations and supplements to CICO consistent with core features of the precise problem statement?	Problem solving: Select CICO adaptations and supplements that (1) modify context to prevent problems, (2) teach and prompt appropriate behavior, (3) minimize the likelihood that problem behavior will be rewarded, and (4) elevate rewards contingent upon desirable behavior.	Precise problem statement Behavior support plan adaptations and supplements to CICO
Are students successful on fading off the CICO intervention?	Identify students ready to fade off CICO, and implement a fading protocol.	Proportion of CICO points per student over the past 6 or 8 weeks

ated with each evaluation question, and the specific data sources that may be used to address each question. The decision by a school or district to adopt CICO requires planning not only for the professional development of staff, but also for the adoption of the data tools and decision-making protocols needed to make CICO effective. Our experience is that most schools already have some of these data sources needed for CICO (e.g., ODR data, FBA protocols). Additions typically include (1) a formal measure of CICO fidelity, (2) a specific referral form (or process) for nominating students to enter CICO, and (3) a computer application that allows for both the easy and efficient entry of CICO daily data (DPR) and the generation of reports summarizing the DPR data. In the following sections, we review examples of how data are used to address evaluation questions and guide CICO decisions. We start this discussion with the evaluation question related to the fidelity of implementation for two reasons: (1) because schools struggle the most to plan for and use fidelity to determine the effectiveness of CICO and (2) gathering fidelity data takes time, as there are no web-based applications to collect these data; therefore, school teams will need to plan ahead for who will efficiently collect these data and how often, who will examine the data, and how effectiveness will be determined. There are, however, many data sources and computer applications that may be used to facilitate CICO student outcome decisions. We use the summary reports from the School-Wide Information System (SWIS; May et al., 2018) as examples in the chapter, but we recognize that any computer application that generates similar data outputs will be effective.

IMPLEMENTING CICO WITH FIDELITY

The first decision that a school or district team faces is to determine if CICO is being used as intended (with fidelity). Both when CICO is first adopted, and at least annually thereafter, a school team should assess whether the core elements of CICO are in place and are being implemented as intended. This assessment need not be cumbersome and can occur as part of a regular PBIS or MTSS leadership team meeting. If concerns or deficits are identified, then the assessment should result in an action plan for improving CICO fidelity. There are two productive ways to assess CICO fidelity. The first is to assess CICO fidelity as part of a larger, annual PBIS fidelity assessment using the Tiered Fidelity Inventory (TFI; Algozzine et al., 2014; McIntosh et al., 2017). The TFI is used by school leadership teams to assess if Tier 1, Tier 2, and/or Tier 3 PBIS practices and systems are being used as intended. A school using CICO would focus on the Tier 2 elements of the TFI, such as Item 2.6 (increased instruction on behavioral expectations, improved structure in daily schedule, and increased opportunity for adult feedback); Item 2.7 (matching CICO with students who find adult attention rewarding); and Item 2.8 (team access to appropriate data). The TFI results provide a summary score for each tier (with 70% used as the level needed to achieve fidelity; see Figure 7.1). For any school with a Tier 2 summary score below 70%, there should be a careful review of the TFI Tier 2 Items Report and the development of an action plan to address unimplemented or underimplemented items (e.g., if the team scored Item 2.8 (data) "not in place," then the team would create an action item for addressing this deficiency within the next 3 months).

The second, and more detailed, assessment of CICO fidelity is to use the formal Fidelity of Implementation Measure (FIM) that has been designed specifically for CICO (CICO-FIM;

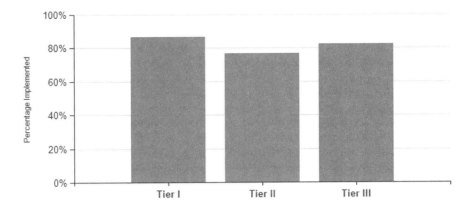

FIGURE 7.1. Example summary scores for each tier on the TFI.

see Figure 7.2 for a sample and Appendix F.1 for a blank copy). Although formal psychometric testing (i.e., reliability and validity) has not yet been conducted with this measure, it has proven helpful to schools implementing CICO. The FIM is composed of 12 items, each rated as 0 = not in place, 1 = partially in place, and 2 = in place. The items assess both the mechanics of CICO ("students on CICO check in daily") and the organizational systems needed for sustained CICO use ("school employs a CICO coordinator . . ."). The FIM produces an overall "total" score, but is most helpful when individual items are reviewed and action plans are developed to address items that are rated a "0" or "1."

The key message is that any school claiming to use CICO will, on a regular basis, document fidelity and formulate relevant action plans to improve CICO implementation when needed. Given the regular level of transition and turnover in education, a regular assessment of whether "core features" are in place is both a useful professional development activity and essential to ensuring that critical elements of any intervention remain available for students.

SELECTING STUDENTS FOR CICO

The second major decision made by teams implementing CICO is to determine which students should receive CICO support. Most schools already have data systems for identifying students who are "at risk." As noted in Chapter 3, one option is to consider any student with two or more major ODRs as a potential candidate for CICO. A more reliable, and more formal, option is to rely on standardized, universal screening tools in which teachers are asked to rate students on a small number of core behavior patterns. Universal screeners, such as the Systematic Screening for Behavior Disorders (SSBD; Walker, Severson, & Feil, 1994) and the Social Skills Rating System (SSRS; Gresham & Elliot, 1990), are available and are well summarized by Kathleen Lane and her colleagues (Lane, Menzies, Oakes, & Kalberg, 2012). These tools identify students whom teachers perceive as needing more than Tier 1 support.

The third data source that teams use to identify students for CICO support is nomination (typically via a CICO referral form) by teachers, administrators, parents, or even the students

School: Hillcrest Middle School   **Date:** 4/7   **Pre:** _____   **Post:** x_____

Evaluation Question	Data Source P = permanent product I = Interview O= Observation		Score 0–2
1. **Does the school employ a CICO coordinator whose job is to manage the CICO (10–15 hours per week allocated)?** (0 = No CICO Coordinator, 1 = CICO coordinator but less than 10 hours per week allocated, 2 = CICO Coordinator, 10–15 hours per week)	Interviews with Administrator and CICO Coordinator	I	2
2. **Does the school budget contain an allocated amount of money to maintain the CICO?** (e.g., money for reinforcers, DPR forms, etc. (0 = No, 2 = Yes)	CICO Budget Interviews	P/I	2
3. **Do students who are identified via screening, ODRs or referred to CICO receive support within a week?** (0 = more than 2 weeks between referral and CICO support, 1 = within 2 weeks, 2 = within a week)	Interview CICO Referrals and CICO Start dates	P/I	2
4. **Does the administrator serve on the behavior team that reviews CICO data on a regular basis?** (0 = no, 1 = yes, but not consistently, 2 = yes)	Interview	I	2
5. **Do 90% of behavior team members state that the CICO intervention has been taught/reviewed on an annual basis?** (0 = 0–50%, 1 = 51–89%, 2 = 90–100%)	Interview	I	2
6. **Do 90% of the students on CICO check-in daily? (Randomly sample 3 days for recording)** (0 = 0–50%, 1 = 51–89%, 2 = 90–100%)	CICO recording form	P	2
7. **Do 90% of students on CICO check-out daily? (Randomly sample 3 days for recording)** (0 = 0–50%, 1 = 51–89%, 2 = 90–100%)	CICO recording form	P	2
8. **Do 90% of students on CICO report that they receive reinforcement (e.g., verbal, tangible) for meeting daily goals?** (0 = 0–50%, 1 = 51–89%, 2 = 90–100%)	Interview students on CICO	I	2
9. **Do 90% of students on the CICO receive regular feedback from teachers?** (randomly sample 50% of student DPR's across 3 days) (0 = 0–50%, 1 = 51–89%, 2 = 90–100%)	CICO Daily Progress Reports	I	2
10. **Do 90% of students on the CICO receive feedback from their parents/caregivers?** (0 = 0–50%, 1 = 51–89%, 2 = 90–100%)	CICO Daily Progress Reports	P	0
11. **Does the CICO coordinator enter DPR data at least weekly?** (0 = no, 1 = 1–2× a month, 2 = weekly)	Interview	I	1
12. **Do 90% of behavior team members indicate that the daily CICO data are used for decision-making?** (0 = 0–50%, 1 = 51–89%, 2 = 90–100%)	Interview	I	2
	Total = 21/24 = 88%		

FIGURE 7.2. CICO-FIM Scoring Guide.

themselves. Remember, this referral process can be initiated in grade-level team meetings (i.e., sometimes referred to as professional learning communities, or PLCs). It should be noted that three commonly used forms of data for identifying students (ODRs, universal screeners, local nomination) can also be used together. For example, it is common for school teams to start with either ODR data or teacher nomination, then add universal screening information or additional nominations if more data are needed to influence the team's decision.

As a final note, we encourage teams to consider ways of making CICO student nomination and entry as maximally efficient as possible, even if the process is an informal one. The team managing CICO should set up clear guidelines for participation for all students receiving CICO support (e.g., level and intensity of problem behavior are not physically dangerous, student is perceived as finding adult attention rewarding, student is more successful when receiving an elevated level of structural prompts and positive feedback). Once clear criteria for participation in CICO have been defined, it is reasonable that a CICO coordinator, in consultation with the school psychologist or counselor who oversees the intervention, could decide to include a student in CICO quickly (e.g., within 2 days), without extensive review or team meetings. Teachers should see CICO as a way to get efficient access to assistance for themselves and "at-risk" students.

IDENTIFYING STUDENTS ON CICO WHO NEED MORE ASSISTANCE

Most behavior support teams managing CICO implementation have more students receiving CICO support than can be discussed during a weekly or biweekly meeting. The team needs a process for identifying which students are benefiting from the current CICO supports and which students are continuing to struggle. Students may be perceived as needing more detailed discussion by the team if (1) they are not experiencing the core elements of the daily CICO cycle (morning check-in, teacher feedback, afternoon check-out, family checks) or (2) they are experiencing the core elements, but have lower than expected daily CICO point totals.

To identify students who need focused discussion by the team, we recommend reviewing a report of a student's average daily points. This report defines a time period (typically the most recent 30 calendar days) and produces histograms that summarize (1) the average daily percentage of CICO points received per student and (2) the number of school days each student has reported CICO data. Figure 7.3 provides a simulated example of the SWIS average daily points by student report for 1 month (November) for a school with 25 students receiving CICO supports. Note that (1) each bar indicates the mean percentage of possible CICO points a student has earned each school day for the days monitored in November; (2) a horizontal line indicates the 80% goal being used for all students (in this example); and (3) an index indicates the actual number of school days that each student reported CICO data (at the bottom of each student's bar). For example, Alec Lexington reported CICO data on 19 school days in November and averaged 82% of CICO points per day. Amanda Franks, Brandy Jones, and Bruce Gil have low percentages of average CICO points per school day, but each of these students reported only 1 day of CICO data in November, so more time on CICO is needed for effective decision making. Brian Bender, however, reported data on 18 days of CICO data in November, yet also has a below-goal level of mean CICO points per day. Brian is a student for whom more detailed discussion is appropriate.

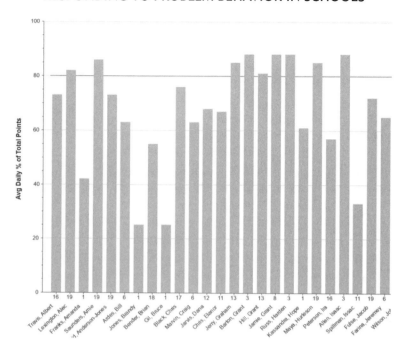

FIGURE 7.3. Simulated example of the SWIS average daily percentage of points by student report for 1 month for a school with 25 students receiving CICO supports.

An efficient behavior support team meeting should begin with a report from one team member (i.e., the "data analyst"), who has the task of reviewing the CICO data before the meeting and helping the team both celebrate the students who are succeeding on CICO and quickly move to a discussion of students who are currently receiving CICO but are not performing as expected (Todd et al., 2012). The first question the team should consider for each of these students is whether they are experiencing the CICO cycle as intended.

One way a student will be identified as not experiencing the core elements of the CICO cycle is if they were expected to be receiving CICO support for more days than are indicated on the average daily points by student report. For example, Amanda Franks and Brandy Jones have only 1 day of data reported, but members of the behavior support team know that each of these students just started CICO in November. The team also knows, however, that Bruce Gil has been on CICO for over 5 weeks, and the fact that he is reporting only 1 day of CICO data suggests that he is not picking up his CICO DPR, is not collecting data, or is not returning his DPR at the end of the day. The key message is that Bruce is not experiencing the key elements of the daily CICO cycle. Team problem solving needs to focus on how to improve the procedural elements of CICO for Bruce so that he is more likely to follow the daily CICO cycle (i.e., self-management protocols, initial positive check-in associated with picking up his DPR, class-by-class self-evaluations and positive feedback from teachers focused on meeting behavioral expectations, and end-of-day check-out used to provide social rewards and prompt performance for the next day). Bruce would be a focus of discussion at the meeting, and the team would need to consider strategies to increase his participation in the daily CICO cycle before considering other changes.

When the behavior support team identifies students who are not experiencing the key elements of the daily CICO cycle, the team also needs to determine whether this is an individual-student or a systems issue. A key indicator may include the number of students not experiencing the core elements of the daily CICO cycle. For example, as indicated in Figure 7.3, if over 40% of the students are not consistently meeting their daily CICO daily point goals, and have been enrolled in CICO for multiple days, this outcome could indicate a systems issue (e.g., how students are oriented, how faculty are included in the process, or how the DPR is used). As part of this level of review, the team may need to consider: (1) reevaluating the CICO training protocol for students and school personnel; (2) the effective use of incentive/reinforcement systems; or (3) whether Tier 1 systems are in place and implemented with high fidelity (i.e., schoolwide expectations are posted, taught, and reinforced in classrooms). As noted earlier, other indicators for determining concerns with CICO systems include completing the CICO FIM (Figure 7.1) or using the TFI (Algozzine et al., 2014), which allows teams to assess and progress monitor the implementation fidelity of tiered behavior systems throughout the school year.

Individual student and systems problems could also be identified when behavior support team members, such as the CICO coordinator, meet with individual students to troubleshoot daily challenges. For example, if a student is inconsistently completing the morning check-ins with the CICO coordinator, the coordinator could find a time to meet with the student (e.g., before lunch or class) to identify the barriers preventing the student from completing the morning check-in. If a student forgets to check in with the coordinator upon arriving at school, the CICO coordinator may work with them to identify additional support strategies for ensuring that these check-ins occur. Strategies could include having the coordinator meet the student at the bus stop or having the bus driver prompt the student to check in with the coordinator. If the CICO coordinator has to adjust the daily CICO cycle for multiple students struggling to complete their morning check-ins, a systems issue may be the problem. For example, the behavior support team may need to reevaluate how students are being trained to complete the daily CICO cycles and what additional training may be needed (e.g., student–teacher walkthrough of CICO cycles, role playing, modeling).

Alternatively, the team also needs to consider additional supports for students who are engaging in the daily CICO cycle but are still having behavioral challenges. The data in Figure 7.3 suggest that Brian Bender fits this description and is a likely candidate for a focused team discussion. He has reported 18 days of CICO data, but his CICO point data indicate that challenges remain. The behavior support team data analyst would not only identify that Brian has low levels of CICO points, but also would drill down in the database to define Brian's behavior with greater precision. For Brian, the process of defining the problem more precisely means first determining if the pattern of behavioral problems occurs regularly or episodically (e.g., multiple days with problem behaviors vs. occasional days with problem behaviors), and if the behavior problems are occurring across all classes, or only in some. The team will then want to examine the data in greater detail to identify what Brian is doing that is limiting his CICO points, where and when this problem behavior is most and least likely, and what possible consequences (what he gets or avoids) may be maintaining his problem behavior. To do this task well, the data analyst and the entire behavior support team need access to more detailed data summaries about Brian's low CICO performance patterns. Identifying CICO problems with functional precision is the next decision challenge for the support team.

PRECISE ASSESSMENT OF LOW CICO PERFORMANCE

An effective CICO data system allows the behavior support team (including the data analyst) to assess patterns associated with low CICO performance by sorting the CICO points for an individual student, first by days and then by school periods. Figure 7.4 provides a summary of Brian's daily CICO points that allows a quick assessment of whether he is having mainly "good days," with only a few "bad days," or if he has a pattern of consistently low CICO points. Brian's data in Figure 7.4 indicate some positive days (above 80%), but show a general pattern of recurring challenges, with a decreasing trend over the past 2 weeks. These data support the need for adding or altering supports within CICO to help Brian.

It is also helpful to determine if Brian's behavior is consistent across class periods. Brian typically has six class periods each day in his middle school. The CICO-SWIS data summary provides a simple process for sorting CICO points by students across classes or periods. Figure 7.5 summarizes the average CICO points per class period for Brian Bender for November. The two sets of numbers under each bar indicate the class period (top number), and the number of school days with CICO data (bottom number in parentheses) from that class period. From the data shown in Figure 7.5, the team can quickly identify that the major challenge for Brian occurs in Class Period 3. A confirmation of this hypothesis is provided by examining the Daily CICO points per day for Period 3 shown in Figure 7.6. Together, the data in Figures 7.5 and 7.6 document that Brian is consistently receiving an unacceptably low level of CICO points in Period 3. The team can now use this knowledge of Brian's problem behavior patterns and focus on specific support variables unique to Class Period 3 that could be addressed to improve his

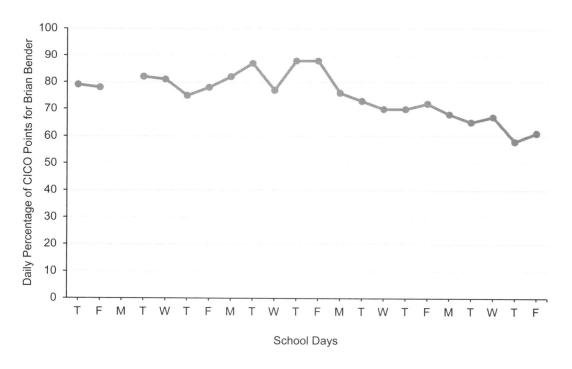

FIGURE 7.4. Daily percentage of CICO points for Brian Bender.

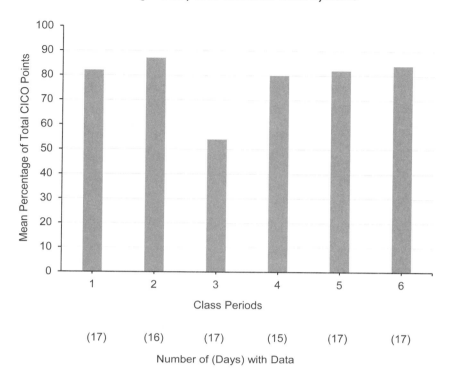

FIGURE 7.5. Average CICO points per class period for Brian Bender.

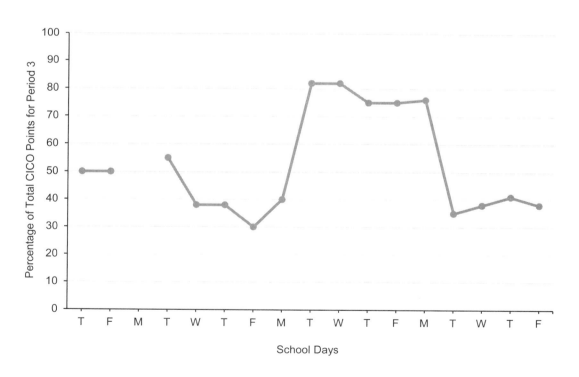

FIGURE 7.6. Daily CICO points per day for Period 3 for Brian Bender.

success. Defining CICO "problems" with precision improves the ability of a school team to develop practical and specific solutions (Horner et al., 2018).

PROBLEM SOLVING

From their knowledge of Brian's problem behavior, and the data provided in Figures 7.4–7.6, the CICO team is able to formulate a statement that identifies Brian's specific problem behavior (i.e., what it is, when it is most and least likely, and the consequences that maintain the behavior). The team's initial discussion would focus on identifying what Brian obtains or avoids in Period 3 when he engages in this problem behavior. With this information, the team would collaborate with the teacher in Period 3 to either recommend minor modifications to the CICO process (e.g., incorporate peer supports or alter the schedule or type of recognition for positive behavior), or determine if he would benefit from a social skills group or a full FBA and access to Tier 3 individualized supports (see Chapters 8 and 9 for more detail). The general pattern would be to use the staff's knowledge of Brian, the school, the faculty, and the social context to (1) identify ways to minimize events that prompt problem behavior, (2) teach socially and educationally appropriate ways for Brian to handle difficult situations, (3) elevate the recognition and reward that Brian receives for correct behavior, (4) limit the likelihood that problem behavior is inadvertently rewarded, and (5) continue to monitor both whether planned support procedures are being used and whether they are effective.

FADING STUDENTS FROM CICO SUPPORTS

An underappreciated component of CICO decision making is the process for fading CICO supports when a student has been successful. There is always a temptation to "leave well enough alone" and simply continue a student on CICO indefinitely when the student's behavior has improved. This is a reasonable choice, but over time it will result in too many students receiving CICO supports. As a general guideline, teachers should not have more than three students on CICO at the same time. An overabundance of students on CICO decreases team effectiveness and challenges the efficiency of CICO for teachers.

The decision to fade a student from CICO supports is also difficult if the team is concerned that a student is succeeding only because of CICO supports and that removing the supports will result in a return to undesirable behavior. This concern is matched, however, by the mirror worry that if we do not build the self-regulation skills needed for the student to be successful in the future, we have only postponed problems, and not really shifted the social and educational trajectory for the student. Given the complexity and importance of the decision to fade CICO supports, we address this decision in more detail.

In terms of criteria, consider students for fading from CICO supports if and when they have demonstrated earning an average of 80% or more of their CICO DPR points per day after 6 to 8 weeks on CICO. Note that access to these data should be available to the team by constructing a summary report on the average daily points per student (Figure 7.3) and extending the time frame to a 2-month window. The decision will be influenced by the fluency and consistency of the student's performance and a consideration of the opinion of those who know the student best (e.g., are knowledgeable about the host of moderating factors). Students should be checking in, both in the morning and with class teachers, and demonstrating success in prompting and recruiting feedback from adults.

The first step in fading CICO supports is to shift the DPR from being completed only by the teacher to being completed first by the student and then confirmed by the teacher. Note that in high schools, we often start at this point in the process (but with much more attention to training the self-monitoring skills). In middle and elementary schools, during fading it is often helpful to start by having the student recruit teacher feedback first to learn the standards expected by each teacher. Once a student has learned what behavior is expected, it is helpful to teach them to self-monitor and self-evaluate. Using the DPR, students can self-evaluate their performance in meeting their behavior expectations and then recruit feedback from teachers, which provides them with additional training in self-management. For data accuracy, only the teacher's ratings on the DPR should be recorded by the CICO coordinator and used to assign points. More advanced data management options are being developed and tested by Flannery and her colleagues (Kittelman, Monzalve, Flannery, & Hershfeldt, 2018) that will allow a CICO coordinator or team to assess not only the teacher's ratings, but also the proportion of ratings on which the teachers and student agree (e.g., the extent to which the student is mastering the self-management skills).

To encourage accuracy in the student's DPR ratings, the student can earn small rewards for having the same score as the teacher. For example, if a student gives themselves a rating of 2, 2, 1, 2 on the four schoolwide behavioral expectations and the teacher gives the same rating, the student could earn a schoolwide token or bonus. Note that this reward is focused not on the absolute score, but on accurate self-assessment (matching the score given by the teacher). Once the student can consistently rate their behavior reliably (i.e., 80–85% agreement between teacher and student), the rewards for accuracy can be faded, and the rewards for appropriate behavior can be reinstated.

The second step in CICO fading is to remove the teacher rating component, which means that the number of times the teacher provides a rating is gradually reduced. For example, during the first week of CICO fading, the teacher will provide a rating feedback on all days. Over time, teacher feedback may only be required for one or two class periods. Fading this component gives the teacher more flexibility to support new students beginning participation on CICO.

In addition to fading teacher ratings, the student's participation in the CICO process can be faded as well. When the student is learning to self-assess their own behavior, they continue to check in and check out and to turn in a DPR. The CICO coordinator continues to collect, enter, and analyze the student's CICO data during the time that they are learning to rate their own behavior. Data collection at this point is critical. The CICO data demonstrate whether the student's behavior stays the same, improves, or significantly worsens, as CICO is gradually faded. In the case of worsening behavior, the team should discuss whether or not the student is ready to move to self-management. The worsening behavior may be an indication that it is too early to remove CICO support. Alternatively, it may be an indication that the CICO fading process has not been adequately explained to the student or effectively implemented.

The third step in CICO fading is to eliminate the DPR but retain the daily check-in and check-out with the CICO coordinator (or designated adult). The student is asked if they are "ready" each morning and asked to provide a summary of their day in the afternoon. Rewards may still be used for checking in, but only morning and afternoon check-in data are collected, coupled with the normal attendance, behavioral, and academic data available through the school data systems. A helpful prompt during this phase of CICO fading is to encourage the student to continue to check in with teachers when they enter and leave class (or start/end a class period), but it is important to make it clear to the student that this check-in is voluntary and less formal. The goal is to have the student engage in typical student–adult interaction but continue to receive the feedback and support that they have found helpful. The student should fade out the artificial elements of CICO (e.g., the DPR), but not the ability to recruit and obtain support from adults in the school.

The final step in CICO fading is to make the morning and afternoon check-in voluntary. We find that it is common for students to continue to check in even after this process has started, but then they may shift to checking in with another adult. In schools where CICO is working well, some students like CICO supports and view the intervention positively. Other students may view CICO fading as a punishment, rather than as a recognition or promotion. It is important to talk about fading during the initial student training on the CICO process. In addition, as mentioned previously, we have found that providing students with alternative ways of gaining adult attention, such as becoming the CICO coordinator's helper, allows them to continue to feel supported without needing full access to the intervention.

If a middle school or high school student wants to stay on CICO, they could continue to check in and check out with the CICO coordinator (unless, of course, the additional check-in/check-out overburdens the coordinator). At the middle school or high school level, continuing this contact should not pose an unnecessary burden on the resources of the behavior support team since the student would continue to rate themselves using the DPR, rather than taking up a teacher's time. Although the student may elect to continue to check in and check out, the behavior support team no longer enters, analyzes, or responds to the data. The student can continue to have daily contact with a person they enjoy, without creating any additional workload for the behavior support team. This makes it possible for a new student to begin CICO.

One final consideration for fading students from CICO is the amount of time remaining in the school year. Often, the easiest transition is to discontinue CICO at the end of the school year. Rather than implementing the self-management process, we have found that treating the end of the school year as a natural fade has worked with many students. A celebration is provided at that time, and students are told that they will begin the next school year as CICO alumni. This type of natural fading works well with the majority of students who have demonstrated success on CICO. Some students will continue to need CICO support the following school year, and this end-of-year option is workable if CICO has not reached the maximum number of students it can support. If there are already 30 students on the intervention, and 3 additional students need to be added, the fading procedures described above should be implemented so that the CICO coordinator is not overwhelmed with too many students at one time.

SUMMARY

The focus of this chapter is on types of problem-solving and decision-making processes that improve success with CICO. Start with clarity about the presumed process by which CICO alters student behavior. When students are clear not just about the behavioral expectation wording (e.g., be respectful) but about what the words mean for behavior in class, in the hallways, and on the bus, they are more likely to behave in ways that are successful. Students who start each day and each class with positive interactions and a highly predictable schedule are more likely to sustain positive behavior and academic engagement. When angry, discourteous, and noncompliant behavior is ineffective (i.e., does not result in rewards or allow avoidance of aversive events), these behaviors become less likely.

CICO is not a behavioral panacea. It is an intervention that is very efficient and easy to implement and produces significant outcomes for many, but not all students. It is important to note that students with more severe problem behavior, major mental health and disability challenges, and long histories of problem behavior will likely need more individualized and more intensive behavior support (although CICO may be a part of these more intensive supports).

The success of CICO depends a great deal on the ability of school personnel, and especially the behavior support team, to collect, summarize, and use data for effective decision making. Our experience with implementing CICO in several thousand schools indicates that asking a team to adopt CICO without providing the team with regular, accurate, and summarized data decreases the potential value and effectiveness of the intervention. Although there are many

TABLE 7.2. Data System Features and Criteria for CICO Implementation

Data system feature	Criterion
Ease of student data setup.	Student information for CICO should be directly transported from the schoolwide data system.
Ease of daily CICO data entry per student.	CICO data are uploaded automatically when an electronic app is used, or entered daily with minimal, but dedicated time from a school staff member.
Access to average daily CICO points per student: *These data will be used to identify students needing more assistance.*	Team can produce the average daily CICO points per student graph within 1 minute.
Access to average CICO points per school day per student: *These graphs will be used to assess the consistency of problem behavior patterns.*	Team can produce the average daily CICO points per school day within 1 minute.
Access to average CICO points for a student per class period: *This graph is used to assess the pattern of problem behavior across class periods.*	Team can produce the average daily CICO points per student per class period within 1 minute.
Access to the percentage of CICO points for a student for one class period: *These data are used to confirm the need for intervention focus on particular class periods.*	Team can produce the average daily CICO points per student per class period within 1 minute.

computer applications and data summary protocols that can be effective, we strongly encourage any school adopting CICO to arrange for a data system with the features summarized in Table 7.2.

CICO is an evidence-based intervention for enhancing the self-regulation and behavioral success of at-risk youth. A central component of CICO is the collection, summarization, and use of data for decision making. Teams adopting CICO will be most successful in CICO implementation when they are trained and provided with an efficient and effective data system to guide team meetings and shape team problem solving.

CHAPTER 8

Adaptations to Basic CICO

In Chapter 3 we introduced the features of and implementation process for basic CICO. The basic version of CICO can be adapted by making some slight adjustments to the intervention process and the DPR to target a variety of behaviors in addition to frequent minor misbehaviors. We highly recommend that schools design and implement basic CICO prior to developing and implementing adapted versions of CICO for several reasons. First, schools need to acclimate to the basic CICO model and work out any systems issues that may prevent the intervention from being effective with the majority of the students. As we mentioned in previous chapters, if CICO is not effective with 70% of the students who receive the intervention, schools need to examine the systems features (e.g., check-in, teacher feedback, check-out) to resolve any implementation issues. Second, once schools have successfully implemented basic CICO, the staff typically have bought into the intervention and are more open to using this technology with other types of problem behaviors. Experiencing success with CICO with students who have externalizing behaviors helps build behavioral momentum for teams to introduce adaptations to basic CICO.

In addition, schools need to make sure that they are implementing this intervention with fidelity and getting the outcomes they desire prior to making any modifications. One of the biggest mistakes we see is that schools view CICO as a simple intervention and quickly adapt the core features. In adapting CICO, they often lose the efficiency of the intervention by individualizing DPRs and other features to target specific student needs. It's important to implement basic CICO with fidelity in order to be successful with adding adaptations. Schools should also use a systematic process when adapting CICO to maintain efficiency and fidelity. For each adapted version of CICO (such as for academic and/or organizational skills), schools should develop screening criteria, determine how progress will be measured, and use a schoolwide, universal DPR to record these targeted behaviors. As we discussed in Chapter 3, including the same expectations for all students, and in this case targeted behaviors, helps ensure intervention efficiency and feasibility. Schools should develop a universal DPR for each adapted version of CICO, so that all students receiving a particular version of CICO use the same DPR, rather than individualizing the DPR for each student.

The purpose of this chapter is to outline some of the adaptations that can be made to basic CICO to expand the types of behaviors the intervention can be used to address. Specifically, we will discuss the extent to which CICO can be adapted to target the following: (1) academic and/or organizational skills, (2) absences and tardies, and (3) problem behavior during recess. We also address how CICO can be adapted for use with a wider range of students, including younger elementary and preschool students. Another adaptation to CICO that we discuss in a later chapter involves targeting students who experience internalizing problem behaviors, such as anxiety, depression, or withdrawal symptoms. More detailed implementation information, as well as a review of the research on CICO for internalizing behaviors, is presented in Chapter 12.

CICO FOR ACADEMIC AND/OR ORGANIZATIONAL SKILLS

Basic CICO targets students with externalizing problem behavior, including students who engage in acting out, disruption, noncompliance, and similar behaviors. These students are typically identified as at risk based on ODRs. Other students are considered at risk and struggle because they lack the organizational skills to effectively navigate the academic environment. They are students who may or may not have a disability, such as attention-deficit/hyperactivity disorder (ADHD), or who struggle to keep up with the demands of an academic environment. Although these students may not typically act out, they may fall behind in work completion and credits earned (if in high school) and have poor grades. It is important to implement interventions to support the academic success of students with poor organizational and/or academic skills, because their challenges may lead to further academic difficulties and increase their risk of engaging in problem behavior (Algozzine, Putnam, & Horner, 2010; Kittelman et al., 2018).

Adapting CICO to support academic and/or organizational skills involves minor adjustments, primarily related to the DPR. First, the expectations on the DPR can be revised to refer specifically to academic and/or organizational behaviors, such as asking for help, completing assignments, staying on-task, and turning in homework (Turtura, Anderson, & Boyd, 2014; see Figure 8.1 for an example of an elementary school academic/organizational DPR). For older students, especially those in middle or high school, the DPR can be adjusted to include a space for students to record information related to assignments, such as the materials needed to complete the assignment, the assignment due date, and a brief description of the assignment (see Figure 8.2 for an example of a middle school academic/organizational DPR). This assignment tracker can be added to the back of the DPR to provide more space to record information, and students can have the opportunity to earn a certain amount of points for completing their assignment tracker each day. The expectations on the DPR can be either the basic CICO expectations (especially if students are engaging in minor misbehaviors) or can be academic/organizational expectations as described in the elementary school example. The daily process of CICO for academic and/or organizational skills is the same as that for basic CICO, in which the students

SOAR Card
<u>S</u>ummary <u>O</u>f <u>A</u>chievement & <u>R</u>esponsibility
"WATCH ME SOAR!"

Name _____   Date _____

Time	Follow directions	Work completed or asked for help	On-task	Materials ready	Turned in my homework	
Before A.M. recess	2 1 0	2 1 0	2 1 0	2 1 0	2 1 0	
After A.M. recess	2 1 0	2 1 0	2 1 0	2 1 0	2 1 0	Teacher Initials
Before P.M. recess	2 1 0	2 1 0	2 1 0	2 1 0	2 1 0	
After P.M. recess	2 1 0	2 1 0	2 1 0	2 1 0	2 1 0	
Totals points	/8	/8	/8	/8	/8	

Today's point total: _____   Goal: _____ %   Today _____ %

2 = Excellent: Consistently follows rule. Needs 1 or fewer reminders (80–100% of the time).	1 = OK: Follows rule most of the time. Needs 2–3 reminders (60–79% of the time).	0 = Poor: Does not or rarely follows rule. Needs more than 3 reminders (0–59% of the time).

Successes: _____

Coordinator Initials _____

Parent Signature _____

FIGURE 8.1. CICO for academic and/or organizational behaviors—elementary school example.

check in and check out with the coordinator and receive feedback at designated times throughout the day.

How Are Students Screened for Academic and/or Organizational CICO?

Schools can develop a data-based decision rule to determine which students qualify for this type of CICO. As of this writing, only one study has examined similar adaptations made to CICO to support students' academic and organizational skills (Swain-Bradway, 2009), and the school in which this study was implemented did not use universal academic screening. As such, there are no definitive screening criteria or cut scores for identification to use for determining which students would benefit most from CICO adapted for academic and/or organizational behaviors. However, many schools have implemented and have reported success with this type of CICO. With this in mind, schools need to develop their own criteria for accessing the intervention, as many students could use the support of an academic/organizational CICO. Some indicators that schools may choose to use in determining which students are in need of CICO for academic and/or organizational skills could include a certain percentage of missing work; a

Name _____

Kennedy Card

Date _____

Class period	Brought materials to class	Worked and let others work	Followed directions the first time	Assignment tracker and feedback	Teacher Initials
1	2 1 No	2 1 No	2 1 No	Assignments: Wow,	
2	2 1 No	2 1 No	2 1 No	Assignments: Wow,	
3	2 1 No	2 1 No	2 1 No	Assignments: Wow,	
4	2 1 No	2 1 No	2 1 No	Assignments: Wow,	
5	2 1 No	2 1 No	2 1 No	Assignments: Wow,	
6	2 1 No	2 1 No	2 1 No	Assignments: Wow,	

Goal: _____ % Total: /36 = _____ %   Assignment tracker: Goal: _____ % Total: /6 = _____ %

Parent Signature: _____

FIGURE 8.2. CICO for academic and/or organizational behaviors—middle school example.

TABLE 8.1. Risk Factors to Consider for Academic and/or Organizational CICO

- Grade point average (GPA)
- Failing at least one subject/course at midterm of grading period, primarily associated with missing or incomplete work
- Percentage of in-class work completion
- Percentage of homework completion
- Missing academic credits
- Frequent tardies or absences
- Off-task behavior during class (e.g., sleeping, on phone, talking)
- Observable disorganization (e.g., messy and cluttered notebook/backpack, frequently loses or misplaces assignments)

---

failing grade in at least one class/subject at the midterm of the first grading period; evidence of lack of organization (e.g., notebook and/or backpack are disorganized and student often cannot find assignments); minor attendance issues; and off-task behavior during class (e.g., failure to complete work, sleeping in class, phone use, talking; Swain-Bradway, 2009). Table 8.1 includes some risk factors that may be helpful to consider when determining which students would benefit from this adapted version of CICO.

Measuring Progress

Measuring progress on CICO for academic and/or organizational skills is very similar to measuring progress on basic CICO, but can also include additional measures to assess the response to the intervention. The percentage of points on the DPR can be used as a progress monitoring tool for students on this type of adapted CICO. In addition, several measures can be used to assess pre–post outcomes, such as the students' grade point average (GPA) per grading term. However, depending on how long the student is on the intervention, a cumulative GPA may not be sensitive enough to show change. More sensitive pre–post measures may include the percentage of work completed in class, the percentage of homework assignments turned in, and the average assessment scores.

It's important to note that for students who are struggling academically, *CICO alone will not improve academic performance,* especially for students who are experiencing significant struggles with academic content. Students need research-based instruction, and possibly more intensive interventions, in the subject areas in which they are struggling in order to improve academic performance. The purpose of CICO that targets academic and/or organizational skills is for the student to track assignments and to get more feedback on work completion and their academic engagement in class. For this reason, CICO could be combined with an academic intervention, particularly for students whose academic difficulties seem to be more related to challenges with content rather than with organization and engagement alone. More information is presented on how to layer interventions, including academic interventions, onto basic CICO in Chapter 9.

CICO FOR ATTENDANCE

Some students are identified as at risk on the basis of their attendance behavior. Students who miss more than 15% of school days are at greater risk for engaging in disruptive behavior, experiencing anxiety and/or depression, struggling academically, being held back a grade, dropping out of school, and being involved in the criminal justice system (Skedgell & Kearney, 2018). Based on these risk factors, schools should prioritize implementing Tier 2 interventions for students who miss 10–15% of school days and Tier 3 interventions for students who miss more than 15% of school days (Skedgell & Kearney, 2018). Students who are also regularly missing a portion of the academic day because they are late for school or who are skipping classes (at the secondary level) should also be considered at risk. Basic CICO should be able to target externalizing and attendance behaviors that students struggle with. However, for students who are mainly absent frequently and/or chronically late for school and/or for specific class periods, CICO for attendance may be an appropriate intervention.

In elementary school, CICO for attendance involves having the student check in each morning with the CICO coordinator to ensure that the student is on time and ready for the school day. In schools we have worked with, check-in for attendance can either be done using a paper-and-pencil type of format as shown in Figure 8.3 or by using a Google doc format and having students check in on an iPad. See Figure 8.4 for a screenshot example of one of the schools we worked with. Checking in using an iPad provides a time date stamp for each student so that on-time behavior can be measured. One of the goals for CICO for attendance is to increase the number of minutes the student is attending school. Even if the student is not missing an entire school day, missing 10–20 minutes of instruction daily can have an impact on academic performance.

At the time of writing, no studies have evaluated the effectiveness of CICO adapted to support attendance behavior in middle or high schools. However, CICO adapted to improve attendance and reduce tardiness may be effective at the secondary level because, similar to basic CICO, the intervention can provide a foundation for establishing communication and

Park View Elementary
Check-in, Check-Out for Attendance & Tardies

Student: _____ Teacher: _____
Date:

			Time In	Minutes Missed
Monday	Great Job!			
Tuesday	Great Job!			
Wednesday	Great Job!			
Thursday	Great Job!			
Friday	Great Job!			

Total: _____

Weekly _____%   Parent's Signature _____

FIGURE 8.3. CICO DPR for attendance—elementary school example.

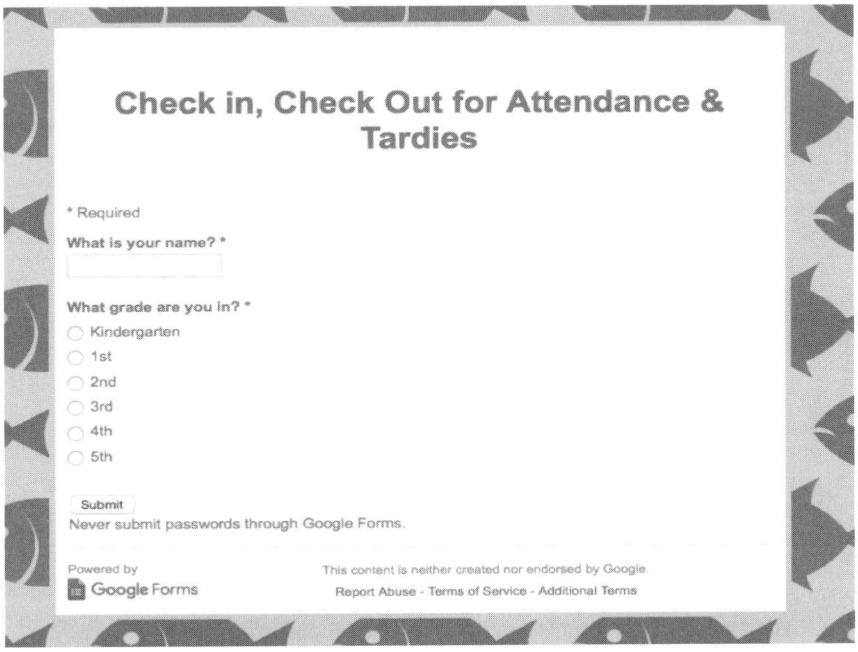

FIGURE 8.4. CICO electronic DPR for attendance—elementary school example.

cultivating relationships between students and teachers and may help hold students accountable for their actions. For secondary schools interested in adapting CICO to target attendance and tardiness, attention should be paid to incorporating reinforcers that are highly motivating. These reinforcers are essential for intervention success because the intervention will need to compete with other highly reinforcing contingencies for skipping class or arriving late for class, such as social time with friends or an escape from nonpreferred classes.

In secondary settings, students may struggle to get to school on time and may also have high rates of tardiness or instances of skipping certain class periods throughout the day. To fit within the secondary school context and allow for consistent tracking even when a student is absent, we recommend using an electronic DPR, which should include spaces for scoring whether a student is present, tardy, or absent for each class period each day throughout the week. An electronic DPR can be created using either a spreadsheet or a document in Google Drive to facilitate shared access for all of the student's teachers and the CICO coordinator. The student could check in with the CICO coordinator on Monday morning, at which time the coordinator could assist the student in setting goals for attending class and arriving on time, and remind the student about specific actions they are working on to improve their attendance. The student could self-evaluate their attendance and tardiness on a paper DPR (see Figure 8.5), and teachers, using the electronic DPR, could rate the student's attendance and on-time behavior for each class every day.

For ease of implementation, a rating system for each class period could be used, with a 0 indicating that the student was absent, a 1 indicating that the student was tardy, and a 2 indicating that the student was on time and present. At the end of the week, the student could check out with the CICO coordinator, who would help the student to determine whether they

I Can Be on Time!

Name: _____   Week of: _____

	Period 1	Period 2	Period 3	Period 4	Period 5	Period 6	% P*	% O-T*
Mon.	0 1 2	0 1 2	0 1 2	0 1 2	0 1 2	0 1 2		
Tues.	0 1 2	0 1 2	0 1 2	0 1 2	0 1 2	0 1 2		
Wed.	0 1 2	0 1 2	0 1 2	0 1 2	0 1 2	0 1 2		
Thurs.	0 1 2	0 1 2	0 1 2	0 1 2	0 1 2	0 1 2		
Fri.	0 1 2	0 1 2	0 1 2	0 1 2	0 1 2	0 1 2		
% P								
% O-T								
0 = absent; 1 = tardy; 2 = present and on time								

*%P = percentage of class periods present; %O-T = percentage of class periods on time.

Goals:	Progress:
Class attendance: Attend at least _____ % of classes	Classes attended this week _____ %
On-time behavior: Be on time to at least _____ % of classes	Goal met?
	Classes on time to this week _____ %
Student signature:	Coordinator signature:

FIGURE 8.5. CICO DPR for self-evaluation of attendance—middle school example.

met their goals and to deliver a student-selected reinforcer. The CICO coordinator should also obtain a weekly attendance report from the school's attendance office to verify ratings on the DPR.

How Are Students Screened for Attendance CICO?

CICO for attendance is very similar to basic CICO in that it needs to be considered a Tier 2 intervention and is appropriate for students who are at risk. Students may be identified as in need of CICO for attendance on the basis of the percentage of school days they have been absent or tardy, starting within the first month of school. Students who are missing approximately 10–15% of the school days or are tardy approximately 1 day per week would be appropriate candidates for attendance CICO. At the secondary level, students who miss 10–15% of the school days or class periods or who are tardy on average for 10–15% or more of their classes may benefit from attendance CICO. Students who are chronically absent, who are missing greater than 15% of the school days, or who are skipping school daily will likely need a more intensive intervention, which may include home visits or wraparound services. Adapted CICO for attendance is best for students who are just starting to demonstrate problems with attendance behavior (Kladis, Hawken, & O'Neill, 2018).

Measuring Progress on CICO for Attendance

Schools can measure progress on CICO for attendance using several different indicators, depending on how the student was identified as at risk and as appropriate for the intervention. For students who are missing full school days, their attendance rates before and after CICO can be compared. For students who are both absent and tardy to school in elementary school settings, schools can examine both full-day absences and the percentage of the school day missed. Figure 8.6 provides an example of how these two pieces of data can be displayed on the same graph. The percentage of school days missed is calculated by the subtracting the number of minutes the student missed by being tardy from the total number of minutes in a week for full attendance, and then dividing the result by that same number. For example, if a typical school day is 375 minutes, then a typical 5-day school week is 1,875 minutes. Therefore, if a student misses 1 school day, then the student misses 20% of the school week ($[375/1{,}875] \times 100$). Student data can be graphed by the percentage of the school week missed and the number of whole school days missed. Looking at Kaida's tardy and attendance data, it can be determined that on average she was missing about 21.1% of the school week prior to intervention (see Figure 8.6). Following the implementation of CICO for attendance on week 11, her percentage of the school week missed was reduced to an average of 2.9% per week.

There are a few options for evaluating progress on CICO for attendance at the secondary level. First, if the DPR used for this version of CICO includes numerical ratings (as described in the discussion of the DPR shown in Figure 8.2), student progress can be evaluated in the same way as it is for basic CICO by graphing the total number of DPR points. Higher scores would indicate that the student is more frequently attending and getting to class on time. These data could be graphed on a daily or weekly basis. Alternatively, the percentage of classes the student attends and/or the percentage of classes the student is on time for could be graphed in a similar way, as displayed in Figure 8.6. In this format, the left y-axis could be adjusted to measure the percentage of classes attended, and the right y-axis could be adjusted to measure either the number or percentage of classes for which the student was tardy.

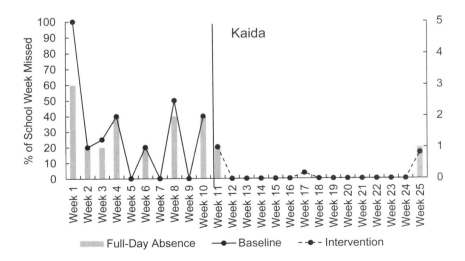

FIGURE 8.6. Sample graph of data for CICO for attendance—elementary schools.

CICO FOR RECESS

Students who are good candidates for basic CICO typically have mild problem behavior throughout the school day in classroom settings. We highly recommend that schools *not* place unstructured settings on the DPR for student feedback. In these settings, there is typically not enough supervision to provide the level of feedback that would be meaningful to the student to motivate changes in behavior. However, there are students who only struggle with behavior on the playground during recess. In this case, CICO for recess may be appropriate. In this section, we will describe two CICO options for recess problem behavior. The first option is intended for use with students who only display problem behavior during recess. The second option is intended for students who are good candidates for basic CICO and also exhibit problem behavior during recess.

CICO for Recess Only

When CICO is adapted to target behavior that only occurs during recess, a DPR that is specific for recess expectations can be created (see Figure 8.7 for an example DPR one school used for daily lunch recess). Schools can decide if additional recess times should be included on the DPR.

SOAR Card
Summary Of Achievement & Responsibility
"WATCH ME SOAR!"

Name _____   Date _____

Time	Respect everyone	Stay safe	Think before you act	Daily total points	Weekly total points
Monday	2 1 0	2 1 0	2 1 0		
Tuesday	2 1 0	2 1 0	2 1 0		
Wednesday	2 1 0	2 1 0	2 1 0		
Thursday	2 1 0	2 1 0	2 1 0		
Friday	2 1 0	2 1 0	2 1 0		

Goal: _____

2 = Excellent: Consistently follows rule. Needs 1 or fewer reminders (80–100% of the time).	1 = OK: Follows rule most of the time. Needs 2–3 reminders (60–79% of the time).	0 = Poor: Does not or rarely follows rule. Needs more than 3 reminders (0–59% of the time).

Successes: _____

_____

_____

Coordinator Initials _____
Parent Signature _____

FIGURE 8.7. DPR for CICO recess.

Unlike other versions of CICO that include a daily DPR, the DPR for CICO recess includes all days of the school week. The expectations are listed across the top. Students' behavior during each recess is typically rated by a paraprofessional or educational assistant, who should receive training on how to provide feedback to the students. The information from Chapter 4 can be used to help guide schools about what features should be included in that training.

CICO for recess can include a check-in at the beginning of the day to receive prompts for appropriate behavior and a check-out at the end of the day to talk about progress. In our work with schools implementing CICO for recess behavior, we have found that students are more likely to be successful in following expectations during recess if an educational assistant can deliver the DPR to the student right before recess and prompt appropriate behavior. In addition, many of the students on CICO for recess with whom we have worked are required to play close to the person who is supervising the playground. Students are taught to hand their DPR to the adult on recess duty at the start of recess and to play within a certain parameter, so that it is possible to rate their behavior at the end of the recess.

Basic CICO plus Recess CICO

As stated previously, for basic CICO we recommend that schools not place unstructured settings, such as the lunchroom or recess, on the DPR because most schools do not have the necessary supervision to provide meaningful feedback in these settings to the 10 to 15% of students who may be receiving CICO. As we have described, CICO for recess addresses students who only have problems at recess. In our work with schools, we have found that it can be possible for schools to support a small set of students who are on basic CICO during recess as well. In these cases, rather than changing the universal schoolwide DPR that was developed for basic CICO, we recommend using a separate DPR for recess times and incorporating the student's points into the student's overall DPR. We provide an example of a recess DPR for a student who is on basic CICO and also on CICO for recess in Figure 8.8. The schoolwide expectations are listed as goals (Be Respectful, Be Responsible, KYHFOOTY = keep your hands, feet, and other objects to yourself), and the three recesses during which the student receives feedback are listed across the top. The recess DPR would be used in addition to the basic CICO DPR for the student in use at the school.

Highlander Elementary School

	A.M. recess	Lunch recess	P.M. recess
Be respectful	2 1 0	2 1 0	2 1 0
Be responsible	2 1 0	2 1 0	2 1 0
KYHFOOTY	2 1 0	2 1 0	2 1 0

Recess CICO

Staff Initials _____   _____   _____

FIGURE 8.8. Basic CICO plus CICO for recess.

How Are Students Screened for Recess CICO?

Students can be identified as in need of CICO for recess by examining specific ODR details. Students whose majority of ODRs have occurred for misbehavior at recess are good candidates for recess-only CICO. Students who have frequent ODRs throughout the school day as well as during recess are good candidates for basic CICO plus recess CICO. In addition to ODR data, schools may also wish to implement a referral system based on the observations of adults on recess duty in case students are engaging in frequent misbehavior that doesn't typically result in ODRs, but is significant enough to warrant receiving an intervention.

Measuring Progress on CICO for Recess

Student progress on CICO for just recess can be measured and evaluated using the same process that is used for basic CICO. Students' total percentage of DPR points can be graphed on a daily and weekly basis to evaluate whether students are earning more points as they participate in the intervention. Similarly, for students receiving CICO for recess in addition to basic CICO, we recommend that the recess DPR data be graphed and evaluated in this way separately from the basic CICO DPR data. It is important to evaluate each of the versions of CICO separately, because student behavior could improve in one setting and not in the other. Including recess DPR points with basic classroom DPR points may artificially lower the students' scores, which could hinder their motivation and investment in the basic CICO intervention, especially if they are making consistent improvements in the classroom but not at recess.

CICO FOR PRESCHOOL AND YOUNGER ELEMENTARY-AGE STUDENTS

CICO for Preschool Students

Students who are in preschool are not too young to benefit from CICO, and implementing CICO for students engaging in misbehavior at this early age may help them develop the behavioral and social skills that are important for success in kindergarten and in later elementary school grades. The primary adjustments for CICO implemented at the preschool level involve slightly restructuring the DPR as well as the daily check-in/check-out process. Figure 8.9 provides an example of how the DPR could be structured for preschool settings. Rather than listing school-wide expectations on the DPR, the programwide or individual preschool classroom expectations should be listed. To provide additional support for preliterate, preschool-age children, it is helpful to include pictures that illustrate the expectations. Rather than using a numerical rating system such as 0, 1, and 2 that is often used in elementary and secondary settings, a preschool DPR can utilize drawings of sad, neutral, or smiley faces to correspond to these rankings. Some preschools prefer to use a color-coded system, such as green, yellow, or red. One problem with this alternative is that a color-coded ranking system will increase duplication costs, because the DPR will need to be produced in color versus black and white. To decrease copying costs, the teacher could use a green, red, or yellow crayon to color in a black-and-white form to indicate how the child had performed for that time period. In addition to the smiley-face ranking system, the DPR in Figure 8.9 includes a model for the student to know what ranking is desired.

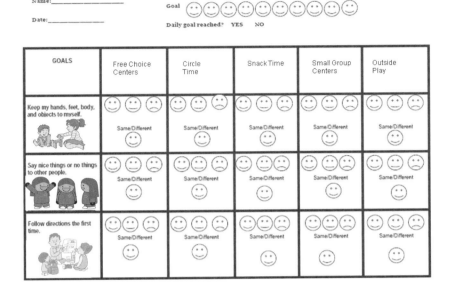

FIGURE 8.9. Example DPR for CICO for preschool students.

These preschool students are working on matching skills and on the concepts of same and different. The figure has a model of a smiley face, so the teacher can ask if the rating that was given is the "same" or "different" from the smiley-face model.

The daily CICO process should be adjusted to fit within the context of preschools. Instead of checking in or out with a separate CICO coordinator, the student can check in and out with their classroom teacher or a classroom aide. Across the top of the DPR in Figure 8.9 there are different times of the day specific to preschool settings (e.g., outside play, snack time). As in basic CICO, the preschool student should receive feedback from a classroom teacher or aide at these designated natural transition points throughout the day. In terms of setting a goal for the student, rather than having a percentage-of-points goal as implemented in elementary and secondary settings, the number of smiley faces that the student must earn is listed across the top of the figure. In this example, there are a possible total of 15 opportunities to receive smiley faces, and the student's goal is 10 smiley faces. During the check-out session, the student can practice additional skills, such as counting and matching. For example, the student can practice one-to-one correspondence counting skills during check-out, with the support of the teacher or aide, by counting up the number of smiley faces earned. Then the student can count the number of smiley faces listed as the goal. At this point, concepts such as more or less can also be introduced: "Did you earn more smiley faces than your goal?" The other components of the daily process for preschool CICO can be implemented as they are with basic CICO.

Screening Process to Identify Students for Preschool CICO

Preschool CICO can be implemented on either a program or classroom level, depending on the structure of the preschool in which it is implemented. If the preschool tracks behavioral data such as ODRs, screening and referral processes that are similar to those used for basic CICO in elementary schools can be used. If preschools do not track behavioral data, we recommend that a referral process be established to allow teachers and/or parents to refer specific students for the CICO intervention. It is important in preschool settings to distinguish between developmentally appropriate misbehavior, versus more severe misbehavior that is in need of intervention.

Measuring Progress on Preschool CICO

The main adjustment needed for measuring progress on preschool CICO compared to basic CICO is to graph the total number of smiley faces earned, as opposed to the percentage of DPR points earned. Schools can also consider using a bar graph that displays the total number of smiley faces earned per day if they would like to show the student their data summary, because bar graphs tend to be easier for younger students to read and understand compared to line graphs.

Modifications for Younger Elementary-Age Students

In order to build efficiency as we've outlined throughout this book, it is important for the DPR to be the same for all students, or as we've discussed in this chapter, for the target behaviors (e.g., academic and/or organizational, attendance) involved. Many of the schools we work with have pointed out that the numeric rating system of 0, 1, and 2 is not as meaningful for younger students, particularly those in kindergarten and first grade. In these situations, we recommend that schools continue to use the schoolwide Tier 1 positive behavioral expectations and that the ranking system be adjusted to be visually similar to that of the preschool version presented in Figure 8.9. In Figure 8.10, we provide an example of a DPR for younger students from one of the elementary schools we worked with. In this case, the school used a smiley-face rating system but also added a numeric rating to the smiley-face system, so that data could be summarized for the CICO intervention across grades. This adjustment to CICO for younger students affects

RAM Report									
	Follow Directions the first time			KYHFOOTY			Be Kind		
I am working on... (write specific behavior)									
Morning bell–first recess	☺ 2	☺ 1	☹ 0	☺	☺	☹	☺	☺	☹
First recess–lunch	☺	☺	☹	☺	☺	☹	☺	☺	☹
Lunch–afternoon recess	☺	☺	☹	☺	☺	☹	☺	☺	☹
Afternoon recess–end of day	☺	☺	☹	☺	☺	☹	☺	☺	☹

FIGURE 8.10. Example DPR for CICO for younger elementary students.

only the visual layout of the DPR. The screening process and the way that CICO progress is measured remain the same as the process used on a schoolwide level with other grades.

SYSTEM-LEVEL CONSIDERATIONS FOR ADAPTED CICO

As mentioned previously, we highly recommend that schools implement basic CICO before implementing the adapted versions discussed in this chapter. Once basic CICO has been implemented with fidelity as measured by the tools provided in Chapter 7, schools can begin to target additional problem behaviors. In doing so, schools will want to adapt the flowchart that was presented in Chapter 3 in order to assign students to the appropriate version of CICO. These decisions should be based on data. If the student is only struggling with getting assignments completed but not with problem behavior in the classroom, CICO for academic and/or organizational skills would be an appropriate first start. If the student is only having issues with getting to school on time and/or attending school regularly, CICO for attendance would be appropriate. These decisions can be made during a grade-level team meeting with the approval of someone from the PBIS leadership team, or the decisions can be made at the behavior-support team level if schools are using behavior support teams to access CICO. Figure 8.11 depicts a revised flowchart that was first presented in Chapter 3.

It should be noted that the same CICO coordinator for basic CICO can check students in and out for these adapted versions. The check-in and check-out process remains the same for students participating in most of the adapted CICO versions we have described, so it is most efficient to include all students receiving any type of CICO intervention in the standard procedures for check-in and check-out. However, including these adapted versions will increase the number of students receiving the CICO intervention. Schools should pay particular attention to the total number of students receiving any type of CICO intervention and the amount of time each check-in and check-out session is taking to determine if they need to include more than one CICO facilitator or coordinator. See Chapter 4 for guidelines related to how many students one CICO facilitator can support.

The biweekly and quarterly features of CICO discussed in Chapter 3 remain the same for any of the adapted versions of CICO. Schools will find that it is most efficient to embed these biweekly and quarterly features in the process they use for basic CICO (i.e., the same people should complete the same tasks for each adapted version of CICO that they do for basic CICO, and each adapted version of CICO should be discussed alongside basic CICO at any team meetings). At least once every 2 weeks, the student data for each version of adapted CICO should be summarized to determine the percentage of students responding to the intervention. As with basic CICO, if fewer than 70% of students receiving one specific adaptation of CICO are responding to the intervention, the fidelity with which the intervention is implemented and other system-level features should be examined. In addition to examining overall intervention effectiveness, individual student data should be examined to determine which students are making appropriate progress, which students are ready for the intervention to be faded, and which students may be in need of additional support. On a quarterly basis, each adapted version of CICO should be included in the basic CICO feedback reports provided to teachers, school staff, and parents.

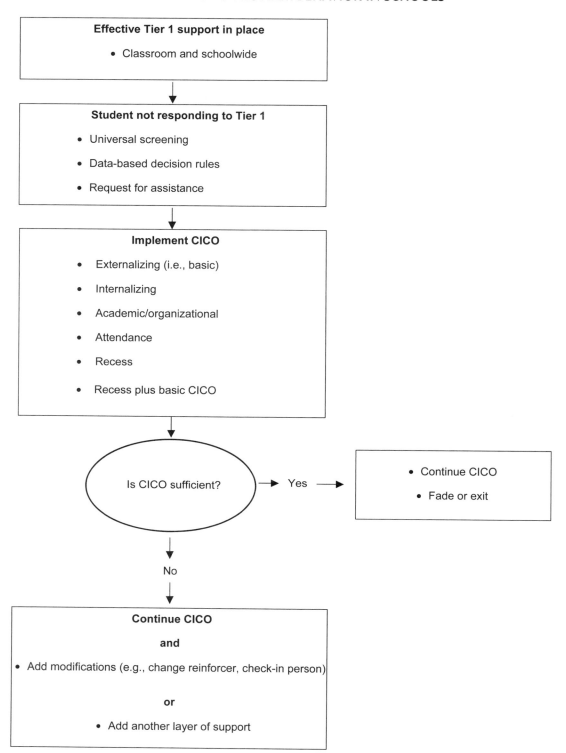

FIGURE 8.11. Process for selecting CICO interventions for each student.

SUMMARY

Schools can expand their use of CICO by making small but systematic adjustments to the intervention. In this chapter, we described important considerations and specific adjustments for adapting CICO to support academic and/or organizational skills, attendance, appropriate recess behavior, and younger students. We recommend that schools prioritize ensuring the efficiency and feasibility of each adapted version of CICO by maintaining universal components (i.e., implementing them the same way for all students and/or specific behaviors) and by following the same biweekly and quarterly routines used for basic CICO. It is important for schools to remember that each adapted version of CICO is designed to be a Tier 2 support and to identify appropriate interventions that can be implemented in addition to adapted CICO to help students in need of more intensive supports.

CHAPTER 9

Layering More Intensive Interventions onto Basic CICO

Leanne S. Hawken, Kimberli Breen, Kaitlin Bundock, and Deanne A. Crone

In Chapters 3–6 we provided the information and tools that schools need to implement basic CICO. Chapter 8 outlines adaptations that can be made to address specific target behaviors. In addition to implementing basic CICO or CICO with adaptations, schools can also add layers of additional support to basic CICO. In this chapter, we describe how to embed CICO within the context of PBIS or, more specifically, a multi-tiered (i.e., layered) systems of support (MTSS). In addition, we will describe how and why CICO should be used as the first Tier 2 intervention within a tiered system of support and how additional interventions can be layered onto CICO when students are not fully responding to Tier 1 plus basic CICO. F, we outline ways to add academic and social skills groups to basic CICO, as well as how to use functional assessment to add function-based support for students who need a more intensive intervention than CICO plus a skills group.

In previous editions of this book, we recommended conducting an FBA early on in the process with students who were not fully responding to basic CICO. An FBA is the process of gathering information about the events that predict and maintain problem behavior (Crone, Hawken, & Bergstrom, 2007). In essence, behavior serves a particular function for the student; functions include getting attention from peers or adults, getting access to a tangible reward (e.g., food, a better place in line, a preferred toy), and/or escaping a task or unpleasant situation (e.g., a difficult math class or noisy environment). Since the publication of the previous version

Kimberli Breen, MS, CAS, MA, is a behavior change agent affiliated with the University of Kansas SWIFT Center, KOI Education and Affecting Behavior Change Inc. She implements, trains, and coaches the Multi-Tiered System of Support framework, with a focus on positive behavior supports and family partnerships.

of this book (Crone et al., 2010), our recommendation about when to introduce an FBA into the process of CICO implementation has changed. This change is based on the research into CICO and the real-life application of this intervention throughout thousands of schools worldwide. Some researchers argue that an FBA should be conducted early in the CICO implementation process (McIntosh, Campbell, Carter, & Dickey, 2009). However, there are many limitations to conducting an FBA early in the CICO implementation process as well as advantages to delaying an FBA in order to provide students with Tier 2 support more quickly. The purpose of this chapter is to describe how and why interventions can be layered onto basic CICO prior to conducting an FBA within a context of intervening with problem behavior for students at risk. In turn, we provide recommendations for how CICO can be embedded into more intensive types of behavior support typically found at the Tier 3 level, including individualized behavior support plans (BSPs).

IMPORTANCE OF IMPLEMENTING CICO PRIOR TO FBA

When implementing an MTSS, schools begin with Tier 1 academic and behavior support. For comparison, it is helpful to consider the screening process schools typically use when identifying students in need of academic intervention. For example, when teaching reading, schools typically begin with teachers implementing a core evidence-based reading curriculum. Once Tier 1 is in place, some students may be identified as needing Tier 2 support based on universal screening, data-based decision making, and/or teacher request for assistance. In elementary school, one set of widely used universal screening measure is the Acadience Learning Assessments (formerly known as the Dynamic Indicators of Basic Early Literacy Skills, or DIBELS; Acadience Learning, Inc., 2019; Good & Kaminski, 2002). The Acadience Learning Assessments for Reading assess the five critical reading skills, including phonological awareness, the alphabetic principle, accuracy and fluency with connected text, comprehension, and vocabulary. Once students are screened for reading difficulties with the Acadience Learning Assessment and the concern is quickly validated (i.e., each assessment takes less than 5 minutes) using different versions of the screener, students can be placed in small groups according to their targeted needs. Placement is usually done without intensive diagnostic testing; in essence, little time is spent diagnosing the problem at this level of support. So, for example, if a student is low in phonological awareness as indicated by the Acadience Learning measure Phoneme Segmentation Fluency, the teacher can target that skill in a small-group format with other students who have that identified need.

In terms of behavior, the foundation of Tier 1 support includes implementing schoolwide and classroom systems of PBIS. Schools identify students who may need additional support either through universal screening or data-based decision rules by using, for instance, office ODRs. At this point in the process some researchers have recommended that an FBA be conducted to ensure that schools are matching the intervention to the function of the problem behavior (McIntosh, Campbell, Carter, & Dickey, 2009). In our experience, conducting a full or a brief FBA at this point (1) is too time-consuming for the identified low-level need; (2) is at odds with the response to intervention logic that students first need an intervention to respond to prior to conducting more intensive assessment (Bruhn et al., 2014; Sugai & Horner, 2009a); and (3) most important, delays the at-risk student's access to an evidence-based intervention. It should also be noted that schools struggle to conduct FBAs and implement BSPs with students who have the most severe problem behavior and need Tier 3 support (Crone et al., 2007). Therefore, asking schools to conduct FBAs with all of the students who need Tier 2 behavior support (i.e., potentially 15–20% of the student population according to the MTSS model) is not only unnecessary, but also an unrealistic expectation given the time and resources required.

In addition, in a recent review of function-based adaptations to CICO, several findings provide support for our decision to conduct an FBA later in the process. First, after reviewing 11 studies with 41 participants, Klingbeil, Dart, and Schramm (2019) concluded that FBA-based modifications cannot be deemed an evidence-based practice at this point, whereas basic CICO has been found to be evidence based (e.g., Maggin et al., 2015). In addition, to make the FBA-based modifications documented in the studies, researchers on average spent 90 minutes collecting direct observation data as part of the FBA process. These findings are counter to the statement by McIntosh, Campbell, Carter, and Dickey (2009), who recommended a quick FBA screener, such as the Functional Assessment Checklist for Teachers and Students (FACTS; March et al., 2000; see Appendix G.1), which can be used to match students with appropriate Tier 2 interventions based on a hypothesized function of the students' behavior.

Some have argued that implementing CICO can be considered "contraindicated," in that it may make the problem behavior worse because it is not based on behavioral function. We have several responses to this argument. To begin with, although some research indicates that CICO is more effective for students who have attention-maintained problem behavior (e.g., McIntosh, Campbell, Carter, & Dickey, 2009; Smith et al., 2015; Wolfe et al., 2016), other research indicates that CICO can be effective across behavioral functions, including escape-maintained behavior (e.g., Hawken, O'Neill, & MacLeod, 2011; Swoszowski et al., 2012). Also, although some researchers have documented a larger effect size (range = 0.78–1.04 across behavioral outcome variables) for CICO when students have attention-maintained problem behavior (e.g., McIntosh, Campbell, Carter, & Dickey, 2009), the same researchers summarized effect sizes that ranged from 0.05 (no effect) to 0.42 (small effect) for CICO with students who have escape-maintained problem behavior. In essence, although there were not substantial effects for CICO with escape-maintained problem behavior in this one study, it did not appear to make the problem behavior worse. Finally, some research has shown that a powerful enough reinforcer, such as interacting daily with a preferred adult, can override behavioral function (Hawken et al., 2011; Shore, Iwata, DeLeon, Kahng, & Smith, 1997; Zhou, Goff, & Iwata, 2000).

Advantages of Implementing CICO before Conducting an FBA

The purpose of MTSS for academics and behavior is to efficiently and effectively provide all students with the level of support they need to succeed. Although an argument can be made for getting a more perfect intervention "fit" with lengthy and highly individualized assessments, it's not efficient to do so. In fact, taking too much time too early on to solve issues with interventions for some students can contribute to many other students not having their needs addressed. For example, if teams spend precious meeting minutes investigating access to low-level Tier 2 behavior support such as CICO, there is less time available to discuss more complicated Tier 3 behavior support for students who truly need the problem-solving expertise of a team. The most valuable resource in schools today is time, and our goal is to help schools use time wisely. By being more efficient in getting students access to evidence-based interventions, such as basic

CICO (without lengthy assessment), schools can optimize the response to intervention (i.e., MTSS) logic, and layer on additional interventions as needed to increase overall effectiveness.

In a recent book *Essentials of Intensive Intervention,* Kuchle and Riley-Tillman (2019) summarize the process of how to integrate behavior and academics in an MTSS model for students with significant academic and behavior support needs. In their chapter, they argue that schools need to start with an evidence-based intervention (e.g., CICO), monitor progress, and then conduct more diagnostic testing (such as an FBA), once students have shown a lack of response to the evidence-based intervention. If students demonstrate a lack of response, then an FBA is recommended to determine why the student continues to engage in the problem behavior. Once the FBA is conducted, the authors recommend adapting "the intervention to better address the factors underlying the behavior" (p. 53). This logic is exactly what we are proposing in this chapter.

An additional reason we advise that function-based adaptations be used later in the CICO intervention process is because CICO coordinators/facilitators (possibly in partnership with a counselor and/or school psychologist) could make adjustments to the intervention that are often cited as function based by researchers in the field (Klingbeil et al., 2019). For example, after a brief time period of implementing CICO, the facilitator may find out through the daily check-in and check-out process that a student is more reinforced by escaping tasks and by asking for breaks from class. This is an easy change in reinforcement that can be a simple modification to basic CICO. Another example is perhaps the student who is always losing their DPR by the end of the day, but is engaging in other parts of the intervention. The student may need an additional reinforcer (e.g., token) for each day they bring the DPR to check-out. It should be noted that one of the reasons we do not advocate that schools modify basic CICO from the beginning is that for each feature that is modified, the ease and efficiency of similar implementation for other CICO students is decreased.

Finally, many features of basic CICO should be included in more advanced levels of behavior support that are function based, including high-frequency progress monitoring, direct instruction, and feedback on behavioral skills, and that focus on antecedent manipulations to ensure that the student is set up for a positive day. Implementing basic CICO allows schools to begin with these core features of behavior intervention and more readily introduce function-based adaptations, as students demonstrate the need for more advanced levels of behavior support.

Now that we have described the benefits of implementing basic CICO prior to conducting an FBA, as well as the drawbacks of conducting an FBA early in the CICO/Tier 2 process, we now describe a model of how CICO can be used flexibly to gradually increase support or provide more specific targeted support for students who are not responding adequately to basic CICO alone. This model was originally developed by the Illinois PBIS network and has been articulated in a Technical Assistance Brief on best-practice Tier 2 and Tier 3 intervention implementation (Eber, Swain-Bradway, Breen, & Phillips, 2013). The model has been replicated and further articulated by Breen and colleagues in multiple states, including California, New York, Arizona, and Utah (Breen, 2016, 2017; Bundock, Hawken, Kladis, & Breen, 2020; DeGeorge, 2015; Hawken, & Breen, 2017) and is detailed in this chapter.

For the remainder of this chapter, it is helpful to refer to the flowchart, originally introduced in Figure 3.4 (Chapter 3) and expanded upon in Figure 8.1 (Chapter 8), that schools can follow to guide their implementation and intensification of CICO. As is shown in the flowchart, schools should begin by implementing basic CICO and engage in the established data-based decision-making process to continuously evaluate whether the intervention is being implemented with fidelity and to determine which students are responding adequately to the intervention. In the next part of this chapter, we discuss the flowchart's components (see Figure 9.1) that guide schools in determining what to do to help students who are not adequately responding to CICO.

CICO AS THE FIRST LAYER WITHIN TIER 2

For the reasons described earlier, we highly recommend that basic CICO be implemented as the first layer of Tier 2 support and that implementation begin without gathering FBA data. After basic CICO has been implemented for several weeks (usually 6–10 weeks, or as determined by each school), the team (or CICO coordinator) should evaluate whether it is sufficient to support the student. For students who are not responding sufficiently (i.e., based on the predetermined data-based decision rules), small adjustments to CICO, such as changing reinforcement, may provide the necessary modification to support the student, as we have described. Figure 9.2 displays a version of the DPR that can be used to support students on basic CICO. Several adjustments can be made to CICO without changing the DPR, including increasing the frequency of prompting and delivery of feedback and of reinforcement delivery, allowing a student to select specific reinforcers, using peer mentors, having the student check in and out with a preferred adult other than the assigned CICO facilitator, and many more. Other adjustments may require small additions to the basic DPR. We use the DPR in Figure 9.2 to demonstrate how interventions can be layered onto basic CICO, while maintaining the same DPR with minor additions.

After modifications to basic CICO are made and the data indicate that the student is still not responding sufficiently to the intervention, we advise adding an additional layer of support. Support can be provided at the end of the recommended length of basic CICO (i.e., 6–10 weeks), or anytime sooner if the student's response is sufficiently low. Note that rather than terminating the student from basic CICO, we advise keeping the intervention and adding another layer of support (such as a skills group) to provide more targeted instruction on either academic and/or behavioral skills.

CICO PLUS SOCIAL OR ACADEMIC GROUPS

Basic CICO provides at-risk students with more instruction and feedback on the Tier 1 school-wide and classroom expectations that have already been taught. For students who do not respond sufficiently, small-group instruction on academic and/or organizational skills or on more targeted social skills may improve intervention responsiveness (Ross & Sabey, 2014). These small groups typically consist of three to seven students who have similar needs for more targeted (Tier 2) instruction. The groups can be implemented by a school counselor, social worker, or psychologist. However, in our experience, with enough training, coaching, feedback, and a scripted curriculum, paraprofessionals and other adults can be trained to provide this instruction.

Many different scripted curricula, or lessons written by personnel within the school or district, can be used to deliver CICO plus social-skills group instruction. Typically, schools can address these groups in one of three ways: (1) use a packaged curriculum designed for "group"

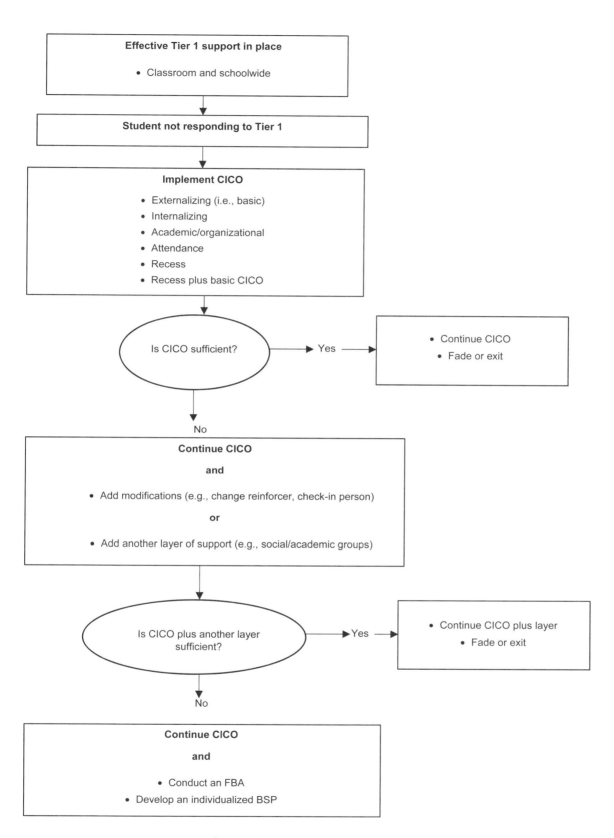

FIGURE 9.1. Layering CICO support.

127

Butler Middle School
Rams Achieve More (RAM) Card

Name: _____   Date: _____

Expectations	Period 1	Period 2	Period 3	Period 4	Period 5	Period 6	Period 7
Safe (KYHFOOTY)	2 1 0	2 1 0	2 1 0	2 1 0	2 1 0	2 1 0	2 1 0
Respectful	2 1 0	2 1 0	2 1 0	2 1 0	2 1 0	2 1 0	2 1 0
Responsible	2 1 0	2 1 0	2 1 0	2 1 0	2 1 0	2 1 0	2 1 0

Teacher's Initials   _____ _____ _____ _____ _____ _____ _____

KEY	Hooray!!!: _____
2 = YES!!! 0–1 reminders	
1 = Almost 2–3 reminders	Goal for Today: _____ %
0 = Try Again 4+ reminders	Total for Today: _____ %

Note: KYHFOOTY = keep your hands, feet, and other objects to yourself.

FIGURE 9.2. Sample basic CICO DPR.

delivery, such as Skills Streaming (McGinnis, 2011; McGinnis, Sprafkin, Gershaw, & Klein, 2011); (2) use lessons from the schoolwide Tier 1 behavioral or social–emotional learning curricula like Second Step (Committee for Children, 2011) so students get an additional dose; or (3) use the schoolwide behavioral matrix and behavioral lesson-plan template to create a series of 4–10 school-specific lessons. It is important to remember that at this point in implementing an MTSS model, these students just need additional skills instruction, and not group counseling or therapy. To implement CICO plus academic-skills instruction in groups, the school should target the academic and/or organizational skills that all students are taught and/or are expected to have, which include study skills, asking questions, asking for academic help, and having organized folders and backpacks,. Just as with behavioral, social, and emotional skills, schools can use the lesson plans from Tier 1, buy a packaged curricula, or create their own lessons when providing targeted instruction for academic and/or organizational skills.

Whether receiving additional academic or social skills instruction, we believe that the student should remain on CICO to (1) continue to receive regular prompts and feedback throughout the day, (2) give teachers reminders about what these students are being taught in the group, and (3) provide a method for progress monitoring to determine if the addition of a group to CICO is providing an added benefit to the student. For a CICO plus group intervention, the DPR can be modified to include the additional behavioral or academic targets that are being taught in groups. Continuing students on CICO and using the DPR to monitor progress allow for a comparison to be made between student progress on CICO alone and student progress on CICO plus academic or social-skills groups. The student outcome variable, or the percentage of points, remains the same across the implementation of basic CICO and CICO plus groups. Figure 9.3 is an example of a DPR for a student who received CICO plus social-skills group instruction. Additional behavioral targets are added below the schoolwide Tier 1 behavioral goals.

Social and Academic Instructional Groups	Butler Middle School Rams Achieve More (RAM) Card						

Name: _____ Date: _____

Expectations	Period 1	Period 2	Period 3	Period 4	Period 5	Period 6	Period 7
Safe (KYHFOOTY) • Stay in assigned area • Use handshakes and high fives	2 1 0	2 1 0	2 1 0	2 1 0	2 1 0	2 1 0	2 1 0
Respectful • Follow directions the first time • Use kind words	2 1 0	2 1 0	2 1 0	2 1 0	2 1 0	2 1 0	2 1 0
Responsible • Be on time • Complete planner • Turn in class homework	2 1 0	2 1 0	2 1 0	2 1 0	2 1 0	2 1 0	2 1 0

Teacher's Initials _____ _____ _____ _____ _____ _____ _____

KEY
2 = YES!!! 0–1 reminders
1 = Almost 2–3 reminders
0 = Try Again 4+ reminders

Hooray!!!: _____

Goal for Today: _____ %

Total for Today: _____ %

Note: KYHFOOTY = keep your hands, feet, and other objects to yourself.

FIGURE 9.3. Sample CICO plus social and academic skills.

CICO PLUS FBA-BSP

For students who are not fully or sufficiently responding to CICO plus academic or social groups, conducting an FBA and using the information to develop a BSP may be warranted. This information can be used to determine the reason that a student acts in a certain way under certain conditions. The FBA helps identify the *function* of the problem behavior. There are a wide variety of methods to conduct an FBA, ranging from a brief, semistructured interview to a comprehensive interview coupled with observations in the classroom. Although the process of conducting an FBA and developing a BSP are beyond the scope of this book (see Crone et al., 2015, for more detailed information), we discuss how information from an FBA-BSP can be used to layer additional supports onto CICO.

Students' problem behavior can be broadly grouped into two categories: (1) problem behavior that is maintained by obtaining access to desirable stimuli (e.g., attention, activities, objects) and (2) problem behavior that is maintained by escaping or avoiding undesirable stimuli (e.g., activities, events, demands). The goal of conducting an FBA is to determine the function or reason why a student is engaging in the problem behavior and to develop alternative or replacement behaviors that can be taught, prompted, and reinforced to replace the problem behavior. FBAs can be fairly simple and brief or complex and time-consuming. The complexity of the assessment depends on the complexity and severity of the problem behavior. In essence, when intervening at this level (i.e., after insufficient response to CICO plus groups), we recommend that schools establish guidelines as to which specific FBA process is warranted, based on the time and resources available, and then make exceptions when needed according to the severity of a student's behavior. We advise that schools first conduct a brief FBA for most students who are not responding fully to CICO plus groups; however, an exception to the guidelines can always be made if the team feels that a full FBA should be conducted earlier for any particular students.

A brief FBA consists of interviewing one or more teachers. Typically, the referring teacher is the one interviewed. Often, older students (i. e., in upper elementary, middle, or high school) can explain why they are engaging in problem behavior. In these cases, a brief student interview is also advisable.

A student whose behavior is complex or severe and who requires a full FBA (for the difference between a full FBA and a brief FBA, refer to Crone et al., 2015) will need more intensive behavior support, which may include mental health and or wraparound support (Eber, Sugai, Smith, & Scott, 2002). We highly recommend that CICO continue to be a part of this more advanced level of behavior support for the same reasons already noted: (1) to continue to receive regular prompts and feedback throughout the day, (2) to give teachers reminders about replacement behaviors the students are working on, and (3) as a method for progress monitoring if "CICO plus group plus FBA-BSP" is providing an added benefit to the student. In this next section, we examine the main functions of problem behavior and identify some examples of alternative/replacement behaviors that the student should be taught.

Functions of Problem Behavior

Behavior Maintained by the Desire to Obtain Something

Students in this category engage in problem behavior because it results in obtaining something that they want. Students may want to obtain a toy, time to play on the playground, or attention from their peers or adults. The desire to obtain attention is a common function of misbehavior. Attention can be either positive or negative. For example, a teacher might reprimand the student in front of the class (negative attention) or a peer might laugh along with an inappropriate joke (positive attention). Some problem behaviors of these students might include talking back to the teacher, arguing or fighting with students, refusing to work, or disrupting the class.

Escape-Maintained Behavior

The problem behaviors exhibited by students in this category are often indistinguishable from problem behaviors that are maintained by the desire to obtain attention or other stimuli. The difference between the two groups is the function that the behavior serves for the student, which can be gleaned by examining the events that occur both prior to and following the instances of the behavior. Students in this group may be disruptive, talk back to the teacher, and argue with their peers in order to get out of a situation or to get away from a person. For example, a student who dislikes male teachers may throw frequent tantrums in male-led classes if they have discovered that tantrums in class result in being sent to the office (and away from the male teacher). A student who has difficulty interacting with peers may be disruptive during lunch so that they can be sent to the principal's office. By engaging in disruptive behavior, the student has been removed from (i.e., escaped) an unpleasant social situation. Students may also engage in disruptive behavior in order to escape a task that it too difficult, long, or boring for them.

How to Use a Brief FBA to Identify and Add Function-Based Supports to CICO

The brief FBA includes a short (i.e., less than 20-minute) semistructured interview. The interview is conducted with the teacher(s) or staff member(s) who referred the student to the behavior support team. The interview can be conducted by a behavior support team member, school psychologist, behavior support specialist, or other person with adequate training and skill. The desired outcomes of the brief FBA are to (1) obtain an observable and measurable description of the problem behavior, (2) identify the setting events or antecedents that predict when the behavior is most likely to occur or not occur, (3) identify alternative behaviors that should be taught to the student to replace the problem behaviors, and (4) identify the consequences that maintain the problem behavior (O'Neill, Albin, Storey, Horner, & Sprague, 2014). This information can be used to determine if the student's problem behavior is escape motivated or attention motivated.

There are several FBA interview instruments in print; one instrument commonly used in schools implementing CICO is the Functional Assessment Checklist for Teachers (FACTS; March et al., 2000; available at *pbis.org*). Schools may choose to use different FBA interview protocols, but should ensure that the interview includes the following critical features:

1. It can be completed in 20 minutes or less.
2. It identifies the specific problem behavior.
3. It identifies the routines that support the problem behavior.
4. It identifies the likely function of the problem behavior.

Schools then use this information to determine what alternative/replacement behaviors will be taught, so that students can access the same reinforcer (i.e., attention or escape) in an appropriate way instead of by engaging in problem behavior. Table 9.1 includes a list of problem behaviors that were identified for one student, who we will call Charlie, using a brief FBA interview, as well as some alternative replacement behaviors that can be taught to help Charlie replace the problem behavior.

Once replacement behaviors are identified, they can be included on the student's DPR to prompt teachers to provide specific feedback on replacement behaviors and to continue to progress monitor the student on CICO plus additional support. In Figure 9.4, we have added specific replacement behaviors identified for Charlie onto the DPR. We recommend that students continue in their social and/or academic groups in addition to receiving FBA-BSP interventions, because having students participate in these groups regularly is a good way to continue to teach and reinforce replacement behaviors identified in the FBA process.

TABLE 9.1. Charlie's Function-Based Problem Behaviors and Replacement Behaviors

Antecedents	Problem behaviors	Replacement behaviors	Function served
Student prompted to complete work during independent work time for mathematics.	Student yells, swears, and crumples up worksheet; sometimes leaves class when frustrated.	Teach student words to communicate that he needs help (e.g., "I'm getting frustrated; I think I need some help with this"). Teach student to use deep breathing/count to 100 when frustrated and use calm space in classroom if needed.	Escape from academic tasks.
Student prompted to work with his group during group work time for social studies.	Student yells and smacks other students.	Teach student to keep an arm's distance when agitated or upset. Teach student the appropriate voice level to use when frustrated.	Escape from either academic tasks or social interaction with peers.
Student prompted to follow directions during whole-class reading instruction.	Student yells and throws objects at peers and teacher.	Teach student to ask for breaks using break cards. Teach student to self-monitor appropriate behavior by self-rating behavior on the DPR.	Escape from academic tasks and/or social interaction in class.

Extending the CICO Model: Cumulative System-Level Benefits of Intensifying CICO

Thus far, we have provided a framework for how to embed CICO into the MTSS system for academics and behavior. Once again, we advise schools to build a solid basic CICO system of support, and then link this intervention to existing Tier 2 support groups and function-based Tier 3 supports. We do not advocate that schools begin with a function-based or individualized level of support for students initially referred for the basic CICO intervention. Implementing basic CICO as a standardized Tier 2 intervention helps ensure that the MTSS system is efficient and effective for the majority of students who receive the intervention. Layering additional Tier 2 interventions or function-based Tier 3 supports onto basic CICO for students who are not adequately responding ensures that an efficient and effective lower-level intervention is maintained, while the student accesses additional targeted or individualized supports. This process of implementing and intensifying CICO provides not only the maximum benefit for students, but also additional benefits to the MTSS system overall, as we have described (and depicted in Figure 9.1), primarily with regard to the efficiency and equity of intervention delivery across the tiers.

Individualized DPR FBA-BSP Based	Butler Middle School Rams Achieve More (RAM) Card

Name: _____   Date: _____

Expectations	Period 1	Period 2	Period 3	Period 4	Period 5	Period 6	Period 7
Safe (KYHFOOTY) • Stay in classroom and use calm space if frustrated • Keep an arm's distance when frustrated	2 1 0	2 1 0	2 1 0	2 1 0	2 1 0	2 1 0	2 1 0
Respectful • Use calm voice when upset or frustrated • Request help when needed	2 1 0	2 1 0	2 1 0	2 1 0	2 1 0	2 1 0	2 1 0
Responsible • Self-monitor with DPR • Use break cards to ask for break	2 1 0	2 1 0	2 1 0	2 1 0	2 1 0	2 1 0	2 1 0

Teacher's Initials   _____ _____ _____ _____ _____ _____ _____

KEY
2 = YES!!! 0–1 reminders
1 = Almost 2–3 reminders
0 = Try Again 4+ reminders

Hooray!!!: _____

Goal for Today: _____ %
Total for Today: _____ %

Note: KYHFOOTY = keep your hands, feet, and other objects to yourself.

FIGURE 9.4. Charlie's individualized DPR after FBA-BSP.

Efficiency of MTSS

Within any multi-tiered system, there is the risk that system-level challenges will result in inefficiency and ineffectiveness. This risk is one of the main reasons why we advocate for implementing and layering CICO as we have described. One component of MTSS that is vulnerable to inefficiency (and can result in a decrease in effectiveness) is how appropriate interventions are selected for students. As discussed in Chapter 2, we recommend that schools primarily utilize the system-level team meetings they establish (i.e., an MTSS team should meet periodically to review and discuss Tier 1 systems, a Tier 2 and/or student-support team should meet at least once per month), and that meetings with relevant personnel should occur regularly for any students receiving individualized Tier 3 supports. Regular meetings of these established teams allow schools to consistently review the effectiveness of interventions that have been implemented within the MTSS system and to facilitate rapid access to interventions for students in need of additional support.

However, schools should avoid establishing a process in which a meeting has to occur in order for an intervention to be selected for a particular student (e.g., a student is referred for

CICO but cannot start the intervention until the behavior support or Tier 2 team meets to review their data, or a student is referred for CICO, but a team has to first be gathered to conduct an FBA). In this type of process, a student may be referred for additional support, but must wait a month or longer before an intervention is implemented to help them. By implementing basic CICO first as we have advocated throughout this book, students can begin to receive an evidence-based intervention within days. If, after a period of weeks, a student is not responding adequately to basic CICO, additional modifications can be made, or other Tier 2 interventions can be layered onto CICO with little delay as well. If a school establishes clear data-based decision rules for determining which students are responding to CICO adequately, the CICO coordinator can adjust CICO quickly and flexibly without the need for a full team to meet.

Equity of MTSS

One of the strengths of MTSS is that the system involves establishing clear and objective guidelines for data-based decision making. If schools establish and use clear and objective guidelines when determining how to respond to student behavior, they may prevent the disproportional use of punishments as well as the disproportional referral for interventions (McIntosh, Girvan, Horner, Smokowski, & Sugai, 2014; Whitford, Katsiyannis, & Counts, 2016). These problems are well documented; schools have a tendency to implement overly harsh punishments for students of color and male students, even when these students have engaged in identical or similar problem behaviors as white or female students (McIntosh et al., 2014; Whitford et al., 2016). Additionally, student demographics such as race, language, and gender are associated with which students tend to be referred for academic and/or behavioral interventions and supports (Cruz & Rodl, 2018). An example of this bias can be found when researchers examined data related to discipline (e.g., number of ODRs) and access to CICO for black, Hispanic, and white students. In 41 middle schools, researchers found that although black students were overrepresented in the number of ODRs, they were less likely to be referred to CICO than white and Hispanic students were (Vincent, Tobin, Hawken, & Frank, 2012). The researchers further documented that although black students were less likely to be referred to CICO, those students who were referred early in the school year responded favorably (e.g., had reductions in ODRs); therefore, it is unfortunate that more black students did not have early access to this support (Vincent et al., 2012).

While disproportionality in discipline and intervention practices are complex issues, recent research indicates that implicit bias may play a role in each one (Whitford et al., 2016). A well-established MTSS system may help decrease the influence of implicit bias at these important decision points by establishing clear data-based decision-making criteria and by creating conditions for consistent application of these criteria for all students (McIntosh et al., 2014). Clear and consistent application of criteria decreases the chance that implicit bias plays a role in determining how to respond to student behavior, because it removes the ambiguity from the myriad situations that can occur in schools. It is in ambiguous situations that school personnel are the most likely to make decisions based on their implicit bias (McIntosh et al., 2014).

In the context of CICO, establishing and following a clear implementation and layering process can help ensure that students engaging in low-level problem behavior are treated equitably. Without such a system, it is easy for personnel to unknowingly allow implicit or explicit bias to play a role in determining which students exhibiting low-level problem behaviors get referred for intervention, receive a consequence, or are ignored. Similarly, following clear data-based decision rules when determining which students are responding adequately to CICO or are in need of additional support can also help to ensure that students receive additional targeted or individualized support when needed (McIntosh et al., 2014). It is important to bear in mind that simply establishing and following clear data-based decision rules will not eliminate implicit bias. We recommend that schools take other actions to minimize implicit bias throughout each of the tiers. For more information, we suggest exploring the resources available on equity and PBIS at *pbis.org*.

CONCLUSION

In this chapter, we have described the benefits of implementing basic CICO as the first response to students identified as in need of Tier 2 supports, along with the advantages of conducting an FBA later in the CICO process for students whose behavior has not improved after modifications and additions have been made to CICO. This process maintains the efficiency of CICO, and most important, ensures that students can quickly access support without having to wait for lengthy assessments or a team to create an individualized intervention. The process we describe here also allows schools to efficiently utilize other Tier 2 interventions already in place at the school, such as social, or academic, or organizational skills groups, to add targeted supports onto basic CICO for students whose data indicate an inadequate response to intervention. If small modifications and additions have been made to basic CICO and a student is still engaging in problem behavior, we recommend that schools conduct a brief FBA to identify the likely function of the behavior and replacement behaviors that can be taught and reinforced through the existing CICO intervention. By following this process, schools can efficiently and effectively support the academic and behavioral needs of their students.

CHAPTER 10

Considerations for Caregiver Partnership and Culturally Responsive CICO

Sara C. McDaniel and Allison Leigh Bruhn

HOME AND COMMUNITY SYSTEMS

While most of this book focuses on systems within schools for implementing CICO, this chapter focuses primarily on including caregivers as key stakeholders and influencers in students' academic and behavioral success as it relates to CICO. Since school-age children are involved in both home and school environments each school day that can vary drastically from each other, it is important to leverage caregiver input and participation when addressing school behavior with CICO. Further complicating this situation, often there is no direct interaction between a student's school and home beyond the basic information sharing that occurs more often in the elementary grades (e.g., bringing home a school note, report card, or newsletter). It is critical that these two environments be inclusive of each other, functioning in a way that facilitates a shared responsibility for students' development and well-being. This means that stakeholders in each system engage in two-way communication and collaboration (Muscott, Mann, & LeBrun, 2008). Several researchers highlight the connections between students, educators, home, and community (e.g., in ecological systems theory; Bronfenbrenner, 1979) and the ways in which students learn behavior (e.g., in social learning theory; Bandura, 1963), which emphasize the importance

Sara C. McDaniel, PhD, is a Professor of Special Education in the Department of Special Education and Multiple Abilities at the University of Alabama and is the Director of the Center for Interconnected Behavioral and Mental Health Systems. Dr. McDaniel conducts research and teaches in the areas of: (1) positive behavior supports; (2) classroom management assessment and coaching; (3) Tier 2 social, emotional, and behavioral supports; and (4) preventative treatments for diverse populations of students placed at high risk.

Allison Leigh Bruhn, PhD, is an Associate Professor of Special Education at the University of Iowa. Her research focuses on assessment and intervention for K–12 students with challenging behavior.

of the parent as a collaborative member and the need for strong partnerships between home and school environments.

The ecological systems theory is a developmental theory that highlights the different systems that affect students (Bronfenbrenner, 1979). Figure 10.1 depicts an adapted example of this theory related to child development and education. The ecological systems theory identifies child development as a process that occurs between the child and their environments, which include classrooms; culturally responsive instruction; peer groups; and relationships with teachers, home, and the community. This theory also points to the importance of understanding how changes and conflicts in one environment (e.g., the home) impact development and progress in other environments (e.g., the school). In fact, different environments can become interconnected when parents and caregivers are members of the same team (Neal & Neal, 2013).

Given the importance of the interactions among home, community, and school environments, school partnerships between caregivers and the community are critical. The importance of these strong collaborative partnerships has been documented in existing foundational research (Christenson & Sheridan, 2001; Pianta & Walsh, 1996; Sheridan, Clarke, Marti, Burt, & Rohlk, 2005). This foundational research led to the more recent work of developing and implementing culturally responsive practices that honor students' and caregivers' varying backgrounds (Bottiani, Larson, & Debnam, 2017; Bradshaw et al., 2018). In response to the highlighted need for culturally responsive practices, we present recommendations for culturally responsive adaptations to CICO, while leaving intact the core components that make CICO an evidence-based intervention (e.g., an adult mentor, goal setting, explicit expectations, ongoing feedback, contingent reinforcement, and home–school communication).

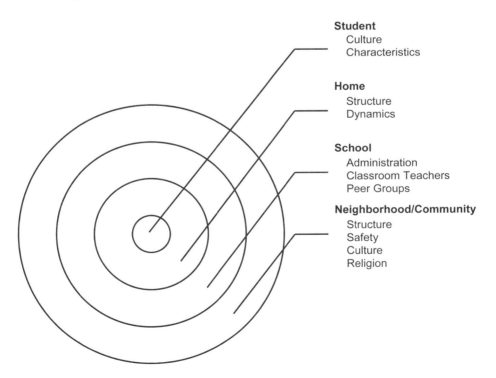

Student
Culture
Characteristics

Home
Structure
Dynamics

School
Administration
Classroom Teachers
Peer Groups

Neighborhood/Community
Structure
Safety
Culture
Religion

FIGURE 10.1. Modified ecological systems theory for education.

CULTURALLY RESPONSIVE PBIS

When implementing tiered systems of PBIS, schools should attempt to embed culturally responsive teaching into all three tiers of support. Culturally responsive teaching is designed to improve educational equity in which all students receive the instruction and supports that they require to be successful, and to incorporate an understanding of varying cultures, races, ethnicities, religions, language minorities, and income groups (Gay, 2000). Multicultural education leads to culturally responsive teaching practices. According to Gay (2000):

> Interactions between students and teachers as well as among students in the classroom are frequently identified as the "actual sites" where learning success or failure is determined. They are prominent among the major attributes of culturally responsive teaching. Conventional wisdom and research studies suggest that teachers play a pivotal role in these interactions. In fact, the tone, structure, and quality of instruction are determined largely by teachers' attitudes and expectations, as well as their pedagogical skills. (p. xv)

Universal Tier 1 culturally responsive teaching practices include (1) truly knowing students and caring about their cultures; (2) using communication strategies that are culturally informed and promote learning; and (3) incorporating culturally diverse and congruent content (e.g., providing an instructional example of geography from a student's home country or geographic region; Gay, 2000). Common strategies for schools to become more familiar with student and caregiver cultures and backgrounds include inviting caregivers and other family members into the school and classroom, holding town halls for family members to air their concerns to educators, and conducting universal student surveys that provide background information of interest as well as students' perceptions of the school's climate and cultural responsiveness. Additionally, caregivers should be represented on the Tier 1 PBIS leadership team, and PBIS should be discussed regularly during school and classroom meetings with caregivers.

In culturally responsive Tier 1 procedures, schoolwide expectations and behavioral goals are culturally informed, and are not solely created from the perspective of the majority of the student body or the culture of the educators. Schools should ensure that the three to five positively stated schoolwide expectations reflect students' home and community cultures as part of existing culturally responsive Tier 1 schoolwide PBIS practices. For example, many schools use "Be Respectful, Be Responsible, and Be Safe" as standard schoolwide expectations. Culturally responsive schoolwide expectations should reflect culturally relevant issues in the school building and community and use culturally responsive wording. One example of a culturally responsive expectation from a rural school with a high percentage of students from low-income backgrounds is the RODEO expectation: "Respect others," "Organized and ready," "Demonstrate a positive attitude," "Engaged," and "Own your actions." RODEO expectations represent the primary concerns of students in a rural low-income middle school about being late to school and not prepared to learn (e.g., a lack of adequate sleep, food, and necessary school materials). Similarly, an example from an urban school that identified physical and verbal aggression (e.g., fighting among peers, angry outbursts toward peers and adults) as the primary areas of concern established culturally responsive schoolwide expectations of SOAR behaviors that were aligned with the community mascot, the falcon, and were defined as students who "Solve problems peacefully," "Own your actions," "Accept responsibility," and "Respect others."

CULTURALLY RESPONSIVE TIER 2 CICO

These elements of culturally responsive teaching should apply to all schoolwide Tier 1 practices and then be incorporated into or extended to CICO implementation. One of the most critical strategies to ensure culturally responsive CICO is to gain an understanding of the (1) student (e.g., race, ethnicity, religion, culture, language, family orientation to education, socioeconomic status, trauma history); (2) home structure (e.g., single-parent household, temporary grandparent guardianship, shared-custody dual household, foster care); (3) home culture; and (4) neighborhood and community characteristics (e.g., socioeconomic status, crime prevalence, culture, structure). Culturally informed communication strategies recognize that students (e.g., Spanish speaking) who do not use the communication styles of those in the majority experience more obstacles in communication than students who do communicate in mainstream styles and languages (Gay, 2000). An understanding of whether educators and school systems require students to "code switch" in order to match their communication style with the mainstream or majority communication style is important. Because communication is a key component of CICO (i.e., between the CICO coordinator and the student and between the coordinator and caregivers), CICO coordinators should facilitate interaction and interpret or modify written and spoken communication with caregivers and students. Examples include providing the CICO DPR and all feedback in the student's native language. Finally, culturally diverse and congruent content aligns content and teaching with the students' cultures, rather than with the teacher's own culture or the majority culture of the school. Content across the academic and behavioral domains should seek to represent the cultures of all students with diverse materials and examples.

The three main tenets of culturally responsive teaching (i.e., relationships, communication, and content) can be used to guide specific culturally responsive adaptations to CICO. Culturally responsive CICO requires (1) intentional CICO coordinator matching, (2) culturally responsive behavioral expectations, (3) prioritized daily goals with culturally informed corrective feedback and praise, and (4) responsive reinforcement strategies.

Matched CICO Mentor/Facilitator and Relationship Building

Mentoring literature highlights the importance of pairing mentors and mentees (when possible) who are similarly matched in terms of race, age, gender, and interests (Grossman & Bulle, 2006; Hanlon, Simon, O'Grady, Carswell, & Callaman, 2013). Mentor matching enhances the opportunity for mentees to have a mentor who serves as a relevant model. To properly match a CICO mentor/facilitator to a student receiving the intervention, educators must have foundational information about students' backgrounds and interests as a Tier 1 culturally responsive practice. Learning more about students' backgrounds becomes even more important as they begin to demonstrate problem behavior meriting the need for a Tier 2 intervention, such as CICO. Therefore, by the time a student is identified to participate in CICO, there should be adults in the school community who know and understand the student.

Culturally Responsive Expectations and Language

Implementing Tier 1 PBIS culturally responsive practices, such as schoolwide surveys and procedures for translating text and communication, helps to build a foundation of truly knowing a student. With a better understanding of a student's culture, background, family structure and parenting style, and strengths, the CICO mentor/facilitator and classroom teachers can use responsive strategies to set, define, and explicitly teach expectations, and provide examples and nonexamples that are representative of the student's culture and native language. After the behavior support team determines the need for CICO (or the student is identified via screening or nomination), and a mentor/facilitator match is found for the student, the facilitator and classroom teachers should discuss strategies for providing culturally responsive expectations and teaching practices of the expectations on the DPR. For example, the DPR may need to include a student's native language alongside English.

Finally, students from diverse, nonmajority backgrounds benefit from examples and nonexamples of the expected behaviors that represent their culture, race, and/or gender. The DPR may include brief, culturally aligned examples, or definitions, under each behavioral expectation, which is a simple, effective adaptation for schools that use culturally responsive practices when teaching schoolwide expectations. For example, if the schoolwide expectation is "take responsibility," a student may benefit from real-world examples of taking responsibility. In another instance, if the schoolwide expectation is "be respectful," a female middle school student would benefit from examples and nonexamples that illustrate what respect looks like for female peers, male peers, and adults, instead of one example that demonstrates respect for adults.

Culturally Responsive Feedback and Reinforcement

A third culturally responsive adaptation for CICO is providing feedback and reinforcement that is aligned with cultural or individual preferences, which can boost the effects of feedback and reinforcement. Like previous components, this adaptation is a natural extension for schools using culturally responsive practices as part of their Tier 1 PBIS. Using the adaptations made for Tier 1, administrators can share with teachers of students receiving CICO examples of culturally responsive decision making, feedback, and reinforcement. One primary component of CICO is the ongoing performance feedback throughout the school day. For some students, frank, specific feedback provides a clear message about performance of behavioral expectations. However, for other students, feedback, especially the corrective kind, may need to be modified in order to be effective. Some students may respond better to private discussions of performance feedback. Others may require extra praise when providing corrective feedback (e.g., "today you did a great job working with your reading partner, but I did notice that when you had a disagreement about turns you raised your voice"). Similarly, for other students, a more nonverbal feedback conversation may be needed. In this instance, a teacher rating the behavior would reduce the perceived embarrassment of receiving feedback in a conversation with a student and by relying on nonverbal cues, such as a thumbs-up or high five, when going over the ratings. Feedback may also be written on paper or electronically and given to the student. This method is specifically helpful for students who find adult interaction to be aversive and may attempt to avoid or escape adult attention (positive or negative).

Just as some students react differently to teacher feedback, students and their caregivers may also require adapted approaches to providing contingent reinforcement. Culturally, one student may best be positively reinforced through a positive parent phone call or home note, while another student may be reinforced by personally receiving recognition, a privilege, or a token. It is important to survey the students and their caregivers to determine the most effective reinforcers. Refer to Chapter 6, Figure 6.6 for a sample reinforcer checklist that can be used to assess student preferences.

CICO and Caregivers

The previous description of culturally responsive practices is extended in this section to include involving caregivers in more active ways, further improving the effectiveness of CICO. Both providing culturally responsive CICO and involving caregivers require (1) understanding the varying environments that the student navigates, (2) appreciating how these environments are similar and different, and (3) determining how best to support the student and differentiate instructional strategies to promote positive outcomes. Caregivers can participate in students' education in a variety of ways, such as communicating with school personnel, attending individualized education plan meetings, following through with school-based interventions at home (e.g., implementing home components), and attending school open house. These examples represent (1) communication, (2) teaming, (3) participation/implementation, and (4) partnership. A majority of home–school activities center on basic one-way communication, such as school newsletters, homework assignments, and report cards. Although these forms of communication are vital in relaying information to caregivers, they represent a surface-level involvement in that the communication is not two way and reciprocal. Other typical home–school activities are participatory in nature, such as serving on the Parent Teacher Association (PTA) committee, attending field trips, volunteering in the classroom, and attending student-led learning conferences. A deeper level of involvement is required for teaming and partnership. Examples of teaming activities include participating in individualized education plan teams and problem-solving teams (e.g., MTSS). To be included in a teaming activity, a caregiver must be invited to attend and participate as one team member of the group. On the team, the caregiver may serve as an advocate for their student and share an important perspective about the student's needs, strengths, struggles, and patterns of behavior. The most in-depth home–school activities are true collaborative home–school partnerships. Partnerships between caregivers and educators require both parties to view the responsibility of supporting the student as shared, in which communication is frequent, clear, and bidirectional. It should be noted that of the existing CICO research, 94% of studies included the review of DPR data by the parent as a component of CICO (Wolfe et al., 2016). Caregiver participation in CICO beyond the DPR review is possibly the least understood and implemented element of the intervention, although students still benefit when caregivers are not actively involved beyond reviewing the DPR.

CICO Home–School Communication

Basic CICO includes two primary forms of home–school communication. First, the caregiver is notified of the school's decision to provide CICO for the student. Second, the DPR is sent home to (1) make the caregiver aware of their child's performance throughout the day and progress toward daily goals, (2) give the caregiver an opportunity to provide feedback, and (3) have the caregiver sign the form as an acknowledgment of the DPR. Although not ideal, this type of home–school communication tends to be a one-way response if DPRs are not returned to school, an occurrence that happens approximately 40–50% of the time based on some studies (e.g., Hawken et al., 2007). On the CICO DPR, the caregiver can write their signature on the lines at the bottom of the form, hence notifying the mentor/facilitator that the DPR was reviewed at home. The signed form is then sent back to school with the student the next day. Using the DPR as a guide for facilitating conversation, the caregiver may encourage student progress, praise the student for meeting set goals (or offer an additional form of reinforcement), discuss the mentor/student relationship, and/or review the schoolwide expectations on the DPR at home. These extension activities at home can be taught and encouraged by the CICO mentor/facilitator, although some caregivers may naturally incorporate these strategies in their parenting approaches.

Advanced CICO Partnership

One model intended to promote caregiver and educator partnerships is the Teachers and Parents as Partners (TAPP; Sheridan, 2014) intervention, previously known as the Conjoint Behavioral Consultation approach. This evidence-based consultation model requires caregivers, educators, and other service providers to meet students' needs by working collaboratively to address student deficits or concerns, to promote learning by determining a common interest, and to build the skills and strengths of caregivers and educators in working as a team. The partnership comprises caregiver(s), classroom teacher(s) and other educators and one leader or facilitator who is typically a school psychologist or counselor. The team identifies culturally responsive, mutually agreed upon goals for the student, and uses data-based decision making and a team problem-solving approach for identifying interventions, strategies, and needed adaptations. The TAPP approach requires collaboration across four stages, which can be adapted in developing partnerships with caregivers in a Tier 2 intervention such as CICO: (1) needs identification, (2) needs analysis, (3) plan development, and (4) plan evaluation. This model takes a strengths-based approach toward student and caregiver interviews to collaboratively understand students' needs and parental priorities, characteristics, and teacher goals.

An advanced partnership through CICO implementation builds on the basic CICO communication strategies previously noted to include bidirectional communication, feedback, collaborative efforts, and adapted TAPP intervention components for caregiver partnerships within CICO.

Establishing Relationships

As presented earlier, often the student is the communicator between school and home. Teachers communicate through the student, and the student informs caregivers about what happens at school. The first strategy in developing an advanced partnership through CICO implementation is to shift the student's role from that of a communicator bridging school and home, to that of team member. In this scenario, the student is not a partner in the middle between school and home, as demonstrated in Figure 10.2. Instead, educators and caregivers should be established as partners within a collaborative relationship, helping to support the student, as shown in Figure 10.3.

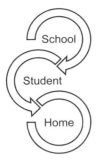

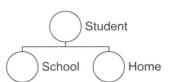

FIGURE 10.2. Example of a student serving as communicator between home and school.

FIGURE 10.3. Example of a partnership between student, home, and school.

In this modified partnership structure, home and school are viewed as allies working together to support the student, and communication between home and school exists independently of the student. This structure leads to more appropriate roles and responsibilities for educators, caregivers, and students. The student serves as the focus for support, while the school and home maintain a shared responsibility for communication about and support of the student. Specifically, educators in the school create a safe, supportive environment during the school day and communicate directly with caregivers. Educators are responsible for providing school-based intervention, collecting and analyzing data about student progress, and making data-based decisions. Caregivers are responsible for ensuring a safe, supportive home environment and for communicating directly with educators at the school.

Expectations at Home

In an established partner relationship, educators and caregivers can work together to provide consistent terminology about the schoolwide expectations listed on the CICO DPR. In most cases, schoolwide expectations are taught as part of Tier 1, throughout all of the settings in the school building, but are not part of the behavioral expectations that are adhered to at home and in the community. Educators and caregivers should discuss schoolwide expectations and how to interpret them for the existing home structure, parenting approach, and culture of the community. It is important to note that the home and community do not have to align their behavioral expectations with what is expected at school. Rather, the caregiver and educator partners should discuss the similarities, differences, and strategies for using consistent terminology throughout home, community, and school settings to enhance an understanding of behavioral expectations. It may be necessary for educators and caregivers to codevelop a behavioral matrix (e.g., a list of behavioral expectations and what they look like in each setting) that includes home and/or community expectations. Importantly, understanding how behavioral expectations may be defined differently in home and community settings is a culturally responsive practice.

Figure 10.4 represents a high school parent brochure for teaching and supporting PRIDE (privacy, respect, involvement, dignity, and empathy) behaviors at school, at home, and in the community. Figure 10.5 represents a home PBIS matrix, which can also be used.

North High School Expectations

Restrooms:
- Use restroom for the appropriate purposes and give others privacy.
- Use restrooms between classes and during lunch.
- Use the nearest restroom and report back to class swiftly.
- Wash hands and keep surfaces graffiti free.
- Pick up any litter or trash on the ground.

Hallways:
- Use appropriate language and volume.
- Be aware of your surroundings.
- Walk swiftly to class and avoid conflict with others.
- Keep hands, feet, and objects to yourself.
- Report spills and hazards to nearest adult.
- Pick up any litter or trash on the ground

Cafeteria:
- Use appropriate language.
- Stay in line.
- Keep all food and drink in the cafeteria.
- Keep hands, feet, and objects to yourself.
- Report spills to staff and place trash in bins.
- Pick up any litter or trash on the ground and throw it away.

Parking Lot/ Bus:
- Park in designated areas.
- Use appropriate language and volume.
- Locate and board bus immediately after dismissal.
- Follow all traffic laws.
- Drive slowly while on campus.

Classrooms:
- Be an active listener.
- Participate in classroom activities.
- Be prompt.
- Be prepared with appropriate materials.
- Stay in personal space.
- Keep hands, feet, and objects to yourself.
- Follow all classroom procedures.
- Be an active listener.
- Pick up any litter or trash on the ground.

Community / Home:
- Look, listen and respond respectfully
- Be helpful at home and in the community
- Think ahead and be responsible
- Help maintain a clean home and community.
- Make positive choices and model good behavior
- Make adults aware of where you are and who you are with
- Spend money responsibly
- Take care of responsibilities and chores before social or recreational time
- If you see or hear about unsafe or unlawful behavior, report to an adult

PBIS Tips for Parents:
1. Remember 5 positives to 1 negative.
2. Set the stage for success and reward the effort.
3. Give clear, specific directions.
4. Stay calm, use a calm voice- *Nagging gets you nowhere.*
5. Set reasonable limits- *Avoid using "always" or "never".*
6. Be CONSISTENT- *Yes means yes and no means no.*
7. Set the example- *Actions speak louder than words.*

FIGURE 10.4. High school parent brochure for teaching and supporting behaviors at school, at home, and in the community.

Co-Creating Goals

Similar to the aforementioned discussion of culturally responsive practice, prioritized goal setting and advanced home–school partnerships within CICO promote the ability of all partners to use progress data, background information, and caregiver preference in establishing attainable daily goals. In basic CICO, the daily goal is focused on earning 80% or more of the total points possible. Through advanced partnerships in CICO, mentors/facilitators and classroom teachers can determine if additional clarification or wording of the schoolwide goals is necessary. For example, a parent may express the importance of improving in the area of accepting negative feedback or error correction for a child who tends to argue with the decisions of authority figures. In this case, the wording "accepts feedback" could be listed under the schoolwide expectation "Be Respectful" and would help narrow the focus on whether the student was able to accept corrective feedback, rather than arguing with the classroom teacher or mentor. Prioritizing this goal may be especially important given the amount of feedback from teachers the student receives throughout the day; and thus by having the student write their goal underneath the schoolwide expectation individualizes the goal, which also helps provide a daily prompt for them to follow the expectation.

	Morning Routine	Bed Time Routine	Meal Time	Riding in the Car
Caring	Help your mom, dad, brother, and sister get ready if they need it Give your family a kiss and hug goodbye Tell your family to "Have a great day!"	Give your family a kiss and hug goodnight Tell your family, "Sweet dreams!"	Share your last bite Make sure others have enough before taking the last helping of food Ask people at the table about their day	Open the car door for someone
Respectful	Say "Good morning!" Say, "Please" and "Thank you" Listen to directions from your parents	Say, "Good night!" Listen to directions from your parents	Say, "Please" and "Thank you" Use good manners. For example say, "Excuse me." Thank the person who prepared the food	Take your turn talking and avoid yelling or interrupting Play music at appropriate level Avoid saying negative things to other drivers or passengers
Responsible	Eat breakfast Brush your teeth Make your bed Get dressed according to the weather and school activities	Brush your teeth Get your pajamas on and put your dirty clothes away Read for 15 minutes before going to bed Turn off all electronics	Help set the table Help prepare the food Clean up after yourself	Wear your seatbelt Clean up any messes—avoid littering out the window! Lock your door after exiting When you get out of the car, pay attention to other cars and people
Ready	Get up on time Make sure your backpack has everything you need for school (homework, lunch, cold weather clothes, gym shoes)	Make sure your backpack has everything you need for school (homework, lunch, cold weather clothes, gym shoes) Go to bed on time	Wash your hands before eating	Have all of your stuff on (e.g., coat, shoes) when it's time to go Bring all necessary materials (e.g., bag, water)

FIGURE 10.5. Home PBIS matrix.

Collaborative Feedback

Similar to co-creating and prioritizing CICO goals, in an advanced caregiver–educator partnership, performance feedback can be provided in the context of a team approach. Corrective and positive feedback are provided to the student, caregiver(s), and the mentor as a team, and not just to the student. The educators providing DPR ratings and performance feedback may meet to discuss feedback with the student and the mentor/facilitator. An electronic DPR format may be used in order to generate more detail and enhanced transparency within a rating period, or a summary of daily performance feedback may be given along with the numerical ratings. For example, a school that assigns Google email addresses for all teachers and students may also request a Google email address for the caregiver, so students' daily performance can be entered in a Google form and shared with the whole team in real time. This team approach to corrective feedback increases opportunities for caregivers and the mentor to support the feedback process, and improves alignment in performance feedback as the student progresses through CICO with more specific positive and corrective notes for the student.

Contingent, Consistent Reinforcement and Consequences

The inclusion of a DPR in CICO allows for (1) contingent reinforcement for meeting a prioritized daily goal and (2) communication about performance within an advanced home–school partnership. First, sending the DPR home allows caregivers to reinforce and celebrate the times when students meet their daily goals at school. Caregivers can use verbal praise and additional contingent reinforcement systems (e.g., if you meet your goal for 2 days this week at school, you can choose a movie to watch on Friday) at home. The DPR also encourages discussions at home about favorable and unfavorable ratings received throughout the day. For example, a caregiver could point out "it looks like today you did a great job being responsible for your own learning during algebra," and similarly, "I see Mrs. Carter rated your respectful behavior a '0' during world history class; can you tell me more about that?" Finally, the CICO DPR also allows for educators and caregivers to be consistent with consequences when behavioral expectations or goals are not met. Although receiving corrective feedback and not meeting goals at school can be instructional, without follow-through at home, school misbehavior may be unintentionally reinforced by caregivers who are unaware of daily performance. For example, if a student demonstrates improved behavior at school and meets daily goals throughout the day, but this performance is not recognized at home, student motivation to demonstrate improved behavior at school may decrease. Conversely, if responses at home are aligned with school performance and include access to additional privileges at home for meeting CICO goals, students receive a consistent message regarding behavioral expectations.

Reciprocal Communication

In advanced home–school CICO partnerships, ongoing communication between the partners (e.g., school administrators, CICO mentors, classroom teachers, caregivers) is a two-way, reciprocal channel. Communication may require weekly phone calls, additional meetings, or daily email communication to discuss progress, or group discussions, such as the "Group me" app, in which partnership members can discuss student strengths, setbacks, setting events, and community, home, or cultural activities and events. This open communication eliminates the student as the information or communication agent. Once free of this obligation, the student can focus on goals and progress, and the partnership members can carry out effective, collaborative communication and problem solving.

All of these suggested adaptations for an advanced caregiver–educator partnership are efficient and require minimal additional resources. In some cases, more resource-intensive approaches are needed. The final three adaptations require additional participation on behalf of the caregiver, which is at times difficult to recruit.

Home Visits

Home visits may be conducted as part of a school's traditional practices in response to students who demonstrate problem behavior. For instance, a Tier 2 team may designate a counselor or social worker to conduct home visits to obtain additional information about the student's circumstances or to facilitate communication with caregivers. Home visits are particularly beneficial for educators and also can be helpful for the student and the family. Most home visits can be conducted in less than an hour and include a few open-ended questions for the caregiver, while the educator is actively engaged in listening and observing. If this practice is already in place, the home visit information can be shared with the Tier 2 team and the CICO facilitator/mentor.

Problem-Solving Team Participation

Similar to requesting and conducting home visits, in some cases it may be necessary for the caregivers to be invited to the school during the biweekly or monthly reviews of progress, with the caregivers serving as an ad hoc member of the problem-solving team. Their role on the behavior support team or Tier 2 PBIS team during the discussion of their child is to (1) inform the team of their child's school progress and contextual factors; (2) receive data updates on the child's progress; and (3) engage in problem solving with the team (e.g., how to get their student to participate in the intervention, what the team may try to use as contingent reinforcement). Working as a team increases shared responsibility, communication, and ownership of the intervention plan and student outcomes. Since most team meetings occur during the school day, it may be necessary to allow caregivers to attend virtually or over the phone. It may also be helpful to provide a translator in order to communicate with caregivers who do not speak the majority language.

Caregiver Needs Assessment

Finally, if a student is not responding to CICO, the CICO facilitator may need to determine if caregiver needs, such as receiving the paper DPR or understanding DPR data, are not being met. In these cases, the facilitator or mentor may request that the caregiver complete a needs assessment that addresses the perceived needs for successful communication, culturally responsive adaptations, and effective collaboration. The information gathered from a needs assessment may help the team to identify and target simple supports for caregivers. For instance, a needs assessment would help identify if caregivers need help with parenting skills and with basic necessities, such as free and reduced-price lunch services, weekend meal services, and access to community mental health care. In a supportive advanced partnership within CICO, the caregivers become integral change agents and entry points for providing support. A simple assessment can assist in efficiently identifying these needs.

CONCLUSION

Students spend a substantial portion of their waking hours at school with teachers who are responsible for providing academic instruction as well as supporting students' social, emotional, and behavioral development. Despite teachers' incredible responsibility to deliver comprehensive educational supports, the caregivers and the community should not be neglected in the process. Research has shown that parental involvement, in particular, has a significantly positive impact on the achievement of students who have a variety of backgrounds, ages, and abilities (Jeynes, 2007, 2012). By including caregivers in the CICO process and considering the culture of the home and community, implementers of CICO are acting in culturally responsive ways that will hopefully enhance student outcomes. It is important to note that the strategies described for improving caregiver partnerships with the school, and in turn for improving CICO implementation, do not change the core components of basic CICO. That is, basic CICO remains intact, while considerations are given and acted upon for improving the role that caregivers play in the process.

FREQUENTLY ASKED QUESTIONS

Can CICO Work without Caregiver Partnerships?

Although this chapter focuses on the strategies for encouraging caregivers to participate as partners and on the benefits of building this partnership, CICO can be implemented without the general or advanced-level partnerships described. Without caregivers as partners, all basic CICO procedures remain in place, with the CICO DPR being sent home to make the review of the report possible. If caregivers do not participate as partners in CICO, you can encourage the student to obtain a caregiver signature, but the student should not be punished if the caregiver does not sign the report. Similarly, the DPR may not be returned to the school after it is sent home. If this practice becomes common, teachers can make a copy of the report prior to sending it home, or record the DPR percentage total before sending the report home in an effort to be able to make data-based decisions from the report data.

What Strategies Should Be Used for a Resistant Caregiver?

Caregivers may be reluctant to participate in CICO for several reasons. One is the presence of eroded relationships between the school and caregiver. For caregivers who are disengaged from school or from specific teachers, intentional relationship building and encouraging more positive, consistent feedback may be helpful. Another common reason for caregiver resistance is caregiver disbelief in the school's identified needs for their child and/or the CICO intervention as a beneficial strategy. Some caregivers may (1) not see challenging behavior at home, (2) have a hard time understanding their student's behaviors and the rationale for CICO, and (3) not understand the need for a partnership with the school. In this case, we advise patiently and explicitly explaining to caregivers how their student was identified for CICO and what CICO is and what to expect, as well as answer any questions that caregivers may have. A third common reason for caregiver resistance is that many caregivers lack the time to support the intervention. Caregivers are often busy with taking care of other children and family members and with working. If a caregiver expresses resistance owing to a lack of time, schools can find more simple and efficient means for them to participate (e.g., text-message updates; weekly updates) or can require less participation throughout the intervention (e.g., signing the DPR).

What If a Child Lives between Two Separate Households?

It is important to recognize that many students transition between households throughout the week or month. This chapter focuses on "caregivers" in general, which can include single-parent households, dual-parent households, split households, grandparents and other family members, temporary custodians, and foster parents. As such, when a child has more than one caregiving household, the parent as a partner model should be expanded to include all of the student's caregiving partners. Having multiple households and multiple caregivers can complicate communication, so setting up a chain of communication, in which one identified caregiver communicates directly with the school and the remaining caregivers communicate in sequence can eliminate confusion and miscommunication. Similarly, educators should allow for multiple caregivers to participate in CICO and sign the DPRs to be returned to school. Finally, in multiple caregiving households, aligning the expectations and procedures for all caregivers can provide structure and continuity and improve student outcomes.

CHAPTER 11

CICO in High School Settings

Kaitlin Bundock and K. Brigid Flannery

Thus far in this book, we have primarily focused on the implementation of CICO in elementary and middle school settings. Students in high schools also experience behavioral difficulties that can be effectively addressed through interventions such as CICO. These students benefit from targeted Tier 2 interventions like CICO for many of the same reasons that students in elementary or middle schools do: CICO provides students with a structured prompting of appropriate behavior, specific feedback on their behavior, opportunities for positive contact with adults in the school, a process for self-evaluation, and acknowledgment for behavioral improvements (Mitchell et al., 2017; Wolfe et al., 2016).

RESEARCH ON CICO IN HIGH SCHOOLS

Although the majority of research on CICO has been conducted in elementary schools, a growing number of CICO studies have been performed in middle and high schools, with most of them having been performed in middle schools (Drevon et al., 2018; Hawken et al., 2014). Although there are distinct differences between middle and high schools (i.e., maturity level of students, academic demands), the *organizational structure* of middle schools is typically more similar to high schools than to elementary schools. For example, middle and high school students typically attend multiple class periods with different teachers. Because of these structural similarities, research on intervention implementation in middle schools can be valuable and pertinent when considering implementing the intervention in high schools. Therefore, in the following review of CICO research pertinent to high school implementation, we include research conducted on CICO in middle as well as in high school settings.

Only one study has evaluated CICO specifically in the context of high schools (Swain-Bradway, 2009). In this study, CICO was implemented with six students in grades 9 through 11. Implementation of CICO was supplemented with a daily 45-minute study-skills class, in which students were provided with instruction on specific skills and strategies to improve their organizational abilities, effective studying and test taking, goal setting, assignment completion, recruitment of adult feedback, and appropriate technology use. Over the course of the intervention, all six of the students demonstrated significantly increased rates of academic engagement and also had improvements in assignment completion. The students also had slight decreases in problem behavior, and four of the students had slight improvements in attendance. Overall, this study provides evidence that CICO, with an additional study-skills support class, can result in positive changes for high school students at risk for problem behaviors.

Two studies evaluating CICO in alternative education settings have included high-school-age students (Ennis et al., 2012; Swoszowski et al., 2012). Ennis and colleagues (2012) determined that CICO was associated with reductions in rates of problem behavior for three students whose behaviors were primarily attention maintained, but the results were less conclusive for three students with escape-maintained behavior. Swoszowski and colleagues (2012) concluded that four of the six students included in their study responded to the intervention, regardless of the function of their behavior. These results indicate that CICO can be an effective way to improve the behavior of high school students with moderate to severe problem behaviors in more restrictive settings.

Even though studies of CICO in high schools are limited, there is a strong research base on CICO in elementary and middle school settings. In a review that included 28 total studies on CICO (including unpublished doctoral dissertations), Hawken and colleagues (2014) found that 10 studies included students in sixth grade and above, and these studies resulted in moderate intervention effects. The following year, Maggin and colleagues (2015) determined that CICO can be considered an evidence-based intervention based on the detection of positive intervention effects for 80% of the students who were included in nine high-quality CICO studies, three of which were conducted in middle schools and one of which was conducted in a high school. Wolfe and colleagues (2016) conducted a review of CICO studies and found that there were 6 studies (out of a total of 12), meeting high-quality research criteria, 2 of which were conducted with students ages 12 years and older. The results of these 2 studies, which included between three and six students each, indicated that CICO resulted in positive changes in student behavior for 64–82% of the data points, the results of which also demonstrated moderate effects.

In an additional review on CICO research, Mitchell and colleagues (2017) found that only 5 of the 13 published studies on CICO met the quality standards published by the Council for Exceptional Children (CEC) related to rigorous research, 2 of which were conducted with students in fifth through eighth grade and in sixth through ninth grade. Mitchell et al. (2017) found that each of the secondary-level studies had neutral to mixed results. In one study, 67% (four out of six) of the participants demonstrated a reduction in problem behavior during the intervention (Swoszowski et al., 2012). In the other study (Simonsen, Myers, & Briere, 2011), there were no significant differences in teacher ratings of behavior prior to or following the intervention (Mitchell et al., 2017).

In the most recent review of CICO research, which included the largest number of studies (a total of 37, with 9 in secondary schools), Drevon and colleagues (2018) found that CICO has a large and significant positive effect on student behavior, with students typically improving by over one standard deviation between baseline and intervention. Drevon et al. (2018) also conducted a moderator analysis in their review to determine if CICO outcomes differed significantly according to factors such as school level (i.e., elementary, middle, or high); function of behavior (i.e., escape vs. attention maintained); gender; or race/ethnicity. In slight contrast to the findings of the prior reviews on CICO, the results of their moderator analysis indicate that there are no significant differences in CICO outcomes based on any of the moderators included. These results indicate that CICO is similarly effective in elementary, middle, and high schools.

In summary, the research base on CICO in secondary schools (and in particular high schools) is growing, but remains limited and currently demonstrates moderate results. Bear in mind, therefore, that the recommendations included in this chapter are informed by the existing research base on CICO in secondary schools (Swain-Bradway, 2009) as well as the work that the authors have conducted directly with high schools that are implementing CICO (Kittelman et al., 2018), and the research related to behavior interventions implemented under a schoolwide PBIS framework in high schools (Flannery & Kato, 2017; Swain-Bradway, Pinkney, & Flannery, 2015).

CICO can be implemented similarly in middle and high school contexts, but the nature of high schools does necessitate modifying specific aspects of CICO to ensure that the intervention matches the high school structure and the particular needs of older adolescents. In this chapter, we first discuss the unique features of high schools that may affect CICO design and implementation. Then we provide a description of the critical defining features of CICO that should be prioritized and maintained, regardless of school level. In the last part of the chapter, we provide specific recommendations for how to design and implement CICO in the high school context to effectively improve student behavior.

UNIQUE ASPECTS OF HIGH SCHOOL CONTEXTS

Fixsen, Naoom, Blase, Friedman, and Wallace (2005) have identified that for successful and sustained implementation of an intervention, it is critical to not only attend to the features and organizational systems of the intervention, but to also attend to the context (i.e., people, environment, culture). These contextual variables will directly affect how the intervention is implemented and sustained and how important student and school outcomes are achieved. Three primary contextual variables unique to high school have been identified: (1) school size, (2) organizational culture, and (3) students' developmental level (Bohanon, Fenning, Borgmeier, Flannery, & Malloy, 2009; Flannery & Kato, 2017; Swain-Bradway et al., 2015).

The first contextual influence to consider is the *size* of high schools—larger campuses with more buildings and physical space than in elementary schools, along with a larger student enrollment and faculty/staff population. A second contextual influence is the *organizational or school culture*, which includes both the shared meanings and values about how the school functions (Lee, Bryk, & Smith, 1993) and the resultant school structure. Foundational to high school culture is the clear focus on teaching academics. Teachers are hired on the basis of their expertise in academic areas, and high schools are typically organized into departments according to these same areas. High school teachers see their roles and responsibilities as defined in relation to academic content and not necessarily in terms of offering social supports to students. Improving social behavior is not often thought to be a high school teacher's responsibility, the assumption being that students should know at this point what behaviors are expected. The last contextual influence that impacts the implementation of interventions is the *student population's age and stage of development*. Secondary students are adolescents searching for increased autonomy from adults, increased independence, and active participation in decision making, especially when the outcome concerns them directly. Adolescents' drive for autonomy and independence also results in a reduced reliance on parents and an increased reliance on peers. Each of these contextual variable needs to be considered when implementing CICO in high schools.

CRITICAL DEFINING FEATURES OF THE INTERVENTION

In addition to attending to the unique characteristics of high school settings to ensure that CICO fits the context, it is important that high schools implementing CICO prioritize maintenance of the critical defining features of the intervention to facilitate the efficiency, effectiveness, and sustainability of the implementation. Next we discuss the key features of CICO (initially described in Chapter 3 and referenced in Table 11.1) within the specific context of high schools. We draw on our previous discussion of the unique characteristics of high schools in describing how to maintain the key features of CICO when implementing the intervention in high school contexts.

First, high schools implementing CICO need to ensure that the intervention is structured as an *efficient system* to support approximately 10–15% of the students in the school who are predicted to be in need of additional supports under the schoolwide PBIS model (Bruhn et al., 2014; Mitchell et al., 2011). High schools may need to adjust the particular roles of the CICO coordinator to ensure that this percentage of the school population can access the intervention regardless of the higher enrollments compared to elementary or middle schools. Ten percent of a high school population could be as large as (or even larger than) 160 students, which will

---

TABLE 11.1. Critical Defining Features of CICO

- Structured as an efficient system.
- Continuous intervention availability.
- Daily check-in and check-out sessions with a respected adult.
- Designed to promote positive interactions between students and teachers.
- Increases the frequency of contingent feedback.
- Designed to require low teacher effort.
- Links behavioral and academic support.
- Is implemented and supported by all school personnel.
- Regular monitoring of CICO DPR data by the school team.
- Use of DPR data by the school team to determine the need for adjustments.

require multiple coordinators and facilitators and possibly multiple behavior support teams. Second, CICO must be *continuously available*, allowing students who need support to access the intervention within 3–5 days of being identified. Third, the intervention is structured with a *daily check-in/check-out session with a respected adult.* It is important to prioritize the check-in session, so that students have an opportunity to start their day with a positive interaction and a reminder of behavior expectations. The check-in may be especially relevant at the high school level because it may be the only time that students receive an explicit review of expectations (academic and behavior) with reminders specific to the behaviors with which they might struggle.

Fourth, CICO is designed to *promote positive interactions between students and teachers.* This feature can be particularly important in high schools, because the student has multiple teachers and class sizes tend to be larger. A brief, positive interaction at the beginning of class can serve as a prompt for appropriate behavior and also as a structured means for teachers and students to establish positive relationships. Fifth, CICO *increases the frequency of contingent feedback* from each teacher about the student's behavior. The developmental level of high schoolers may necessitate providing more specific training or coaching about how to appropriately accept and respond to feedback. Sixth, CICO is designed to *require low teacher effort* to help ensure that the intervention is consistently implemented and that teachers see positive behavior changes with little work on their part. Fortunately, CICO is structured to be low effort, so few, if any, adaptations are needed for this element at the high school level. Yet, owing to the large number of students who might participate in CICO and the limited time between class periods, during which students and teachers have to make transitions, the behavior support team must make sure that teachers do not have too many students participating in CICO in any one period.

Seventh, CICO *links behavioral and academic support.* With the primary focus in high school on academics, this intervention component should be prioritized to ensure that teachers are giving students immediate and constructive feedback so that they can adjust their behavior. CICO expectations can be used to link behavioral and academic support to provide students with a structure for keeping track of their assignments and with a foundation for encouraging conversations about academic progress with teachers. Eighth, *the intervention is implemented and supported by all school personnel*, since each student interacts with several teachers every school day. The ninth feature is that students identified as being in need of support must have the *opportunity to choose to participate* and cooperate with the CICO intervention. Due to the increased freedom students have in high school, this feature is critical in ensuring that students receiving the intervention actually participate in the parts of the daily CICO process that occur outside of class times (i.e., before and after school). Finally, a school-level team *regularly monitors CICO DPR data, and uses these data to determine whether any adjustments are needed* for the intervention as a whole as well as for specific student participants.

HIGH SCHOOL CICO IMPLEMENTATION RECOMMENDATIONS

Given the *size, organizational culture*, and *the age and developmental level* of students that make high schools unique, as well as the importance of maintaining the key features of the CICO intervention, guidance is needed for implementing CICO in high schools. In this section, we feature specific recommendations for designing and implementing CICO in the high school setting. These recommendations prioritize maintenance of the key features and include suggested adaptations of particular elements of the intervention to ensure that they are feasible and appropriate for high school settings (a summary of CICO recommendations is provided in Table 11.2).

Roles and Responsibilities

When beginning any intervention, a school team needs to determine the infrastructure or systems that are necessary to support its implementation. When implementing CICO, the three primary staffing roles that need to be in place are that of the coordinator, the facilitator, and the behavior support team members (e.g., data analysts, teachers). The roles of the school personnel involved in CICO implementation are discussed in more detail in Chapter 5. One difference in personnel roles related to CICO at the high school level should be noted: the CICO coordinator in this setting takes on a more supervisory role, which is made possible by the addition of the CICO facilitator, who is responsible for the daily check-in/check-out sessions.

The CICO Coordinator

The coordinator, who may be a teacher or related service provider (i.e., a counselor or paraprofessional), needs to review the students' data, to check in with facilitators to confirm that students are progressing, and to troubleshoot if things aren't going well. Given that students in high school typically attend classes with four to eight teachers a day, the coordinator must have the flexibility to support the students throughout the day when they initially start the intervention if the facilitator is not available. For example, students will need to develop fluency in completing the teacher–student check-in/check-out cycle for each class and may need prompting to remember. Initially some troubleshooting may be required for an individual student that cannot wait until the next team meeting. As a result, the coordinator must know how to adjust the procedures and reinforcers in order to increase the effectiveness of the intervention.

The CICO Facilitator

The CICO facilitator interacts directly with the students by checking in and out with them in the morning and at the end of the day. This individual, typically a paraprofessional or teacher, starts each student's day and sets the student up for success. Depending on the number of students and the structure of the school, the coordinator may also be a facilitator with some students. The facilitator sets goals with each student and manages the delivery of reinforcers for achieving the goals. Typically each facilitator in a high school can support 5–10 students owing to the size of the student body and time constraints before and/or after school. In addition to developing rapport with the students, the facilitator should present opportunities for them to take a more active role in the intervention based on adolescents' desire for more control and choice. To do so, students could be allowed to select their facilitator from a list of possible candidates, to provide input on the reinforcers and/or the reinforcement system used, and to select what specific information is sent home to parents, among other options. Last, the facilitator is responsible for communicating with the students' family or guardians about their progress.

TABLE 11.2. Summary of Recommendations for Implementing CICO in High Schools

Identification and referral

Student selection	• Actively review incoming freshmen prior to start of school.
	  ○ Use middle school data and other information.
	  ○ Look for significant changes from the previous GPA or other data, in addition reviewing the current GPA.
	• Use behavioral (e.g., ODRs, tardies/attendance) and academic indicators (GPA, credit accrual, citizenship grades, etc.).
	• Include students with attendance issues when the function of the behavior aligns with connecting with adults/organizational skills.
	• Do not include students who are averse to adult contact.

Key roles

Coordinator	• Availability needs to be flexible, especially when student begins the intervention to provide support throughout the day if necessary. • Teach problem-solving routines for students who need additional support (e.g., low teacher fidelity, data collection) or when things go awry (e.g., recovery routines). • May need multiple coordinators if there are more than 30 students.
Facilitator	• Maintain a student caseload that can be served in the time available. • Establish rapport with students quickly. • Use strategies to actively involve students throughout the process. • Support students in choosing a facilitator who will motivate them to check in and out (e.g., have rapport with, near their location at beginning/end of day).

Orientation and training

Orientation for faculty	• Expand the exploration phase to include time to discuss the alignment of social behavior and academic performance as well as college and career readiness or other schoolwide initiatives. • Due to the number of teachers involved, ensure efficient and consistent training is available to address teacher turnover and training for substitutes.
Training for facilitators and coordinators	• Provide basic training in CICO procedures and also in strategies (including referrals elsewhere when appropriate) for dealing with unexpected setting events (e.g., fighting with peers/parents, medication changes).
Orientation/training for students	• Provide a rationale for CICO and explain its value for their time in high school and for the future (e.g., college- and career-ready standards). • Actively include students in the process and in decision making. • Use CICO to teach self-regulation and organizational skills. • Teach a "recovery routine" for when things aren't going well and how to find the coordinator for support.

(continued)

TABLE 11.2. *(continued)*

CICO process	
Daily CICO routine	• Consider multiple check-in and check-out locations in the building. • Meet with student at another time (instead of check-out) toward the end of the day for goal review and acknowledgments; possibly not meet daily if student is on track (e.g., weekly review sessions).
DPR	• Ensure that academics can be addressed through DPR expectations. • Support teachers in using positive and corrective feedback. • Ensure that teachers apply schoolwide expectations in their classroom. • Use a DPR that maintains the key elements but is age appropriate (e.g., small size, electronic). • Incorporate additional academic elements (e.g., homework tracker). • Have students self-assess their performance each period before the teacher provides feedback.
Feedback on performance	• Explicitly teach (e.g., role-play) how to provide and accept feedback. • Involve teachers and students; attend to multiple classroom contexts. • Support students' ability to integrate feedback from teachers and self-monitoring, investigate and implement strategies to adjust behaviors.
Selection of reinforcers	• Students could participate in selecting reinforcers. • Use privileges as well as tangibles; privileges can include things such as a "fast pass" to go to the front of the lunch line. • Link to the Tier 1 schoolwide acknowledgment system when possible. • Reinforcers for both completion of the process (e.g., turning in card, checking in with each teacher) and for meeting goals. • Due to strong ties with peers, the inclusion of fellow students might be considered; have rewards be something they can share with other students, such as gum or coffee cards; have a peer come with them to the daily check-in/check-out.
Family communication	• Send summarized information on performance home weekly. • Send information electronically.

The Behavior Support Team

The use of a behavior support team increases the likelihood that interventions are implemented with fidelity and are more efficient and effective (see Chapter 2 for more information about Tier 2 interventions and Chapter 4 for more information about the role of the behavior support team in CICO implementation). This team establishes access to interventions, evaluates the fidelity of systems and practices, and regularly utilizes data to monitor the progress of students. Members typically include someone from the schoolwide PBIS leadership team, the CICO coordinator, a person knowledgeable about behavior, and a school administrator. The team meets every 2 weeks to review students' progress and resolve any problems.

When implementing CICO in a high school setting, the number of students on the intervention may require multiple teams. For example, because freshmen are often the largest group of students in need of Tier 2 support (Allensworth & Easton, 2005; Kato, Flannery, Triplett, & Saeturn, 2018), a school may consider that at least one behavior support team focus on this group. If this is the case, additional teams can be developed to support students from a mixture of upper-grade levels.

Identification and Referral of Students

Students are typically selected by the behavior support team through a standard selection process (see Chapter 3). Teams often will consider students for CICO who have been brought to their attention by their rate of ODRs or who were directly referred by a teacher or parent. CICO is designed for students with or without disabilities who have a high frequency of low-level behaviors throughout the school day. These behaviors may range from students who need support in organizing their day, to students with minor misbehaviors, such as talking out, talking to peers during class, work completion issues, minor disruptions of the class, and use of cell phone in class. Schools should also consider students who have received suspensions for multiple minor behavior infractions as potential candidates for CICO. Due to the increased focus on academic success at the secondary level, schools may also consider using academic screening criteria, such as a student's overall GPA or the total credits the student earns in progressing toward graduation.

It may also be worth evaluating any discrepancies between students' middle and high school GPAs, because a significant change in GPA could indicate a need for support. As noted earlier, students who find adult contact aversive are not likely to respond to CICO, because of the fact that frequent adult interaction is a key feature of the intervention. High school students change classes on a regular basis, encountering differences in content, teaching styles, and interaction patterns, so it is to be expected that students may have issues in one class and not in another. CICO is also better suited to students who display behaviors somewhat consistently throughout the day and in most of their classes, rather than for those who struggle with one or two particular class periods or teachers. As long as the student exhibits the behavior in the majority of the classes, CICO may be the right choice.

High rates of absenteeism may also indicate a student's need for support. However, it is important to consider that students who frequently skip multiple classes may not necessarily benefit from the intervention because the contingencies may not be strong enough to result in their attendance. Students who have mental health concerns can benefit from CICO if their behaviors are stable, but it would be wise for schools to consider layering on additional supports for these students (refer to Chapter 12 for information about CICO for internalizing behavior problems, and to Chapter 9 for information about adapting CICO for students with more severe behavioral needs). Due to the limited passing time between high school classes, strategically consider each potential CICO candidate's level and type of need, so that no teacher has more than two to three students per period involved in CICO, when possible.

A final recommendation for identifying and referring students for CICO is to especially consider freshmen at the beginning of the school year. These students have many new expectations at this key transition time, so the increased structure and clarity provided by CICO participation can deliver much-needed support. Often, reviewing middle school data and talking with middle school staff can assist in selecting appropriate students.

Orientations and Trainings

Training for All School Faculty and Staff

Before beginning CICO, the behavior support team ought to conduct an orientation for all the faculty and staff to ensure that there is support for and commitment to the intervention prior to implementation. The team needs to agree that there is a problem that can be addressed by providing students with some extra supports, and that they, the teachers, are willing to commit 3–4 minutes at the end of their class periods to check in with the students and provide feedback. This process of commitment may require more than a brief presentation. It may necessitate some discussion with the faculty and staff about (1) their role in social development; (2) how CICO could reduce students' classroom disruptions and thus increase instructional time; (3) how the skills students will be developing are linked to College- and Career-Ready Standards (U.S. Department of Education, 2010) or other professionalism requirements (e.g., citizenship grades, professional standards related to career and technical education classes); and (4) how CICO will help improve academic performance, and thus, help ensure graduation. The faculty also will need to be oriented to the general teacher–student check-in, check-out process and to the importance of positive and constructive feedback, and specifically how to provide that feedback.

When the specific teachers who will be interacting with the student in each period are known, the coordinator should set aside time to discuss, and potentially role-play, troubleshooting examples. Some examples include what to do if there is a substitute teacher, what to do if a student misses a class or doesn't want to check in, what to do if there is no time one day to check out a student, or what to do if a student doesn't accept feedback.

A report by the Learning Policy Institute by Carver-Thomas and Darling-Hammond (2017) found that teacher turnover rates were negatively correlated with school size. This finding means that schools with higher enrollment numbers tend to have higher rates of teacher turnover, and that schools with lower enrollment numbers tend to have lower rates of teacher turnover. Although any school has the potential for staff turnover, the size and demands of high schools create a higher risk for more significant staff turnover. It is therefore essential for high schools to have a strategy for orienting new teachers to the CICO intervention on an ongoing basis. We recommend that teachers new to the school be provided with a CICO training and orientation session at the beginning of the year, and that the coordinator follow up with new teachers to ensure that they understand the rationale for CICO as well as their role in the intervention. The school should also determine what procedures to use for substitute teachers. For example, one option is to have a brief handout on CICO that the front office staff could provide to substitutes when they sign in for the day.

Coordinator and Facilitator Training

Facilitators and coordinators will need the basic training on CICO procedures (see Chapters 5 and 14), but also may have some unique training needs relevant to working with adolescents. These students may have setting events (e.g., medication changes, disagreement with peers/parents, and disruption in romantic relationships) that occur before the school day and thus can be identified or noticed at check-in or during the day. Facilitators will need to have the skills to debrief with these students and get them back on track or referred to others (i.e., counselors) for support.

Student Training

Active participation in CICO will require schools to use an approach that encourages students "buy-in" to the importance of learning these skills and agree to partner in implementing this specific intervention. This training can be more efficient when students understand the rationale for using these skills and their connection to being "career and college ready"—or about how participation benefits them now in high school and how it relates to their future.

One central expectation in high schools is that students take greater responsibility for their academic and social behavior (Schiller, 1999). This increased expectation for self-regulation strategies requires that students rely more on their own skills and less on adult guidance and control (Sheffield & Waller, 2010). This expectation aligns with the students' need to seek autonomy, to control events that affect them, and to actively participate in decision making. With active student involvement, CICO can be a great mechanism for teaching self-regulation skills to students (e.g., goal setting, self-monitoring, receiving of feedback, self-evaluation). The training will require going beyond the typical orientation for students about when and where to check in and check out, about how to use the DPR, and about setting goals. Students can receive explicit short trainings in areas identified as needed in each of the skills in a complete self-regulation process that includes (1) goal setting, (2) self-monitoring, (3) seeking feedback, (4) self-evaluation, and (5) adjustment of behavior based on feedback. It may be helpful for the facilitator to role-play with the student how to have efficient contacts with their teachers at the beginning and end of each class period.

Last, students will need to be taught a "recovery routine" that explains what to do when their day doesn't go well. Students may experience events that set them off (e.g., a disagreement with peers or parents, a negative interaction with teacher, an instance of nonpositive feedback). These disruptive events are typical in the day-to-day life of an adolescent, and many of the students eligible for CICO do not have a set routine to follow in adjusting and maintaining appropriate behavior when these events occur. A recovery routine can be as simple as checking in with their facilitator when they get a break in their schedule or engaging in a quick reset routine to redistribute the negative energy. For example, a reset routine could consist of the following: (1) Take a deep breath (delay your response); (2) do the next right thing (focus on one thing at a time); and (3) loop back when you are in a better mindset and determine your next steps (e.g., Do you need to seek help with this? Are there actions to take? Is it something you can let go of?). The CICO coordinator should teach students a process to follow, including a reset routine, when they encounter highly stressful or upsetting situations.

The CICO Process in High Schools

CICO Routine

High schools that implement CICO may find that they need to slightly adapt the daily check-in, check-out routine. High school campuses can include multiple buildings that span a wide area. Depending on the size of the school, the CICO facilitator's room may be on the opposite side of campus compared to where students have their first or last class. Students will likely be less motivated to check in and/or check out if the routine results in them being late to class or missing the bus home. Another potential barrier to implementing a traditional daily CICO routine in high schools is that students are more independent and tend to be motivated by peer attention and approval. Checking in and out before and after school may take up valuable social time with peers, and the risk of social stigma may cause students to be hesitant to check in and check out when other students are present. Next we describe several options for how the check-in/check-out process can be adjusted to maintain critical components, while maximizing contextual fit.

First, high schools implementing CICO may address these barriers by having multiple facilitators. To implement this recommendation, schools should identify several adults skilled at developing positive student relationships who are willing to serve as CICO facilitators. The CICO coordinator could either assign students to specific facilitators, or provide students with a choice of which facilitator they would like to work with. When determining which students will check in and out with which facilitators, the coordinator should consider the physical locations of each facilitator's classroom or work space, as well as students' first and last period classes, to ensure that they can easily get to class on time after checking in and catch the bus home on time after checking out. Schools could also consider having peers serve as mentors who walk students through the check-in/check-out sessions.

Upper-level students or CICO graduates may be appropriate peer mentors for this role, especially if they have social status at the school. For example, a recent CICO graduate could be assigned to one or two students who are just beginning CICO, and could help with role plays, could remind the students to check in and out, answer questions they have about CICO, or could offer them helpful advice. An upper-level student could also assist with the check-in/check-out sessions by passing out DPRs or by helping students total their points and calculate the percentage of points earned. Peers have been used successfully in similar roles in elementary schools (Dart et al., 2014; Smith et al., 2015).

A second adaptation option is to modify the check-out component. Students may be more likely to skip check-out than check-in, because of access to social time with peers, to after-school activities, or to transportation. The check-out time in CICO is used not only to review the DPR points for the day, but also to provide students with an opportunity to access reinforcers for meeting their point goals. It is incorporated in the intervention because many students benefit from having more frequent opportunities to access rewards. One option would be to have students text their facilitator at the end of the day, indicating how their day went. The text can be in a comment format or a simple "thumbs up, down, or sideways."

However, older students may need less frequent opportunities to access preferred or desirable tangible rewards, especially if they are provided with consistent feedback and positive reinforcement throughout the day by teachers. As an option, the check-out component could be modified to have the student check out briefly with their last period teacher, or to leave their completed DPR in a specified drop box location rather than checking out in person. If students use this modified check-out, it is possible that there might not be enough time during check-in to complete the additional required features (e.g., fully review the student's behavioral and/or academic progress, provide positive/constructive feedback, and deliver rewards earned). With this particular adaptation, students could have a standard check-in and then a longer weekly review session (10–15 minutes) with the CICO coordinator during lunch or study hall, for example.

During the weekly review, the coordinator could discuss with the students their academic and behavioral progress, set goals, and identify specific actions that they will take to reach their goals. The coordinator could conduct weekly reviews on a rotating basis, meeting with a different set of students each day (e.g., with 25 students on the intervention, the coordinator meets with a different set of 5 students per day). These weekly review sessions could provide valuable time for the coordinator to brainstorm unique and complex academic and behavioral challenges with the students.

Daily Progress Report

Another feature of CICO that may be adapted for use in high schools is the DPR. The foundational elements of the DPR should not be modified (see Chapter 6). At the high school level, it is even more important to guarantee that the faculty have agreed on clear schoolwide expectations to achieve consistency for students, given the size and organizational culture of high schools. Additionally, because the focus in high schools tends to be on academic success, the DPR may be adapted to incorporate feedback on academics. Academic content in high school is typically more rigorous and high stakes (i.e., the consequences for failing classes are more severe and long term in relationship to students' options after high school). For example, students who do not pass required classes will need to retake them, potentially delaying graduation.

CICO can link behavioral and academic support so that students have a structure for documenting academic supports under specific expectations (e.g., responsibility includes tracking/completing of assignments) or a foundation for encouraging conversations about academic progress with teachers. Many high schools have a schoolwide expectation that relates to academic success (e.g., "be responsible"), which provides an opportunity to incorporate feedback on academic behaviors on the DPR. If the school does not have an academic success expectation, one may be added to the DPR to help generate faculty buy-in for CICO. Additional academic components, such as a homework tracker, may also be added to the DPR to help build students' organizational skills (see Figure 11.1). Completion of the homework tracker could be worth points that go toward the DPR point totals.

In addition to adding academic components to the DPR, the format of the DPR itself may be adapted to better fit high school contexts. High schoolers may find it stigmatizing or embarrassing to carry around full-page DPRs, and adaptations could be made to reduce this risk. For example, some high schools have reported using wallet-sized DPRs, incorporating DPRs into student planners, or formatting DPRs to resemble grade or attendance check forms used by student-athletes. A wallet-sized DPR is less obvious and may draw less attention (see Figure 11.1). Many schools require students to write down homework in planners provided by the school, and some teachers may initial student planners to confirm that students have done so. Schools with such a system could format the DPR so that it fits easily into the planner. To increase acceptability, another option is to print the DPR on the same size and color of paper used for student-athlete grade/attendance checks. A fourth DPR formatting option is to use an electronic DPR (e.g., Google sheets or an app; see Figure 11.2) that the student, the CICO facilitator, the CICO coordinator, and all of the student's teachers have access to. The main benefit of using an electronic DPR is that the student does not have to carry around a paper version. However, schools using electronic DPRs should implement a system to make sure that students and teachers still discuss behavior ratings at the end of each class period, since one key feature

DPR with Assignment Tracker

Class Period	Respect	Relationships	Responsibility	Name: ____________ Date: ______ Assignments:	Teacher Feedback & Initials:
1	2 1 No	2 1 No	2 1 No		
2	2 1 No	2 1 No	2 1 No		
3	2 1 No	2 1 No	2 1 No		
4	2 1 No	2 1 No	2 1 No		
5	2 1 No	2 1 No	2 1 No		
6	2 1 No	2 1 No	2 1 No		
				□/36 = ____% Goal:_____	

Wallet-Sized DPR

Name:____________ Date:____________

Block	Materials	On Time	Work Complete	Respectful	Teacher Initials
1st	2 1 0	2 1 0	2 1 0	2 1 0	
2nd	2 1 0	2 1 0	2 1 0	2 1 0	
3rd	2 1 0	2 1 0	2 1 0	2 1 0	
4th	2 1 0	2 1 0	2 1 0	2 1 0	
Subtotal	___/8	___/8	___/8	___/8	___/32 Poss
GOAL	Current Goal: ____%			Goal met today? Y / N	

FIGURE 11.1. Example DPR cards for use in high schools.

of CICO is that the intervention provides structured opportunities for students and teachers to discuss behavior performance. If this element of the intervention is lost, students are less likely to make significant behavioral improvements.

Feedback on Performance

In traditional CICO, students receive specific feedback from their teachers at the end of each class period throughout the day. During this time, the student's teachers provide the student with positive and/or corrective feedback on the degree to which they met expectations. These feedback opportunities prompt the student to engage with their teachers, which can help build positive relationships. As noted earlier, it is important to acknowledge that high school is a time during which students develop and practice exercising a greater degree of independence. This independence can also lead to behavioral challenges if students are not provided with appropriate supports. The feedback component of CICO can be adapted to equip students with a process in which they learn and practice self-assessment in a structured way, with opportunities for specific feedback from adults.

First, the process by which students receive feedback from their teachers throughout the day may be adapted to have them self-assess their behavior prior to receiving feedback from their teachers. Self-assessment, which can help increase responsibility, independence, effort,

FIGURE 11.2. Example electronic DPR from a smartphone app. Copyright 2020 Educational and Community Supports, University of Oregon. Reprinted with permission from the author.

and self-reflection (Paris & Paris, 2001), is currently used in the lower grades as a way to fade students off the CICO intervention after they have been consistently meeting their daily point goals (see Chapter 7). In high schools, the student receiving the CICO intervention could first rate the degree to which the behavioral expectations were met at the end of the class period. The student would then share their ratings with their teacher, who adjusts any ratings that they feel need to be revised (either higher or lower) and provides the student with positive and/or corrective feedback. When incorporated into behavioral interventions, similar processes of self-assessment have helped increase students' on-task and appropriate behavior (Sheffield & Waller, 2010).

As previously discussed, when beginning the CICO intervention at any grade level, the CICO facilitator trains students on how to recruit and respond to teacher feedback. This element of the intervention may need to be intensified at the high school level, in part owing to students interacting with several different teachers throughout the day, and in part owing to the increased autonomy of high school students. Prior to starting the intervention, the CICO facilitator may conduct a more intensive training session (or sessions) with the student. During these sessions, the CICO facilitator can use role plays to specifically teach the student how to recruit and respond to feedback from their teachers, taking into consideration the many different classroom contexts the student interacts with throughout the day. Additionally, if the student is self-rating their behavior prior to receiving teacher feedback, time must be allocated during the training session to model how to respond when there are disagreements between the student's and teacher's ratings. We recommend that the focus of the student training sessions be on acknowledging the teacher's feedback, problem solving, and implementing strategies to change their behavior based on teacher feedback.

Selecting Reinforcers

One key component of CICO is that it provides students with frequent opportunities to access contingent positive reinforcement for engaging in the CICO process (i.e., checking in, seeking feedback from teachers, checking out, or turning in their DPRs) and for meeting DPR point goals. The CICO coordinator (or facilitator) and other involved school personnel select age-appropriate reinforcers and incorporate student choice in making selections. The CICO facilitator might give each participating student a survey so they can indicate which reinforcers would be most motivating (see Chapter 6 for examples and resources). Additionally, student choice can be taken into account by setting up a reinforcement system in which students earn points that they trade in for specific items or privileges.

Many school systems that implement schoolwide PBIS already have school stores where students can trade in schoolwide tickets or slips for tangible items and can accommodate a CICO positive reinforcement system. In addition to tangible reinforcers like pens, pencils, and food, high school students are often highly motivated by privileges, such as a "fast pass" to go to the front of the lunch line, the opportunity to use an electronic device at a specified time of the day, free (supervised) time, access to a specific activity, extra credit points, or free homework passes. Because peer relationships in high schools are so strong, reinforcers that can be shared with other students (e.g., gum, other snacks, coffee cards, specific activity, or free time) may be particularly motivating.

Family Communication

In traditional CICO, a copy of the DPR is sent home with the student at the end of each day for the family to review and sign. The student turns in the signed DPR at check-in the following morning. High school students, who are becoming increasingly autonomous, may be less likely to share their daily DPR with their parents, and may find it juvenile to have to return a signed DPR each day. However, communication between school and home is still necessary, especially for students who have behavior or academic challenges. Rather than sending home the DPR every day, the CICO coordinator could instead send home compiled DPR information weekly, and not require the student to bring back a signed copy. Another option is to electronically send DPR information (daily or weekly) directly to parents. To do so, the CICO coordinator or facilitator could scan the DPR (for daily communication) or compile a report of weekly DPR data in a table or graph, and send the information to an email address provided by the parents. These adjustments may more appropriately match the level of independence of high schoolers, while still maintaining consistent school-to-home communication.

CONCLUSION

In this chapter, we described the unique characteristics of high schools that necessitate adjustments to the CICO intervention, provided an overview of the key features of the CICO intervention that should be maintained, and presented recommendations for CICO implementation in high schools. More research on CICO in high schools is needed and is currently being conducted. The results of this research may lead to additional recommendations or adjustments to the recommendations we have described here. High school practitioners implementing CICO should periodically evaluate the new research conducted in this area and make adjustments as needed to align with it. Until additional research on CICO in high schools is available, we recommend that practitioners implementing CICO in this setting attend to the recommendations provided in this chapter to facilitate efficient and effective CICO implementation.

FREQUENTLY ASKED QUESTIONS

What if a student receiving the CICO intervention doesn't attend the high school for all class periods each day (e.g., they don't have a first or last period, or they attend an enrichment program off campus for half the day)?

Be flexible with regard to establishing alternative times to check in and out given that high school students' schedules can vary. For example, consider adding a lunchtime check-in/check-out session, in which students who attended the school for the first half of the day could complete check-out, while students just arriving for the day could complete check-in.

What if the student(s) aren't checking in and/or checking out?

Talk with the students who are consistently missing check-in/check-out to determine if there are outside factors affecting their ability to check in (e.g., arriving late to school because they depend on other people for rides) or to check out (e.g., fear of missing the bus), if they are forgetting to check in/out, or if they just don't like checking in/out. If external factors affect their ability to check in/out, develop procedures to allow the student flexibility with when and how they perform the task. For example, students could check out or leave their DPR with their last-period teacher or drop off their DPRs at established secure locations in the school (lockboxes).

If students are forgetting to check in, employ a text system to send texts to students reminding them to check in/out or help them set an alarm on their phone. If students don't like checking in, problem-solve to adjust the check-in, give them the option of a different facilitator to check in with, or add a reinforcement for checking in. For example, students could receive points or a small item for checking in and/or could bring a friend to check in with them.

What if the student leaves the DPR in a prior class period?

Provide front office staff and teachers with extra copies of DPRs to hand to students who lose them throughout the day. The front office is typically a convenient location to pick up a new DPR, rather than having to track down the whereabouts of any specific facilitator or coordinator in the school. Additionally, provide teachers who have students receiving the CICO intervention in one or more of their classes with extra copies of DPRs for students to use if they forget their DPRs in any other class period.

What if the student doesn't have a positive relationship with their facilitator?

If there is only one CICO facilitator in the school, the CICO coordinator could serve as a substitute for a few students who clash with their assigned facilitator. Alternatively, a second person in the school could be added as a facilitator to work with a specific student (or a set of specific students). If there are multiple CICO facilitators, allow the students to choose the one they want.

What if a student doesn't want to check in/check out with a teacher at a specific class period?

Meet with the student to discuss why they don't want to check in or out with the particular teacher. During this meeting, discuss ways to make checking in/out with the teacher more comfortable for the student, and practice the application of these ideas through role plays. Additionally, meet with the teacher to get more information about the student's behavior in their class and to determine if there are specific things that the teacher could do differently to increase the likelihood that the student will check in/out at the beginning and end of each class period.

What if a student is doing well in several classes—should they still use the DPR in those classes?

If a student has been consistently meeting their DPR goals in all but a few specific classes, there may be a tendency to stop using CICO in the classes in which the student is performing well. However, we recommend that the student continue using CICO in all classes, because doing so provides more opportunities for acknowledgment of appropriate behavior throughout the day. The coordinator and student could also identify what works for the student in the classes in which they are performing well and develop strategies that can be used to adjust to the differences in their other classes. Additionally, the student could work on more advanced behavioral goals related to schoolwide expectations in the classes in which they are doing well. Be aware that a lack of consistency between class periods may cause confusion and potentially affect the fidelity of implementation. The coordinator should work with the student to make sure that they understand how the intervention is being implemented in each class period.

    If a student has been doing well in all of their classes except for one or two, it may be beneficial to evaluate the context of the classes in which the student is not as motivated. Occasionally, classroom teachers may need coaching from the CICO coordinator related to how to provide appropriate feedback to the student and/or how to accurately rate their behavior.

What if the student isn't motivated by or interested in any of the reinforcers we are using?

If the student is motivated to improve their behavior without external reinforcers, no adjustments are needed. Provide the student with specific positive feedback during check-in/check-out, and find out if each of the student's teachers are providing the student with frequent contingent praise. If the student does not appear to be motivated by the reinforcers, but does seem to be motivated to change their behavior, work with the student to identify items, activities, or privileges that they would enjoy having the opportunity to earn.

If the student does not appear to be motivated to change their behavior, discuss with the team whether CICO is an appropriate intervention. Specifically evaluate whether the student has a higher level of need that would be more adequately met through a Tier 3 intervention. It may also be useful to conduct a functional analysis of the students' behavior to determine what function is maintaining their inappropriate behaviors.

CHAPTER 12

CICO for Students with Internalizing Behavior Problems

Kristin Kladis, Kristen Stokes, and Breda O'Keeffe

Educators often immediately notice and respond to students with behavior that is outwardly disruptive to instruction and other students; however, educators also recognize that students who withdraw from instruction and their peers may be having challenges. Internalizing behavior problems are related to mental health diagnoses, such as anxiety and depression (Kovacs & Devlin, 1998). They also include social withdrawal and somatic complaints (e.g., higher than average complaints about physical discomforts, such as headaches, stomachaches, shakiness, and nausea; Hughes, Lourea-Waddell, & Kendall, 2008). Students with anxiety often display excessive worry, fear, and emotional distress or avoidance of situations, sometimes with corresponding somatic complaints (American Psychiatric Association, 2013). Depression is characterized by chronic or cyclical feelings of excessive sadness, emotional "emptiness" or irritability, and corresponding physical and cognitive difficulties that affect daily functioning (American Psychiatric Association, 2013). Although identifying behavioral challenges as "internalizing" does not identify the behavioral function (i.e., behavior directed inward may be escape maintained or attention maintained), using this terminology can help practitioners be aware of the

Kristin Kladis, PhD, has been a member of the Judge Memorial Catholic High School faculty since 2017. As Director of Judge Memorial's Department off Student Services, Dr. Kladis oversees academic and behavioral intervention for students who benefit from Tier 2 and Tier 3 support.

Kristen Stokes, PhD, is currently the Director of Student Services for a PreK through 8th grade school. She has expertise in multi-tiered systems of support and trains teachers to work with students with various academic and behavioral needs.

Breda O'Keeffe, PhD, is an Associate Professor in the Department of Special Education at the University of Utah. Her primary research interests include evidence-based practices in assessment, behavior supports, and reading instruction for diverse elementary students at risk for and with disabilities.

unique characteristics of internalizing behavioral challenges that may be early indicators of more severe mental health issues. In addition, identifying internalizing behavior problems in their early stages, before they meet the diagnostic criteria for anxiety, depression, and related disorders, can help students by providing them with more effective and less-intensive interventions that prevent more severe problems from developing (National Research Council & Institute of Medicine, 2009).

Students with internalizing behavior problems often have lower academic performance in school and are at a higher risk for dropping out of school than peers without these difficulties (e.g., Duchesne, Vitaro, Larose, & Tremblay, 2008; Hughes et al., 2008; Rapport, Denney, Chung, & Hustace, 2001). If left inadequately treated, anxiety and depression can lead to severe behavioral problems, such as social isolation, substance use disorder (e.g., Kendall, Safford, Flannery-Schroeder, & Webb, 2004; O'Neil, Conner, & Kendall, 2011), and suicide (e.g., Fergusson, Woodward, & Horwood, 2000). Clearly, practitioners need to screen for and address internalizing behavior problems as early as possible.

RESEARCH ON INTERVENTIONS IMPLEMENTED TO ADDRESS INTERNALIZING BEHAVIOR PROBLEMS

Internalizing behavior problems can be underestimated and overlooked, while the consequences of failing to treat these challenges can compound over time and become severe. School settings are one of the most common contexts for students to receive mental health services, despite having considerably fewer professionals, compared to clinical settings, prepared to provide these services (e.g., Costello, He, Sampson, Kessler, & Merikangas, 2014; Wu et al., 1999). In addition, research-based practices for treating internalizing behavior problems tend to be highly technical and time intensive, yet are the most effective for students in need of intensive individualized supports (e.g., Compton, Burns, Egger, & Robertson, 2002; Marchant, Brown, Caldarella, & Young, 2010). For example, cognitive behavioral interventions have the most evidence for reducing internalizing behavior problems, but require the mental health expertise of practitioners, and can require many hours outside the classroom (e.g., Compton et al., 2002). Other interventions, such as social skills training and the Strong Kids curriculum, are promising for internalizing behavior problems, but appear to be most effective for students whose internalizing behavior problems are more severe (Marchant et al., 2010; Williams, 2015).

Call for PBIS to Include Interventions for Internalizing Behavior Problems

Research on the effects of schoolwide PBIS with students exhibiting externalizing behavior problems has shown this organizational approach and related interventions to be successful (e.g., Benner, Nelson, Sanders, & Ralston, 2012; Bradshaw et al., 2010); however, McIntosh, Ty, and Miller (2014) found only two studies on schoolwide PBIS at the time that included internalizing behavior as an outcome or intervention target. Although students with internalizing behavior problems experienced improved outcomes in both studies (Cheney et al., 2009; Lane, Wehby, Robertson, & Rogers, 2007), McIntosh et al. (2014) called for increased research and practice to focus on screening and interventions for students with internalizing behavior problems within schoolwide PBIS models. The implementation of schoolwide PBIS encourages practitioners to screen and provide supports for students at risk for academic and behavioral challenges before they become entrenched problems. The focus on prevention and intervention may be more difficult for internalizing behavior problems, because practitioners have fewer screening tools and Tier 2 interventions that specifically target these behavior challenges early in their trajectory.

Previous Research on CICO for Students with Internalizing Behavior Problems

As one of the most widely implemented Tier 2 behavior interventions, CICO is typically used to support students with externalizing behavior problems. However, research is emerging on adapting CICO to address different problem behaviors in addition to supporting diverse student populations, specifically addressing students with internalizing behaviors (Dart et al., 2014; Hunter, Chenier, & Gresham, 2014; Kladis et al., 2020; Mitchell, 2012). Hunter and colleagues (2014) combined CICO with simple cognitive-behavioral strategies to support four elementary students who had been identified as at risk for internalizing behavior problems. The intervention was identical to a typical five-step CICO intervention used for students with externalizing behaviors, with the only difference being that the active engagement behavior goals on the DPR were individualized. Data from the teacher-completed DPRs indicated that all four participants demonstrated increases in active engagement behaviors. Data from the Student Internalizing Behavior Screener (SIBS; Cook et al., 2011) also showed a decrease in each student's level of internalizing behaviors.

In another study, Dart et al. (2014) examined the effectiveness of a peer-mediated CICO for elementary students who had internalizing behavior problems. The DPRs used in this study also had individualized behavior goals that promoted active engagement behaviors. In contrast to how CICO is typically implemented with an adult mentor or coordinator, upper-elementary students served as the coordinators for the target students and facilitated the morning and afternoon check-in/check-out sessions. Using peers to manage the intervention may be an effective alternative to the CICO intervention for schools that lack resources. An adult supervisor was present during both check-in and check-out sessions; however, the student coordinator was responsible for running the check-in/check-out process. Overall, the results from this study suggest that CICO for students with internalizing behavior problems can be effective in increasing active engagement behaviors, as measured by the daily point totals on the DPR forms. Two of the three target students demonstrated significant increases in DPR scores during the CICO intervention, as compared to baseline levels. Furthermore, after the intervention was implemented, all three participants no longer met the criteria for "at risk" on the SIBS, thus indicating that these students would no longer be identified as in need of services beyond the Tier 1 level. The research conducted by Dart et al. (2014) suggests that peer-mediated CICO can be an effective and efficient Tier 2 intervention for students with internalizing behavior problems in schools with limited resources.

Mitchell (2012) examined the effectiveness of CICO on reducing student anxiety, depression, somatization, and other internalizing behavior problems. This study included three students in an elementary school who were identified as at risk for internalizing behavior problems. Initially, the behavioral expectations listed on the DPR aligned with schoolwide behavior expectations, but were further individualized for each student according to teacher-reported areas of need. Teacher perceptions of student internalizing behavior problems improved following the CICO implementation. Postintervention assessment measured by the Behavior Assessment System for Children–2 (BASC-2; Reynolds & Kamphaus, 2004) indicated that levels of anxiety for all participants were reduced. In fact, for two of the three participants, anxiety scores decreased from clinically significant to normal levels. Scores on the BASC–2 depression scale decreased to a level within the normal range for two of the participants. Teacher ratings on the internalizing problems section of the BASC–2 also improved for two of the three participants. Mitchell's study provides support for using CICO to reduce the levels of internalizing behavior problems for students in the elementary school setting.

CICO for Internalizing Behavior Problems with Universal DPR

Researchers in past studies that evaluated CICO for internalizing behaviors have not used schoolwide behavioral expectations as the expectations on the DPR, but rather created individualized behavior expectations for each student based on their areas of need. Individualizing the DPR for each student enables CICO to be implemented with students who have internalizing behaviors more as a Tier 3 rather than as a Tier 2 intervention (Crone et al., 2010). As stated earlier, two important features of a Tier 2 intervention include consistent and similar implementation for all students and consistency with schoolwide behavior expectations. Most recently, Kladis et al. (2020) continued this line of research on the effects of CICO for internalizing behavior problems (CICO-IB) implemented as a Tier 2 intervention. One of the differences between this study and the previous research is the use of one DPR for all students with internalizing behaviors. The DPR listed schoolwide behavior expectations and examples of social and academic engagement behaviors that align with these expectations. For example, if one of the schoolwide behavior expectations on the DPR is "Respect Everyone," the DPR included an example of how to meet this behavior expectation by pursuing an active social engagement behavior of "verbally interact with a friend."

The purpose of Kladis et al.'s (2020) study was to determine if a functional relation existed between the implementation of CICO-IB and subsequent reductions in internalizing behaviors and increases in active academic and social engagement behaviors. A multiple-baseline design across participants was used, because this design allowed for the effects of the intervention on students' DPR scores to be examined. CICO-IB's acceptability was evaluated through the use of teacher, parent, and student ratings following the intervention.

Results from Kladis et al. (2020) provided evidence of a functional relation between CICO-IB implementation and increased active academic engagement for students who exhibited internalizing behaviors. All four participants experienced increases in active academic engagement following the implementation of the CICO intervention, as measured by direct observation and the total percentage of DPR points earned during the intervention phase. Just like basic CICO, the percentage of DPR points provides a snapshot of the students' progress toward engaging in active academic and social behaviors throughout the day. Additionally, overall engagement (active and inactive combined) for all participants increased to nearly 100%, and the DPR points earned increased from an average of 18.5% to an average of 89.5% of points earned during the intervention phase. The data also indicated a functional relationship between CICO-IB implementation and decreases in off-task behavior. During the intervention, all participants demonstrated decreases in off-task behavior, as measured by direct observations during the intervention phase.

Explicitly taught behavior expectations, continuous behavior feedback, consistent routines, positive reinforcement, and teacher–student relationships that foster student connectedness to the school are the foundational research-based principles underpinning the CICO intervention (Crone et al., 2010). Students who are at risk benefit from interventions based on these behavioral principles (Crone et al., 2010). Results from the aforementioned studies provide evidence that CICO-IB may be a promising intervention for decreasing internalizing behavior problems and increasing active engagement behaviors (Dart et al., 2014; Hunter et al., 2014; Kladis et al., 2020; Mitchell, 2012).

HOW TO IMPLEMENT CICO-IB

CICO-IB is an ideal Tier 2 intervention because its flexibility allows it to be adapted to meet the various behavioral needs of students. By using an existing Tier 2 intervention to assist students who are typically overlooked in the school setting, schools are able to support students with internalizing behavior problems within the framework of the school's current service delivery model. Using one universal DPR that has schoolwide behavior expectations and examples of active academic and social engagement behaviors for all students who receive the intervention allows for the immediate and consistent implementation of the intervention (Kladis et al., 2020). In the remainder of this chapter, we outline the specific steps for implementing CICO-IB and highlight the differences between CICO-IB and basic CICO.

Identifying Students for CICO-IB

Schools can use three methods to identify students in need of intervention: ODRs, teacher referrals, or screening tools. First, schools may use their ODR system to identify students (McIntosh & Goodman, 2016; McIntosh, Reinke, & Herman, 2009). However, students with higher rates of ODRs often have externalizing behavior problems rather than internalizing behavior problems (McIntosh, Campbell, Carter, & Zumbo, 2009). For this reason, we do not recommend relying solely on ODRs to identify students with internalizing behavior problems who need intervention.

Teacher referrals can also be used to identify students who need CICO-IB (Crone et al., 2010) and can be an efficient way to identify students with internalizing behavior problems who would have otherwise been missed using schoolwide data systems, such as attendance forms and ODRs (Carter, Carter, Johnson, & Pool, 2012). Teachers should follow the individual school's student support process when identifying students of concern to the behavior support team. Following a schoolwide PBIS model (Sugai & Horner, 2009b), the behavior support team, including the student's teacher, will decide if CICO-IB is the appropriate intervention to meet the student's need.

The third method of identifying students for CICO-IB is to use a formal screening tool (Oakes, Lane, & Ennis, 2016). Universal screening occurs with *all* students and is another method of identifying students with internalizing behavior problems who may be misrepresented or overlooked in other data systems or in the teacher referral process (Tanner, Eklund, Kilgus, & Johnson, 2018). Some examples of assessments that can be used for universal screening purposes are the Student Internalizing Behavior Screener (SIBS; Cook et al., 2011), the Systematic Screening for Behavioral Disorders (SSBD; Walker et al., 2014), and the Student Risk Screening Scale: Internalizing and Externalizing (SRSS-IE; Lane et al., 2012, adapted from Drummond, 1994).

The SIBS measure (Cook et al., 2011) screens students specifically at risk for internalizing behavior difficulties. The measure is a simple, paper-based tool that asks teachers to list the students in their class. Then the teacher rates the frequency ("0 = never, 1 = rarely, 2 = occasionally, 3 = frequently"; Cook et al., 2011, p. 74) with which each student displays or experiences each of seven internalizing behaviors, including "nervous or fearful, bullied by peers, spends time alone, clings to adults, withdrawn, seems sad or unhappy, complains about being sick or hurt" (Cook et al., 2011, p. 74). Students whose total score is greater than or equal to 8 can be considered at risk for internalizing behavior problems (Cook et al., 2011). These students will likely need additional support to develop adaptive skills in this regard.

The SSBD (Walker et al., 2014) is a norm-referenced, gated screening measure for externalizing and internalizing behavior difficulties. First, teachers identify students in their classes whom they consider at the highest risk for externalizing behavior problems, then separately at the highest risk for internalizing behavior problems. For students who have been identified in the first stage, teachers complete a "critical events checklist" for both positive and negative behaviors. The rating for each student is compared to ratings for students in a normative sample, with students rated in the highest 5% for internalizing and/or externalizing behavior problems considered to be at risk. The second edition of this measure can be completed online for automatic scoring and reports (*www.pacificnwpublish.com/online/ssbd.html*).

The SRSS-IE (Lane et al., 2012) includes three subscales: SRSS–Externalizing 7 (SRSS-E7), the SRSS–Internalizing 5 (SRSS-I5) for elementary schools, and the SRSS–Internalizing 6 (SRSS-I6) for middle/secondary schools. The SRSS-E7 behavior items include stealing, lying, behavior problems, peer rejection, low academic achievement, negative attitude, and aggressive behavior. The SRSS-I5 behavior items include emotionally flat, shy/withdrawn, sad/depressed, anxious, and lonely. The SRSS-I6 adds peer rejection to the list of items (which is rated across both internalizing and externalizing scales at the secondary level). Teachers rate their students three times per year, much like they do for academic screening assessments, and they rate the frequency with which each student engages in each behavior item on a Likert-type scale. The summed scores provide an estimated level of risk for each student (Lane et al., 2012). Students who score within the moderate ranges for internalizing behavior problems and within the low ranges for externalizing behavior problems may benefit from CICO-IB (Kladis et al., 2020). For example, if a student scored a 2 or 3 on the SRSS-I5, they would be exhibiting moderate levels of internalizing behaviors (see Lane et al., 2015).

Regardless of the method used to identify students for CICO-IB, it is important to remember that CICO-IB is a Tier 2 intervention; if students need more intensive support, another intervention or a further adaptation may be needed. For example, students who scored 4 or higher on the SSRS-I5 would be considered in need of more intensive support than CICO-IB can provide without further modifications (Lane et al., 2015). In addition, students who are being considered for CICO-IB should exhibit internalizing behavior throughout the school day rather than at isolated times or in specific environments.

Once a student has been identified for CICO-IB, the CICO coordinator will train the student on the same five-step process as the basic CICO intervention (Crone et al., 2010; see

Chapter 5 for information on the training process for CICO). The only adaptation that will need to be made during the training process is explaining the behavior expectations for prosocial behaviors (academic and social active engagement).

Check-In

At the beginning of the school day, the student checks in with the CICO coordinator. The coordinator provides the student with a DPR (see Figures 12.1 and 12.2), reviews the student's goals and expectations for the day, and offers encouragement for active social and academic engagement. In basic CICO, the coordinator typically gives the student some quick reminders about how to meet behavioral expectations in the areas for which they had lower scores on the previous day. In CICO-IB, these reminders are focused on increasing prosocial engagement.

SOAR Card
Summary Of Achievement & Responsibility
"WATCH ME SOAR!"

Student Name: _____   Date: _____

2 = Excellent	1 = OK	0 = Poor
• Needs 0–1 reminders • Consistently meets expectation	• Needs 2–3 reminders. • Usually meets expectation	• Needs 3+ reminders • Rarely meets expectation

Time	Follow Directions: *Request help*	Respect Everyone: *Active social engagement*	On Task: *Active academic engagement*
Before A.M. recess	2　1　0	2　1　0	2　1　0
After A.M. recess	2　1　0	2　1　0	2　1　0
Before P.M. recess	2　1　0	2　1　0	2　1　0
After P.M. recess	2　1　0	2　1　0	2　1　0
Total points	/8	/8	/8

Teacher initials: _____   Coordinator initials: _____

My goal today:										
%	100	95	90	85	80	75	70	65	60	55%	50%
Pts	24	23	22	21	19	18	17	16	15	13	12

Today's Points: _____   Points Possible: _____   Today's Percent _____ %

How I soared today! _____

_____

_____

Parent Signature: _____

FIGURE 12.1. Elementary DPR example for internalizing behaviors problems. Adapted with permission from Bundock, Hawken, Kladis, and Breen (2020).

Hillside Middle School
CICO Daily Progress Report

Student Name: _____   Date: _____

2 = 0–1 reminder   1 = 2 reminders   0 = 3+ reminders

	Be Respectful: *Actively engage in social tasks*			Be Responsible: *Actively engage in academic tasks*			Be Prepared: *Ask for help if you need something*			Be Positive: *Say kind things about self and others*			Teacher/ student initials
Period 1	2	1	0	2	1	0	2	1	0	2	1	0	
Period 2	2	1	0	2	1	0	2	1	0	2	1	0	
Period 3	2	1	0	2	1	0	2	1	0	2	1	0	
Period 4	2	1	0	2	1	0	2	1	0	2	1	0	
Period 5	2	1	0	2	1	0	2	1	0	2	1	0	
Period 6	2	1	0	2	1	0	2	1	0	2	1	0	
Period 7	2	1	0	2	1	0	2	1	0	2	1	0	

Today's Goal: 50%   55%   60%   65%   70%   80%   85%   90%

Today's Points: _____   Points Possible: _____   Today's Percent _____ %

Today's Successes: _____

_____

_____

_____

FIGURE 12.2. Secondary DPR example for internalizing behavior problems.

For example, if the student did not actively engage socially or academically the previous day, the coordinator and the student could quickly brainstorm about ways to be more actively engaged in prosocial behaviors (e.g., "Remember to raise your hand if you know the answer"; "Say hello to your teacher and a friend when you see them"). The CICO coordinator can use a point-tracking sheet to keep track of a student's points and to let the student know when their points can be redeemed for a reinforcer. It is important to remember that reinforcers must vary (e.g., include a variety of tangible and social choices) and be preferred by the student (i.e., be actually motivating and reinforcing).

Teacher Feedback

With CICO-IB, teachers can provide feedback to students specifically on their active engagement behaviors; therefore, they should understand the operational definitions of the behaviors, or "what the behaviors look like and sound like." As in basic CICO, teacher feedback should be positive and explicitly describe the correct behaviors they observed from the student. Additionally, if the student did not participate in an active engagement behavior listed on the DPR, teachers should provide specific examples of the desired behavior. The example DPRs (shown in Figures 12.1 and 12.2) include active engagement behaviors, such as Follow Directions—request help; Respect Everyone—active social engagement; and On Task—active academic engagement. Example operational definitions for the active engagement behaviors are as follows: Follow Directions—the student raises a hand or verbally requests assistance from the teacher; Respect Everyone—the student greets a peer or an adult (e.g., says hello, good morning, waves, and smiles); and On Task—the student responds to a question orally (e.g., individual, choral, partner, or team response). Table 12.1 provides a list of additional operational definitions for the active engagement behaviors.

At naturally occurring breaks in the school day (e.g., recess, lunch) and as designated on the DPR, the teacher(s) provides praise to the student about the observed level of active engagement during that session and awards an appropriate amount of points on the DPR. For example, if the student raised their hand once during a math lesson, the teacher could say, "Jaime, thank you for raising your hand during math class. I will award you 1 out of the 2 possible points for active academic participation. Next time, I would also like to see you share at least one idea with your partner. Keep up the good work." The teacher will then award 1 point on the DPR for that session.

If the student struggled to actively engage socially or academically, the teacher provides brief corrective feedback and encourages the student to try again during the next session. For example, if the student did not raise their hand or talk to a partner when asked, the teacher could say, "Jamie, I didn't see you raise your hand or talk to your partner during the lesson. Dur-

---

TABLE 12.1. Operational Definition of Active Engagement Behaviors

Follow Directions (ask for help)
- Student raises hand or verbally prompts for assistance from the teacher.
- Student verbally prompts for assistance from a peer.
- Examples: "How do I do _____?"; "I don't get it"; "I need help"; "This doesn't make sense"; "Is this right?"

Respect Everyone (active social engagement)
- Student greets a peer or an adult (e.g., says hello, good morning, waves, and smiles).
- Student initiates a social interaction with an adult or peer (e.g., "What are you doing?"; "Will you be my partner?"; "Can I sit here?").
- Student responds to a social interaction initiated by an adult or peer (e.g., verbal response, gesture, facial expression).

On-Task (active academic engagement)
- Student responds to a question orally (e.g., individual response, choral response, partner response, or team response).
- Student uses an action to respond to a question (e.g., hand signals, gestures).
- Student shares a written response to answer a question (e.g., whiteboard, response cards, slates).
- Student uses technology to respond to a question (e.g., classroom response systems).
- Student actively participates during small-group/partner work (e.g., shares an answer with the group, answers a peer's question, passes out group materials, writes an answer on the group paper).

ing the next lesson, I would like to see you raise your hand one time and to share one idea with your group. If you have any questions, please let me know. I can help you, so you can be more actively engaged." In this case, the teacher awards 0 out of 2 points for that session.

Check-Out

As with basic CICO, at the end of the school day, the student returns the DPR to the CICO coordinator. The coordinator calculates the total percentage of points earned for that day. If the student reaches the assigned goal (e.g., 80% of daily points earned), the coordinator praises the student for meeting the goal and actively engaging in class and awards the student the points that were earned on the point-tracking sheet.

Parent/Guardian Participation

The check-out process for CICO-IB is also similar to that used for basic CICO. At the end of the check-out process, the CICO coordinator prompts the student to take the DPR home and share it with their parent(s)/guardian(s). Students are encouraged to return a signed copy of the DPR the following day, but we recommend that no reinforcers or consequences be provided for doing so to avoid putting students with less access to home involvement at a disadvantage. If the student does not return a signed DPR, no consequences are given. In addition, we recommend that schools provide the parent(s)/guardian(s) with a graph showing the student's progress on the intervention on a frequent basis (e.g., monthly).

Measuring Fidelity of Implementation

As part of the process that determines if an intervention is effective, teams must consider the fidelity with which the intervention was implemented. Fidelity of implementation measures allow teams to determine if an intervention is being used as intended (Gresham, 1989; McIntosh & Goodman, 2016). The same process for assessing fidelity for basic CICO can be used to assess fidelity of CICO-IB. Ideally, schools should collect fidelity of implementation data using the basic CICO Fidelity Checklist presented in Chapter 7. Fidelity should be checked at the beginning of the intervention and then on an ongoing basis (e.g., two to three times per school year; Algozzine et al., 2014) to monitor the use of the intervention. Fidelity of CICO-IB can be assessed at the same time as the fidelity of implementation of basic CICO. As detailed in Chapter 7, measuring the fidelity of implementation is especially important if a student is not responding to the intervention as expected, because an additional assessment of fidelity may be needed. These data allow the team to rule out improper implementation as a reason for why the student is not responding to the intervention.

Measuring Response to Intervention

For CICO-IB, the active engagement behaviors listed on the DPR should align with the schoolwide behavioral expectations. As with basic CICO, teachers with students in their classes who are participating in CICO-IB rate students' behavioral performance during multiple time periods throughout the day. The teacher rates each student's performance of active engagement behaviors on a 3-point Likert scale, with 0 for *Poor* (e.g., Does not or rarely engages in the behavior. Needs more than three reminders.); 1 for *OK* (e.g., Engages in the behavior most of the time. Needs two to three reminders.); and 2 for *Excellent* (e.g., Consistently engages in the behavior. Needs one or no reminders.). Just like basic CICO, the total points earned across behaviors and time periods are calculated, and if students reach their daily point goals, they receive a specific number of points at the end of the day. The DPR also has a section for positive teacher comments as well as a section for the parent or caregiver review and signature. Data from the DPRs constitute a record of the teacher's perception of the student's daily behavior in the classroom. The DPRs only focus on the targeted active engagement behaviors rather than on negatively stated internalizing behaviors. The percentage of points earned on the DPR offers snapshots of the students' progress toward active engagement behaviors throughout the day.

Progress monitoring data are necessary to determine if the intervention is working for the student. To measure the student's response to CICO-IB, the percentage of daily DPR points earned should be graphed in an electronic system (e.g., Microsoft Excel or CICO-SWIS found on *www.PBISapps.org*) and reviewed on a biweekly basis. Graphs allow teams to quickly determine if there is an initial increase or decrease in the desired behaviors and to note overall trends of the student's behavior(s) (McIntosh & Goodman, 2016).

CONCLUSION

In this chapter, we described the need for, current research on, and a process for implementing CICO-IB, which is designed to efficiently and effectively meet the needs of students with internalizing behavior problems. Schools need timely screening methods and interventions to identify students with internalizing behavior problems, who often slip through the cracks and experience elevated levels of anxiety, depression, and stress as a result. Research on CICO-IB indicates that the intervention can improve the prosocial behaviors of students with internalizing behavior problems. As with basic CICO, CICO-IB utilizes a universal DPR and includes many of the same components of basic CICO (i.e., check-in, feedback throughout the day, checkout), but focuses on promoting active prosocial engagement behaviors rather than on just meeting standard behavior expectations. Accordingly, coordinator and teacher feedback for CICO-IB is focused on encouraging students to engage in specific behaviors that involve increasing their involvement and participation in academic and social interactions throughout the school day. By implementing CICO-IB, schools can quickly identify students with internalizing behavior challenges who are in need of intervention, and provide them with supports to help them be successful.

FREQUENTLY ASKED QUESTIONS

What if my school does not have schoolwide behavior expectation examples that promote active engagement behaviors?

Typically, most schools do not have schoolwide behavior expectations for students with internalizing behavior problems. You may have to work with your school team to create examples of behaviors that meet the schoolwide behavior expectations and promote active engagement behaviors. Similar to the way your team provides examples of appropriate behaviors for students with externalizing behaviors, your team can determine what examples of behaviors you can provide for students who may benefit from increasing active engagement behaviors. Some example behaviors are featured in Table 12.1.

Do we need a separate check-in, check-out coordinator and location for kids who are on the CICO-IB intervention?

No, students who are on basic CICO and CICO-IB can check in and out with the same CICO coordinator in the same location. Because CICO-IB utilizes one universal DPR like CICO, all students can follow the same format for ease of implementation.

What if a student is identified as being at risk for both externalizing and internalizing behavior problems? Should this student be placed on basic CICO or CICO-IB?

Students may be at risk for both externalizing and internalizing behavior problems. If a student is engaging in externalizing behaviors that are disruptive to the learning environment, that student should be placed on basic CICO. On basic CICO, the student will receive feedback on appropriate classroom behaviors. Through micro-teaching moments, teacher feedback, and access to reinforcers the student should engage in less disruptive behavior and more appropriate behavior conducive to the learning environment. It is recommended that the student should meet their behavioral goal for a percentage of points for at least 6–8 weeks before fading the intervention. Once the student has been faded off basic CICO, if internalizing behavior problems, such as sitting quietly instead of raising a hand to offer answers and/or avoiding or ignoring peers, persist or return, the student may be screened for internalizing behavior difficulties and placed on CICO-IB.

CHAPTER 13

CICO in Alternative Educational Settings

Nicole Swoszowski, Robin Parks Ennis, and Kristine Jolivette

Approximately 2% of students are served in alternative educational (AE) settings, and this percentage is steadily increasing over time (Lehr, Tan, & Ysseldyke, 2009). This percentage is equal to approximately 645,500 students who are served in AE settings annually (Carver, Lewis, & Tice, 2010), with more than 93,000 youth held in secure residential or juvenile detention facilities across the United States (National Juvenile Justice Network, 2009; Office of Juvenile Justice and Delinquency Prevention, 2011). AE settings incalude (1) public and private alternative schools, (2) special day treatment facilities/schools, (3) residential treatment facilities, (4) clinic and hospital schools/facilities, and (5) juvenile correctional facilities. Students qualify for support in AE settings if they have been removed from traditional or "home" school settings to receive more intensive intervention and support in an array of domains (e.g., behavioral, social–emotional, mental health), beyond that which is available in a traditional school setting.

A large percentage of students served in AE settings have diagnosed physical, cognitive, or emotional disabilities (i.e., 12–50% for alternative schools [Foley & Pang, 2006; Gorney &

Nicole Swoszowski, PhD, is an Associate Professor and Head of the Department of Special Education and Multiple Abilities at the University of Alabama. Dr. Swoszowski's research is focused on adapting positive and preventative academic and social interventions within multi-tiered systems of support for students with emotional and behavioral disorders and those with behavioral challenges.

Robin Parks Ennis, PhD, BCBA-D, is an Associate Professor in the Special Education Program at the University of Alabama at Birmingham. Her research and services focus on providing behavioral, social/emotional, and academic supports to students with and at risk for emotional and behavioral disorders,

Kristine Jolivette, PhD, is the Paul W. and Mary Harmon Bryant Endowed Professor at the University of Alabama. Her research focuses on school-age youth with and at risk for emotional and behavioral disorders, adaptations to tiered interventions, and approaches of multi-tiered systems of support for use within alternative, residential, and juvenile justice facilities, and facilitywide applications of trauma-informed frameworks.

Ysseldyke, 1993] and 50–80% for juvenile justice settings [Leone & Fink, 2017; Quinn, Rutherford, Leone, Osher, & Poirer, 2005; Sedlak & Bruce, 2010; Skowyra & Cocozza, 2007]). In addition to the marginalized and vulnerable dynamics of the student population in AE settings, this population often is transient and variable, posing additional challenges for providing appropriate and sustainable supports for students. Researchers have shown that students in AE settings often have poor school experiences given that their academic and social deficits are coupled with ineffective and inconsistent instructional practices (Van Acker, 2007). The need for more systematic and evidence-based practices for these challenging settings (Cook & Cook, 2013) is indisputable.

The use of PBIS has been recommended as a proactive and preventative approach to address the needs of all (Tier 1), some (Tier 2), or a few (Tier 3) students at the facilitywide level (Jolivette, 2016). It has been argued that alternative settingwide PBIS (most commonly referred to as facilitywide PBIS) has great promise for improving the behavior and academics (i.e., engagement) of students served through AE settings (Jolivette, 2016; Jolivette, Kimball, Boden, & Sprague, 2016; Jolivette, McDaniel, Sprague, Swain-Bradway, & Ennis, 2012; Simonsen, Jeffrey-Pearsall, Sugai, & McCurdy, 2011; Simonsen & Sugai, 2013). Often it is assumed that students in AE settings will require the most intensive and individualized supports available, which are commonly associated with Tier 3 supports; however, researchers have shown that this level of support is not necessary (Jolivette, 2016; Jolivette et al., 2012). Many students in AE settings will respond to the universal (Tier 1) supports in place because the environment more appropriately meets their needs across domains (Jolivette et al., 2012; Simonsen & Sugai, 2013), especially when PBIS is adapted to match student and/or facility characteristics (Jolivette, 2016; Jolivette, Kimball, et al., 2016; Leone & Weinberg, 2010).

IMPLEMENTING CICO IN AE SETTINGS

Students in need of more targeted supports within AE settings can benefit from a Tier 2 intervention such as CICO. CICO has been evaluated across numerous, largely therapeutic AE residential settings (Ennis et al., 2012; Melius, Swoszowski, & Siders, 2015; Swoszowski, Jolivette, & Fredrick, 2013; Swoszowski et al., 2012; Swoszowski, McDaniel, Jolivette, & Melius, 2013), with juvenile correctional facilities beginning to also use and adapt CICO (Jolivette, Sprague, & Doyle, 2018; Swoszowski, Patterson, & Crosby, 2011). To date, research regarding CICO in AE settings has included single-case research design experiments and has evaluated the impact of CICO on the problem behavior of students with multiple disabilities, including emotional behavioral disorder, developmental delay, autism spectrum disorder, other health impairments, learning disability, and mild intellectual disability. A majority of studies have included students in grades 1–3; however, students in grades 4–9 also have been represented in the literature.

The perspectives of stakeholders (teachers within AE settings) regarding the utility of implementation of CICO across AE settings has been evaluated (Swoszowski, Evanovich, Ennis, & Jolivette, 2017). These teachers reported (1) ease of implementation, (2) more student awareness of their own behavior, and (3) aid in collaboration as the benefits of implementing CICO in AE. These same teachers identified (1) triggers apart from the educational programming (e.g., conflict in the housing unit) and (2) lack of facilitywide consistency (e.g., across entities within the facility, such as education, therapeutic, and security) as challenges to implementing CICO in AE settings (Swoszowski et al., 2017). Such challenges are commonly seen as the contextual variables and flexible programming needs that are unique to CICO implementation in AE settings (Jolivette, 2016; Jolivette, Kimball, et al., 2016; Leone & Fink, 2017).

There are additional positive aspects of CICO for AE related to the benefits we have noted. First, CICO can be incorporated into existing frameworks of support (e.g., within behavior intervention plans; see the discussion of incorporating BIPs into CICO in the "Frequently Asked Questions" section at the end of the chapter). Second, CICO is resource efficient in terms of the number of students with and without disabilities who may be served at one time. Crone et al. (2010) suggest that, if needed, up to 30 students can be exposed to CICO at one time with support from a single CICO facilitator. In addition, CICO requires materials that are readily available and already in use in the AE setting (e.g., DPR cards; Swoszowski, 2014). Third, CICO can be put into place immediately. Immediate implementation could help mitigate the ongoing history of behavioral and school failure that these students have experienced prior to placement in the AE setting, as well as within the AE environment (Swoszowski, 2014; Swoszowski et al., 2017). Fourth, CICO requires minimal training for the CICO facilitator to implement with high fidelity (Swoszowski, 2014; Swoszowski et al., 2017).

When considering the utility of implementation of CICO in AE settings, the unique features and parameters of alternative schools and residential facilities must be weighed when identifying students appropriate for the targeted support available through the five-step CICO cycle. Each of these components are discussed in the following sections, along with detailed descriptions of possible modifications that facilities may need.

Screening

Some of the noted benefits of Tier 2 interventions, such as CICO, are the systematic identification of students who are not responsive to Tier 1 supports as well as the systematic collection of data across tiers to determine responsiveness in an objective manner (Sugai & Horner, 2002). Historically, ODRs have been used to identify students in need of CICO and to determine responsiveness to the intervention. Given that many schools record ODR data, ODRs are readily available and easy to use, and they can indicate student problem behaviors and patterns (i.e., where and at what time of day they occur or with certain groups of students; McIntosh, Reinke, et al., 2009; Sugai, Sprague, Horner, & Walker, 2000; Wright & Dusek, 1998). It is recommended, however, that ODRs be used alongside other assessment measures and after students have been identified for services or intervention, and not as a solitary means of assessment (McIntosh et al., 2010; McIntosh, Reinke, et al., 2009). This is especially true when identifying students for CICO in AE settings.

Traditionally, the benchmark used to identify students for a Tier 2 intervention within the PBIS framework is the accrual of 2–5 ODRs (Sugai & Horner, 2002; Sugai & Horner, 2009b). This benchmark, however, was derived from research with the general education student population. Student identification in AE settings has not been evaluated exclusively to determine if 2–5 ODRs are appropriate because the number of ODRs may be greater for this group.

Behavioral function also should be considered when determining which students need and are most likely to respond to CICO. It has been noted throughout the CICO literature that students demonstrating attention-maintained behavior are more responsive to CICO (Campbell & Anderson, 2008; Filter et al., 2007; March & Horner, 2002; McIntosh, Campbell, Carter,

& Dickey, 2009) than students with escape-maintained problem behavior (Ennis et al., 2012; Swoszowski et al., 2012; Swoszowski, McDaniel, et al., 2013). CICO can provide a protective, proactive approach, considering that attention is incorporated into the daily routine at both check-in and check-out; thus, the intervention can reduce the need for students to act out to gain attention. Completing an FBA contrasts with the resource-efficient design and approach of CICO. However, most students served in AE settings likely have an FBA on file from the school district in which they were previously enrolled, which is consistent with federal regulations regarding students who demonstrate behavior that impedes their learning or the learning of others. For students who do not have a current FBA on file, completing an informal, brief FBA, such as a functional assessment interview and archival record review, may be a helpful way to identify students with attention-maintained behavior for the CICO intervention (Campbell & Anderson, 2008; McIntosh, Campbell, Carter, & Dickey, 2009). Students demonstrating escape-maintained behavior should not necessarily be excluded from CICO; however, the intervention (specifically the reinforcement component) may need to be altered to more effectively meet the needs of students who generally demonstrate a function of behavior other than attention. Additionally, students who exhibit peer-attention-maintained problem behavior may benefit from peer-led CICO. Note that our brief FBA recommendation for these students at this stage is different from the one provided in Chapter 9 for students served in non-AE settings. The rationale for this change is that, once students have reached the level of needing the support of an AE setting, the selection and implementation of the intervention need to be more precise because multiple previous interventions have failed and the level or severity of the problem behavior exhibited by students in AE settings is too great.

Aside from ODRs, other methods used to identify students for CICO include teacher/administrator referral (Fairbanks et al., 2007; Hawken et al., 2007; Hawken & Horner, 2003; March & Horner, 2002; McIntosh, Campbell, Carter, & Dickey, 2009; Simonsen, Myers, & Briere, 2011) and a family request for intervention (March & Horner, 2002). Within AE settings, such as juvenile facilities, a wider array of data sources are required for a team to determine if a student would benefit from CICO. For example, incident infractions, logbook narratives, mental health/treatment notes, intake/ongoing behavioral assessments, and staff nominations are used in place of ODRs. Each individual facility team determines the threshold for entrance into Tier 2 interventions such as CICO. Many AE settings have regularly scheduled (i.e., weekly or biweekly) treatment team meetings to discuss the behavioral progress of each student served in the facility, which allows for consistent and systematic student assessment.

CICO Coordinators/Facilitators

To the greatest extent possible, we recommend that one CICO coordinator support all students for check-in and check-out as in traditional CICO. In alternative day-treatment schools, this arrangement likely is possible. In residential settings, including residential schools and juvenile detention environments (that have 24-hour per day/7-day per week programming), support by only one coordinator likely is not possible given the round-the-clock scheduling demands. Students receiving CICO supports may require CICO coordinator contact prior to and following the educational programming. Additionally, given the unique needs of students in AE settings, it may be necessary to increase the number of coordinators in each facility to adequately implement CICO and address the necessary adaptations for students in these settings. These potential adaptations are addressed in detail in the next part of the chapter.

The Process

Basic CICO involves a five-step process that includes (1) check-in, (2) teacher feedback, (3) checkout, (4) a home component, and (5) a return to school. Each of the steps for implementing CICO, with a specific focus on adaptations for AE settings, are discussed next. (See Table 13.1 for a list of possible adaptations for AE settings.)

Check-In

As in CICO within traditional school settings, the student checks in each morning with the CICO coordinator/facilitator during the first 10–15 minutes of the school day. During this interaction, several activities occur: (1) the student and coordinator/facilitator review the schoolwide behavioral expectations or other behaviors the student is expected to display in class on the DPR; (2) a behavioral goal (percentage of points) for the day is set based on the total points possible during the school day (e.g., 80% goal); and (3) the student and coordinator/facilitator discuss appropriate problem-solving strategies the student may use if presented with a difficult

TABLE 13.1. Possible Adaptations for CICO in AE Settings

Increased checks (check-up)	Increasing mentor contact through additional checks to allow more frequent contact, feedback, and possible reinforcement.
Individual goal setting	Adapt point sheet to address specific student concerns and/or goals, as opposed to facilitywide expectations.
Longer conversations	Increase length of conversation between student and CICO facilitator/mentor to allow for more brainstorming regarding responses to challenging situations within the facility.
More than one facilitator/mentor	Assign more than one facilitator/mentor to each student to provide CICO across the entire day, as opposed to in educational programming alone and/or to allow for CICO implementation across weekday and weekend shifts (for residential facilities).
Increased reinforcement	Provide additional opportunities to earn an agreed-upon reward (i.e., at check-up) to allow for more frequent reinforcement and to prevent students from delaying gratification from check-in to check-out.
Function-specific reinforcement	Adapt reinforcement to match function, specifically for students displaying escape-maintained or peer-attention-maintained behavior.

task or a challenging situation. Meeting at the beginning of the school day can serve as a positive setting event for a student by establishing a relationship with the CICO facilitator as well as by receiving feedback and encouragement for appropriate behaviors. In addition, during check-in students receive strategies to cope with potentially challenging situations that may occur throughout the school day.

Several adaptations for the check-in portion within an AE setting could be made. First, the initial point of contact with the CICO coordinator may occur at different times in AE settings than in traditional school settings. In AE settings, the student may need to meet with the coordinator when first arriving at school prior to any other activity (i.e., morning routine) to remediate any conflicts or address concerns that happened at home and to help in the transition from home to school. In a residential setting (i.e., therapeutic residential or juvenile justice) the initial point of contact with the CICO coordinator may occur in the housing unit before the student goes to classes or any other facility environment. Second, it is likely in AE settings that, because staff members work in shifts, the same facilitator may not be the one who checks in with the student every day. This is especially true in residential settings where supports are in place 24 hours a day/7 days a week, requiring that multiple facilitators for day, evening, and weekday/weekend shifts will need to be trained on the process. Third, the check-ins are likely to occur every day of the week for residential facilities and may not be limited just to school days; again, different facilitators may serve in this role.

Finally, it is likely that adjustments to check-in may be needed depending on whether a facility has made any adaptations to the DPR. Many AE settings do not use DPRs or have stopped using them owing to staff and student manipulation of the points awarded (e.g., students and staff members engage in power struggles over the points earned). In some cases, a staff member might threaten to remove or withhold points on a DPR, a practice that is inconsistent with the proactive and preventative approach of facilitywide PBIS. Another example of DPR manipulation includes the staff avoiding or negating the problem-solving language included in CICO. Furthermore, paper is considered contraband in many juvenile justice facilities and therefore prohibited. Fifth, if a DPR is used, the 80% goal may not be a realistic expectation for some students in AE settings; they may be performing significantly below the level needed to meet this goal, and setting too high an expectation may frustrate these students, resulting in increased problem behavior instead of improvement. For these students, it may be helpful to collect baseline data using the DPR and to initially set a more achievable yet lower goal (based on current student performance) as well as to use shaping principles for the student behavior to reach the 80% criterion over time (Lane, Capizzi, Fisher, & Ennis, 2012). The check-in process should be adjusted accordingly based on any adaptations a facility makes to the DPR itself.

Point Feedback

As in traditional school settings, the student in AE settings carries the DPR to each class where each teacher awards the student points and gives other oral or written feedback at the end of each class period/block for each expected behavior. This continuous feedback allows the student to view their behavioral progress toward the daily goal throughout the school day. For facilities that do not use a DPR, other means for reporting progress are necessary. Some more restrictive facilities embed feedback toward the goal verbally rather than numerically (i.e., assigning students points per behavior). This method avoids staff and student manipulation and power struggles over earned points, and allows the staff and students to focus on a more natural reinforcement of goal progress and on problem-solving conversations about self-regulation. When points are not being used as the metric in these settings, a clear communication plan between the CICO facilitator and behavior support teams is needed to ensure that progress monitoring is occurring. See Table 13.2 for a description of CICO without the use of a DPR.

Check-Up/Check-Out

During check-out in the basic CICO approach, if the student achieved the predetermined goal, the facilitator responds with praise, encouragement, and an agreed-upon reward (i.e., token or coupon) linked to schoolwide PBIS. This reward is critical for students who have significant behavioral challenges in AE settings, and who may not consistently receive explicit verbal reinforcement for appropriate school behavior. If the student did not reach the expected goal, the CICO coordinator and student brainstorm more appropriate ways to respond to difficult situations in the future. Daily problem-solving sessions with the CICO facilitator provide the student timely feedback on their behavior and a means for addressing it better the next day, without engaging in prolonged accounts of past failures. The most commonly used reinforcer associated with CICO for students who reach their daily goals is typically associated with the schoolwide reinforcement system in place. A secondary reinforcer, such as a token or coupon (e.g., Starbucks card, Cougar card, gotcha card), can be used for reinforcement in this phase, as can computer time, a homework pass, or any other acceptable, agreed-upon reward. In many CICO studies, the reinforcer is given daily during check-out if the student earns the designated number of daily points. In addition, and as previously discussed, for those students with attention-seeking behavior, inherent in the intervention is reinforcement through adult attention.

Students in AE settings who display more frequent, intense, and/or prolonged rates of problem behavior may be expected to require more extensive discussions about their behavior. The brief (1- to 3-minute) feedback sessions used in traditional settings may not allow enough time for the thorough discussion about the points earned or about the progress being made toward their goals. Lengthening the time that the student and facilitator meet for check-out may be a simple modification to address this need. Additionally, given the severity of the problem behavior and the unique needs of students in AE settings, including those with disabilities, students may have difficulty delaying gratification for reinforcement throughout an entire educational programming time period or during an entire day (e.g., if the housing unit is included in monitoring). Therefore, it may be necessary to increase the rates of reinforcement for students within AE settings. Each of these adaptations may necessitate using additional CICO coordinators/facilitators instead of one coordinator to support up to 30 students, as recommended in traditional school settings.

Check-In, Check-Up, Check-Out

One way to create more frequent opportunities for adult contact and reinforcement is by increasing the number of check-ins and check-outs daily. This modification is known as Check-In, Check-Up, Check-Out (CICUCO) and is based on the premise that more frequent contact with

TABLE 13.2. CICO and CICUCO Steps for Implementation

Steps	CICO	CICUCO	CICO/CICUCO without a point sheet
Check-in	Student receives the DPR and the point goal for the day. The discussion ends on a positive prompt, such as "I know you can earn your points today!"	Student receives the DPR and the point goal for the day. The discussion ends on a positive prompt, such as "I know you can earn your points today!"	Student and facilitator review facilitywide expectations and decide what expectation to focus on for the day. The discussion ends on a positive prompt, such as "I cannot wait to hear how you meet expectations today. I know you can do it!"
A.M. feedback	Student receives scores of 0, 1, and 2 after each period of the facility day.	Student receives scores of 0, 1, and 2 after each period of the facility day. Can adjust the frequency of feedback to provide for more feedback throughout facility day (i.e., every 30 minutes).	Student receives praise throughout the facility for meeting facilitywide expectations and engaging in problem-solving conversations for difficulties related to following facilitywide expectations.
Check-up	NA	Facilitator and student discuss point earnings. They have more explicit conversation regarding triggers and problem-solve ways to more appropriately respond to frustrating or difficult situations in the future. If 50% of the point goal is met, the agreed-upon reward is given. The discussion ends on a positive prompt, such as "You are really working hard today to earn your points and I know you can stay on track."	Facilitator and student discuss progress toward meeting facilitywide expectations. They discuss any triggers, as well as consequences earned, and problem-solve ways to address these triggers in the future.
P.M. feedback	NA	Student receives scores of 0, 1, and 2 after each period of the facility day. Can adjust the frequency of feedback to provide for more feedback throughout facility day (i.e., every 30 minutes).	Student receives praise for meeting expectations and engaging in problem-solving conversations for difficulties related to following expectations.

(continued)

TABLE 13.2. *(continued)*

Steps	CICO	CICUCO	CICO/CICUCO without a point sheet
Check-out	Facilitator and student discuss point earnings. If the point goal is met, the agreed-upon reward is given. The discussion ends on a positive note, such as "I am so proud of you for working so hard toward your goal today and I know you will meet your point goal tomorrow."	Facilitator and student discuss point earnings. They have more explicit conversation regarding triggers and problem-solve ways to more appropriately respond to frustrating or difficult situations in the future. If the point goal is met, the agreed-upon reward is given. The discussion ends on a positive note, such as "Tomorrow is going to be another great day for earning points!"	Facilitator and student discuss progress toward meeting the facilitywide expectation. They discuss any triggers, as well as consequences earned, and problem-solve ways to address these triggers in the future.
Home component	Parent/guardian views and signs the DPR, provides feedback on progress, and places the DPR in the folder/bag to be returned to the facility the following day. The discussion ends on a positive note, such as "I look forward to seeing how great you do tomorrow."	Parent/guardian signs views and signs the DPR, provides feedback on progress, and places the DPR in the folder/bag to be returned to the facility the following day. The discussion ends on a positive prompt, such as "I am excited to see you meet expectations and earn your point goal tomorrow."	Staff throughout the facility (i.e., education staff and unit staff) have routine conversations regarding the student's progress toward meeting expectations. The entire staff provide praise and encouragement to the student regarding meeting expectations and engaging in problem-solving conversations to resolve difficult situations.
Return to facility	Student returns the DPR to the facility, and the CICO cycle begins again.	Student returns the DPR to facility, and the CICO cycle begins again.	N/A

the CICO coordinator can result in more frequent opportunities to earn reinforcement. Check-out 1 (referred to as "check-up") could occur before lunch instead of at the end of the day, and check-out 2 (referred to as "check-out") could take place at the end of the day. During check-up, the CICO coordinator/facilitator and student could review the DPR and point goal to determine if 50% of the point goal has been met. For example, if the point goal for the day is 32/40 points, the student and facilitator would determine if 16/20 or more points were earned at the mid-day check. If this point goal were met, the student would receive an agreed-upon reward (e.g., an extra coupon) or a function-specific reinforcer (e.g., time with friends at lunch for students motivated by peer attention) at that time. During check-up, the CICO mentor/facilitator could remind the student of the point goal for the day, discuss any areas of difficulty experienced prior to the midday check, and review strategies to possibly address any future difficult situations. Before and after lunch, PE, and/or recess are recommended check-up times, because these transitions are typically less structured than classroom time and therefore, potentially more difficult for students with behavioral challenges in AE settings. (See Table 13.2 for a detailed comparison of implementation steps for CICO and the adapted CICUCO.)

Parent/Other Guardian Feedback

The home component of traditional CICO occurs when the student takes home the DPR to be reviewed and signed by a parent/guardian. This step provides an opportunity for the family member to view progress, areas of focus, and goal attainment. For the families of students served in AE settings, who often receive negative reports from school regarding their child's behavior, CICO provides a venue for positive school-to-home feedback. In a setting where a DPR is not used, communication/anecdotal verbal reporting between the educational and housing program staff will be necessary to address this component.

The parent/guardian feedback component of CICO is typically implemented with the lowest rates of fidelity in traditional school environments. Conducting CICO in residential facilities allows for this component to be implemented more consistently because the housing/unit staff can be trained to serve in the parent/guardian role and to complete the positive conversation with students about how they performed throughout the school day. Also, the student may have more difficulty in the unit (during unstructured times, for example) than during the more structured educational programming portions of the day. If this is the case, CICO can be altered to include unit behavior, and a staff member or members in the unit would need to be trained to provide the CICO feedback. Given this scenario, check-out would actually occur at the end of the day (just before bedtime), as opposed to at the end of educational programming; thus, the CICO facilitator (at least for the check-out portion of CICO) would need to be available in the housing unit at night. Many juvenile facilities implementing CICO use the morning and nightly unit routines as a means of collectively reviewing the facilitywide PBIS expectations to determine which specific expectations each youth should focus on for improvement and to celebrate the growing displays of these expectations by each youth. Although it may seem logical to "split" CICO into an educational-programming CICO separate from a housing-unit CICO, the evening may be a natural time for the identified youth who is more formally engaged in CICO to have their end-of-day check-out. Conducting CICO across the entire day (from morning-unit routine to nightly-unit routine) ensures communication, collaboration, and consistency across entities (i.e., in education, therapy, security, and housing units) and supports students by identifying and addressing setting events and/or triggers that may impede their progress with CICO during the school day (even though these triggers are outside the educational programming).

Return to School

Fifth, the DPR, once signed by a parent/guardian or the unit staff, is returned the next morning to the CICO mentor/facilitator during morning check-in. The five-step CICO cycle then begins again the next day. Students continue to participate in CICO until they have demonstrated and maintained daily behavioral improvement at a level determined to indicate success by the facility staff.

MONITORING PROGRESS

Progress monitoring involves assessing the effectiveness of CICO or adapted CICO over time. DPRs, when used, can indicate the effectiveness of the intervention, as can ODR data. Regardless of how effectiveness is measured, it is important to have a plan for systematically (e.g., every 2 weeks) looking at the data and determining how each student is responding. It is recommended that behavior support teams in AE settings meet every 2 weeks, at a minimum. Given that the population in these facilities is transient, it may be necessary to meet more frequently. Most facilities have case and/or file review meetings or treatment team meetings scheduled weekly or biweekly, and these meetings are excellent opportunities to review CICO data and to make decisions regarding student response to the CICO intervention. Students receiving CICO with morning and afternoon checks should be exposed to an additional check/additional mentor contact (CICUCO) before a team decides that the student is unresponsive to CICO and requires more individualized (Tier 3) supports. Additional adaptations (those noted previously) also may be helpful to consider to increase student response to CICO. (See Table 13.1 for a description of possible adaptations to aid in making progress monitoring decisions.)

Fidelity

Fidelity of implementation is critical in assessing the accurate implementation of the intervention and the basis for the behavior team's decision making. Comprehensive fidelity analysis is essential when working with students in AE settings because their success requires that interventions, including consistent CICO procedures and reinforcement to minimize the continuation of school failure, are implemented with fidelity. For CICO in AE settings, the analysis would include all five steps and the type of feedback provided during check-in and check-out as well as throughout the educational programming. The basic CICO fidelity of implementation checklist included in Chapter 7 could be adapted to include the midday check-in that is often required for students in AE settings to be successful.

CONCLUSION

In conclusion, CICO is a resource-efficient approach that is effective for addressing the behavioral and academic needs of students in traditional and AE settings. Adaptations to the traditional approach may be necessary for successful implementation in AE settings; however, these adaptations remain resource efficient and allow for implementation at Tier 2 to address the unique needs of our most vulnerable and marginalized students. Furthermore, CICO allows for collaboration and consistent practices throughout entities within these facilities, such as educational, therapeutic, security, and housing units. We conclude the chapter with a case example to further illustrate the concepts we've discussed and provide answers to frequently asked questions regarding CICO implementation in AE settings.

CASE EXAMPLE

Cody is a 16-year-old youth who resides in a secure juvenile justice facility. He has lived in this facility for 5 months and will continue to live there for the next 9 months. His facility has been implementing facilitywide PBIS the past 2 years using the SMART behavioral expectations of Strive for success, Make good choices, Act respectful, Remain safe, Take responsibility. In the past few weeks, the facility staff have noticed that Cody's behavior has progressively worsened from periodic displays of class A behaviors (e.g., nuisance contraband, horseplay, and disrespect) to serious rule violations of class B behaviors (e.g., threats, continued refusal to obey, youth-on-youth physical altercation, and unauthorized presence). In reviewing Cody's behavioral incident data for the past month, his serious rule violations included: (1) three youth-on-youth physical altercations on Saturday afternoons during recreation or prior to visitation; (2) 14 continued refusals to obey during transitions between activities, especially when moving between units; (3) 11 threats to peers, often in combination with transitions between units, and two unauthorized visits to a unit. Also, all but two of these incidents occurred between noon on Friday through dinner on Sunday. The education staff have not observed any serious behavior incidents with Cody during school hours, but they have heard other youth talking about Cody's behavior and about how he is trying to position himself as a leader in the facility, given that he will be there for a long period of time. In looking at these data and in talking with other members of the staff who work with Cody, it was hypothesized that he was using his inappropriate behavior to gain the attention of his peers. The staff decided that Cody may benefit from an adapted version of CICUCO as a Tier 2 support to address some of these behaviors.

The facility staff need to make several adaptations of the original school-based intervention for it to accommodate the facility's policies, staff schedules, and routines. In terms of policies, youth are not permitted to carry paper on their person, nor to have paper in the units, and a daily point card is not used as part of the behavior management system and facilitywide PBIS. Therefore, the facility staff will not be able to use a DPR, either as part of their progress monitoring of the effectiveness of CICUCO or as part of the visual feedback between the facility staff and Cody during the check-ins and check-outs. In terms of facility staff schedules and the time period (i.e., Friday noon to Sunday evening) during which Cody displayed these negative behaviors, several observations emerged: (1) shifts rotate during this time, so there is no consistency with which the facility staff are available for check-ins and check-outs; (2) depending on the events calendar, several different volunteers would be present during activities or in the units; (3) Cody's unit has had staffing issues, resulting in one fewer staff member than specified and a modification of scheduled activities; and (4) because of other issues in the facility on the weekend, the shift-change debriefings have often taken longer than expected, resulting in fewer flexible minutes to do check-ins and check-outs. Owing to these problems, the facility staff did review the facilitywide data to check whether other youth were experiencing behavioral changes like Cody, but none were found. In addition, the facility staff realized that none of the staff who works the Friday through Sunday shifts have been trained on CICO like their counterparts on the education staff. The facility routines and procedures related to staff members' access to units presented an additional complication. Facility staff are only given keys and access to units in the facility where they have assigned shifts. For example, staff members who work on the Bravo Unit do not have access to the Alpha Unit, and vice versa. These routines create uncertainty about which CICO facilitator may be available and about when and where CICO feedback sessions could occur. After thinking through these concerns, the facility staff came up with the following check-in/check-out intervention for Cody.

First, four facilitators were identified. These facilitators were staff persons who (1) had histories of working in Cody's unit on Friday, Saturday, and/or Sunday and doing so consistently (i.e., rarely missed a shift, came to work on time, stayed for their entire shift); (2) had overlapped in shifts with one another; (3) had expressed a desire to be a facilitator and agreed to come in early to their Friday shifts to be trained by facility education staff on the procedural aspects of CICO; (4) had demonstrated competency on the in-place Tier 1 motivational-interviewing and verbal-judo interventions, which called for both verbal communication skills and addressing problems in difficult situations; and (4) had consistently, accurately, and in a timely fashion completed their shift paperwork even when disruptions occurred. The four facilitators were trained to mastery on the CICO procedures and observed each other during the first several check-ins.

Second, the four facilitators brainstormed possible progress monitoring methods that could be used consistently across shifts that did not involve a DPR. They decided to utilize the logbook, in which each staff member is required to write their observations about the activities and behaviors in the unit. All the students are familiar with the logbook because staff members note observations in the book in their presence throughout their shifts. Instead of tabulating a point card for Cody, the facilitators affixed daily scripts inside the front cover of the logbook to use with him during the check-ins and check-outs; they also added notes about their conversations with Cody during the these times. At the end of the notes, the facilitator indicated whether Cody participated in the CICO conversation and in problem-solving dialogue. These notes were written after the conversation, and Cody was not made aware that such notes were being taken.

Third, the facilitators decided on time point ranges when check-ins and check-outs would occur each day, noting that the times must be flexible given scheduling changes due to facility issues (e.g., youth behavior) as well as Cody's own behaviors. For example, based on Cody's data, the following "cycle" was agreed upon: (1) the first check-in would take place during lunch on Fridays since that time was typically when negative behavioral incidents occurred and all the facilitators had keys to the cafeteria based on their shift schedule; (2) subsequent check-ins would occur at natural breaks in activities instead of at preset time points; (3) check-ins would occur in the area Cody was supposed to be in instead of in different areas because of staff ratio issues and would occur without drawing much attention, so as not to stigmatize the youth; (4) depending on Cody's behavior, the facilitators defined the circumstances under which a check-up may be needed to help him self-regulate and modify his behavior in between check-in times, and what the facilitator should say to Cody (e.g., use the facilitywide PBIS SMART reset phrase, review which SMART expectations need to be of immediate refocus, provide encouragement, remind him that he can use SMART to change the path of his behavior); and (5) the culminating check-out prior to lights-out would occur each Friday, Saturday, and Sunday night. These time-point ranges only encompassed the days in which Cody was experiencing difficulties.

Fourth, the facilitator who also worked on Mondays was selected to be the person who would meet with Cody's juvenile detention counselor each Monday to debrief him on Cody's progress and data based on his review of the unit logs. If any changes in the intervention were needed, that facilitator would include the edited script with the changes highlighted in the unit logbook.

A fifth adaptation was the decision to not provide Cody with any additional reinforcement for his participation in the CICO intervention even though as part of their facilitywide PBIS Tier 1 plan, the facility staff used SMART bucks, which were written for students whenever they displayed SMART behaviors. When students merit SMART bucks, they are told why they are receiving one, and the facility staff then directly put a SMART buck into the SMART bin for a raffle. However, the facilitators worried that students would begin to display inappropriate behaviors as a means of accessing the Tier 2 CICO intervention for additional SMART bucks. Instead, they relied on scheduling more behavior-specific praise during the facilitated check-in conversations.

To ensure that the facilitators were delivering the check-in/check-out intervention as written, Cody's juvenile detention counselor would review the unit videos at the Saturday and Sunday time points each week.

FREQUENTLY ASKED QUESTIONS

What if a student does not have a good relationship with their teacher and/or staff—won't this impact feedback and response to the intervention?

A poor relationship certainly could influence the student's desire to check in and check out daily. An adult with a positive or neutral history should be identified.

What if our facility does not have a three-tiered model in place?

CICO may not be as effective without Tier 1 in place, but CICO can still be used by basing it on classwide expectations or on specific behavioral goals for the student.

Should the behaviors tracked be unique to the student?

As a Tier 2 intervention, CICO should be tied to class- and schoolwide expectations, as it can help with the transition to less-restrictive settings (when students are transitioning back to a home school with schoolwide expectations in place; Jolivette, Swoszowski, McDaniel, & Duchaine, 2016). However, if students have unique behavioral challenges, appropriate replacement behaviors can be tracked in lieu of, or in addition to, the class- and schoolwide expectations.

How can CICO be incorporated into an existing Behavior Intervention Plan?

The reauthorization of the Individuals with Disabilities Education Act (IDEA, 1997, 2004) requires behavior intervention plans (BIPs) for all students who demonstrate behavior that interferes with their learning and the learning of others. This means that students with behavioral issues in AE settings should have BIPs already in place; BIPS are designed to address both inappropriate student behavior as well as the role of the educator in remediating the inappropriate behavior (Killu, 2008) through teaching, modeling, and reinforcing more appropriate replacement behaviors. BIPs and CICO are not mutually exclusive approaches toward addressing problem behaviors, so a natural approach would be to include CICO as a component of a

BIP. Furthermore, IDEA (2004) requires the use of an FBA for selecting interventions for a BIP to ensure that the plan is truly individualized and function based. As stated in Chapter 9, replacement behaviors included in the BIP that are taught by educators can be included under the facilitywide PBIS expectations to provide the individualized support required under IDEA. In addition, the reinforcement students earn for meeting goals can be modified to support different functions beyond obtaining adult attention, including escape, tangible rewards, and peer attention.

Can CICO only be used at Tier 2 in AE settings, or can it be used at Tier 1 as well?

Intake data may indicate the need for Tier 2 intervention; however, in juvenile detention facilities, a less-formal, less-resource-intensive version of CICO as well as in an adapted form at Tier 1 has been implemented with success, so that all students in a facility receive CICO support. In this case, CICO is implemented with all students in a facility from intake through release from the facility.

CHAPTER 14

Training Schools on CICO Implementation

A Guide for Coaches/Trainers

The effectiveness of any intervention depends on the quality of the training and coaching that teams receive on how to implement the intervention (Fixsen, Blase, Metz, & Van Dyke, 2013). CICO is the most widely implemented Tier 2 intervention (Bruhn et al., 2014; Mitchell et al., 2011), and with the widespread adoption of CICO, there is a greater need for more school staff and personnel to be able to implement the intervention with fidelity (Mitchell et al., 2011). Although CICO is a relatively simple intervention to put into practice, there are many ways in which schools may struggle with implementation. We have had experiences with many school personnel who have said, "We tried CICO, and it wasn't effective." These instances of ineffectiveness in large part may be due to a failure in implementing the intervention as designed. Over the past 20 years, research has shown that CICO, when implemented with fidelity, can be effective with approximately 70% of the student population (Hawken et al., 2014). We do not expect CICO to work for all students, because the intervention may not be appropriate for everyone, and additional supports, including mental health interventions, are needed for students engaging in more severe problem behaviors. We recommend that if CICO is not effective for least 70% of the students who receive the intervention in your school, it is likely not due to the students or to the intervention itself, but rather due to the way in which the system is implemented.

The purpose of this chapter is to provide best practice guidelines for training new schools in how to implement CICO. Our intended audience includes people who coach schools in implementing PBIS and/or train schools in implementing interventions, whether they work in individual schools, at the district level, or as outside consultants and/or providers. In framing this chapter, it is helpful to consider and refer to a tool developed to evaluate the extent to which professional development is evidence based and implemented at a high-quality level. The Observation Checklist for High-Quality Professional Development (HQPD; Figure 14.1) pro-

The *Observation Checklist for High-Quality Professional Development* was designed to be completed by an observer to determine the level of quality of professional development training. It can also be used to provide ongoing feedback and coaching to individuals who provide professional development training. Furthermore, it can be used as a guidance document when designing or revising professional development. The tool represents a compilation of research-identified indicators that should be present in professional development. Professional development training with a maximum of one item missed per domain on the checklist can be considered high quality.

Context Information

Date:

Location:

Topic:

Presenter(s):

Observer:

Role:

The professional development provider:	
Preparation	**Observed? (Check if Yes)**

1. Provides a description of the training with learning objectives prior to training
  • *EXAMPLE 1: Training description and objectives emailed to participants in advance*
  • *EXAMPLE 2: Training description and goals provided on registration website*
  • *EXAMPLE 3: Agenda including learning targets provided with materials via online file sharing before training*	

Evidence or example:	

2. Provides readings, activities, and/or questions in accessible formats to think about prior to the training
  • *EXAMPLE 1: Articles for pre-reading emailed to participants in advance*
  • *EXAMPLE 2: Book for pre-reading distributed to schools before training*
  • *EXAMPLE 3: Materials made available via online file sharing*	

Evidence or example:	

3. Provides an agenda (i.e., schedule of topics to be presented and times) before or at the beginning of the training
  • *EXAMPLE 1: Paper copy of agenda included in training packet for participants*
  • *EXAMPLE 2: Agenda included in pre-training email*	

Evidence or example:	

4. Quickly establishes or builds on previously established rapport with participants
  • *EXAMPLE 1: Trainer gives own background, using humor to create warm atmosphere*
  • *EXAMPLE 2: Trainer praises group's existing skills and expertise to create trust*
  • *EXAMPLE 3: Trainer uses topical videos to break the ice with the audience*	

Evidence or example:	

(continued)

FIGURE 14.1. Observation Checklist for High-Quality Professional Development (HQPD). From Noonan, Gaumer Erickson, Brussow, and Langham (2015). Reprinted by permission. (See original source for additional notes and references.)

Introduction	Observed (Check if Yes)
5. Connects the topic to participants' context • *EXAMPLE 1: The state leader introducing the presenter explains that the topic is related to the initiative being implemented across the state* • *EXAMPLE 2: Trainer shows examples from classrooms, then asks participants to compare the examples to what happens in their school* • *EXAMPLE 3: Trainer shares participating district data profiles and asks participants to consider how the intervention might affect students*	
Evidence or example:	
6. Includes the empirical research foundation of the content • *EXAMPLE 1: Trainer provides a list of references supporting evidence-based practices* • *EXAMPLE 2: Citations to research are given during PowerPoint presentation* • *EXAMPLE 3: Trainer references key researchers and details their contributions to the training content during presentation*	
Evidence or example:	
7. Content builds on or relates to participants' previous professional development • *EXAMPLE 1: Trainer explains how intervention relates to other existing interventions within the state* • *EXAMPLE 2: Trainer refers to content provided in previous trainings within the sequence* • *EXAMPLE 3: Trainer uses participants' knowledge of other interventions to inform training*	
Evidence or example:	
8. Aligns with organizational standards or goals • *EXAMPLE 1: Trainer shows how the intervention fits in with the Elementary and Secondary Education Act and Individuals with Disabilities Education Act* • *EXAMPLE 2: Trainer discusses how the district selected this intervention for implementation as part of an improvement plan* • *EXAMPLE 3: Trainer refers to the program as part of a federally funded State Personnel Development Grant*	
Evidence or example:	
9. Emphasizes impact of content (e.g., student achievement, family engagement, client outcomes) • *EXAMPLE 1: Participants brainstorm the ways the intervention will impact students, especially students with disabilities* • *EXAMPLE 2: Trainer uses data to show that the intervention is shown to positively impact post-school outcomes and inclusion in the general education classroom for students with disabilities* • *EXAMPLE 3: Trainer shares research that shows that the use of the instructional strategies improved academic achievement for students*	
Evidence or example:	

Demonstration	Observed (Check if Yes)
10. Builds shared vocabulary required to implement and sustain the practice • *EXAMPLE 1: Trainer has participants work together to formulate definitions of the intervention components and then goes overs the definitions as a group* • *EXAMPLE 2: Trainer defines instructional practices according to established literature* • *EXAMPLE 3: Trainer introduces acronyms and mnemonics to help participants remember training content*	
Evidence or example:	

(continued)

FIGURE 14.1. *(continued)*

11. Provides examples of the content/practice in use (e.g., case study, vignette) • *EXAMPLE 1: Trainer provides video examples of the intervention in place within classrooms at different grade levels* • *EXAMPLE 2: Trainer provides hands-on demonstrations of how to use new technology tools* • *EXAMPLE 3: Trainer uses a case study to demonstrate how to implement the intervention*	
Evidence or example:	

12. Illustrates the applicability of the material, knowledge, or practice to the participants' context • *EXAMPLE 1: Trainer describes how the intervention will benefit schools/classrooms* • *EXAMPLE 2: Trainer shows trend data before and after the practice was implemented in a school* • *EXAMPLE 3: Trainer presents a case study of a teacher who has successfully implemented the intervention*	
Evidence or example:	

Engagement	**Observed?** **(Check if Yes)**
13. Includes opportunities for participants to apply content and/or practice skills during training • *EXAMPLE 1: Trainer has participants perform a mock lesson using the new instructional strategy* • *EXAMPLE 2: After receiving training on how to complete a form, participants practice completing the form with a sample case* • *EXAMPLE 3: Participants practice identifying various instructional strategies from sample videos*	
Evidence or example:	
14. Includes opportunities for participants to express personal perspectives (e.g., experiences, thoughts on concept) • *EXAMPLE 1: Participants use their experiences and prior knowledge to fill in a worksheet on the advantages and disadvantages of various instructional approaches* • *EXAMPLE 2: Participants work together to strategize ways to overcome barriers to implementation in their school* • *EXAMPLE 3: In groups, participants share personal and professional experiences related to the topic.*	
Evidence or example:	
15. Facilitates opportunities for participants to interact with each other related to training content • *EXAMPLE 1: Participants independently answer questions, then discuss those answers as a large group* • *EXAMPLE 2: Participants work in groups to assess implementation progress in their building* • *EXAMPLE 3: Participants think/pair/share about questions within the training*	
Evidence or example:	
16. Adheres to agenda and time constraints • *EXAMPLE 1: Breaks, lunch, and dismissal occur on schedule according to written or verbal agenda* • *EXAMPLE 2: Trainer adjusts training content to accommodate adjustments to agenda (e.g., participants arriving late due to inclement weather)*	
Evidence or example:	

(continued)

FIGURE 14.1. *(continued)*

Evaluation/Reflection	Observed? (Check if Yes)
17. Includes opportunities for participants to reflect on learning • *EXAMPLE 1: Participants strategize how to apply the knowledge from the training in their own schools* • *EXAMPLE 2: Participants record three main points, two lingering questions, and one action they will take* • *EXAMPLE 3: Green, yellow, and red solo cups at tables used to visually check for understanding at key points throughout training*	
Evidence or example:	
18. Includes specific indicators—related to the knowledge, material, or skills provided by the training—that would indicate a successful transfer to practice • *EXAMPLE 1: Participants work in district-level teams to use a graphic organizer to create an action plan* • *EXAMPLE 2: Expectations for completing classroom observations outlined for coaches* • *EXAMPLE 3: Materials provided for educators to do mid-semester self-assessment to see if intervention is being implemented*	
Evidence or example:	
19. Engages participants in assessment of their acquisition of knowledge and skills • *EXAMPLE 1: Post-test to assess trainees' grasp of learning objectives* • *EXAMPLE 2: After guided practice on how to complete an observation form, participants use the form to individually rate a video example and compare their responses to the trainer* • *EXAMPLE 3: Participants complete performance-based assessment, illustrating that they have mastered the learning targets.*	
Evidence or example:	

Mastery	Observed? (Check if Yes)
20. Details follow-up activities that require participants to apply their learning • *EXAMPLE 1: Participants complete an action plan with clear activities, a timeline, and individuals responsible* • *EXAMPLE 2: Due dates for steps of student behavioral assessment process reviewed at end of training* • *EXAMPLE 3: Implementation timeline with due dates provided and discussed*	
Evidence or example:	
21. Offers opportunities for continued learning through technical assistance and/or resources • *EXAMPLE 1: Trainer describes future trainings and explains how training fits into the series* • *EXAMPLE 2: Trainer provides contact information for technical assistance including email address and phone number* • *EXAMPLE 3: Trainer shows participants where to find additional materials and readings on the project website*	
Evidence or example:	
22. Describes opportunities for coaching to improve fidelity of implementation • *EXAMPLE 1: Trainer describes follow-up in-building support to be provided by state-level coaches* • *EXAMPLE 2: Trainer provides monthly two-hour phone calls to discuss barriers and strategize solutions* • *EXAMPLE 3: Series of coaching webinars scheduled to provide follow-up support and additional information on how to implement the intervention*	
Evidence or example:	

FIGURE 14.1. *(continued)*

vides trainers with guidelines for planning and delivering evidence-based professional development (Noonan, Gaumer Erickson, Brussow, & Langham, 2015).

GET READY: ASSESS WHETHER THE SCHOOL IS PREPARED TO IMPLEMENT CICO

Before beginning to implement CICO, a school's readiness for implementation should be examined using the readiness checklist found in Chapter 4. One of the readiness criteria is that schools have Tier 1 PBIS in place. In preparing for CICO training, a coach or trainer should evaluate the extent to which the school has established Tier 1 PBIS using either the School-Wide Evaluation Tool (SET; Sugai, Lewis-Palmer, Todd, & Horner, 2005) or the Tiered Fidelity Inventory (TFI; Algozzine et al., 2014). A score of 80% or greater on teaching expectations and 80% or greater overall on the SET indicate that a school has an established schoolwide Tier 1 system in place with fidelity (Todd et al., 2012). A score of 70% or greater on the Tier 1 portion of the TFI indicates that a school is implementing Tier 1 PBIS with fidelity (Algozzine et al., 2014).

In addition to evaluating the degree to which a school is implementing Tier 1 PBIS before implementing CICO, schools should also examine the extent to which they have Tier 1 classroom PBIS practices in place. This primarily includes the extent to which expectations and routines have been translated from the schoolwide level to classroom settings. We recommend that teachers adopt the schoolwide expectations in their classroom behavior management systems and provide explicit instruction on what these expectations look and sound like in classroom settings. Also, effective instructional principles should be instituted to support appropriate behavior and prevent disruption in the classroom. Several tools that evaluate the extent to which Tier 1 classroom supports are being used are available. Figure 14.2 includes a list of components of a successful classroom (Hawken, 2008). Another tool available to evaluate classroom practices includes an assessment of a classroom system, management decisions based on data, implementation of effective instructional strategies, and appropriate curriculum (Simonsen et al., 2015). We recommend that schools evaluate the extent to which Tier 1 classroom PBIS is being used before or in conjunction with the development of a CICO intervention.

A coach or trainer who is conducting the implementation of CICO should next meet with the principal and outline the readiness requirements for effective CICO implementation. Ideally, during this meeting, the coach or trainer should share the overview for administrators document with the principal, so that they know what role they have in implementing and supporting CICO (see Figure 5.5). Far too often the school staff are excited about implementing CICO and the principal has agreed to support the intervention, but all the details required to get it up and running have not been agreed upon. In these cases, schools may unintentionally fail to allocate the time and resources needed to establish and implement CICO successfully. As mentioned in Chapter 5, it is critical for the principal in particular to be on board and be supportive of CICO because of the principal's key role in determining how resources and time are allocated, and can either help or hinder the extent to which other school personnel invest in the intervention.

Depending on the level of initial interest a school has in implementing CICO, typically the next step is to meet with the schoolwide behavior support team, leadership team, or other

In place	Somewhat in place	Not in place	Components
			Tier 1 Classroom Support
			Are the classroom rules/expectations posted (three to five rules, positively stated)?
			Have the rules/expectations been systematically taught and reviewed?
			Are positive consequences/rewards (more than verbal praise) that acknowledge meeting classroom expectations posted and consistently implemented?
			Are negative consequences/punishments that address students who are not following classroom expectations posted and consistently implemented?
			Is a daily class schedule posted large enough for all students to see? Does the teacher refer to/explain the daily schedule and any schedule changes?
			Is *at least* a 5:1 ratio of positive to negative consequences for academic and behavioral responses implemented? Positive examples: verbal praise (e.g., "Good job finishing your work"; "Thumbs-up"; points on point chart; classroom bucks). Negative examples: redirection, error correction (i.e., "Stop it"; "Don't do that"; "Get in your seat").
			Have classroom routines been established and systematically taught (e.g., entering the classroom, bathroom procedures, getting help from the teacher, sharpening pencils)?
			Are transitions between activities structured (moving from one activity to the next)?
			Is unstructured time kept to a minimum?
			Is the academic material presented at the students' instructional level? How do you know?
			Is students' academic and behavioral performance monitored by circulating among students (e.g., walking around the room while students are working in groups or independently vs. standing/sitting at the front of the room)?
			Is there an attention signal to get students on task in less than 5 seconds (e.g., "May I have your attention please?"; "One, two, three—eyes on me")?
			Is the classroom environment arranged to effectively support students (i.e., students can transition easily from area to area; items posted on walls are not overly distracting; materials, chairs, and tables are organized)?
			Are there mechanisms established for frequent parent communication particularly for *positive* events that occur (i.e., good note home; "Caught you being good" phone calls)?

After completing the self-assessment, please create three professional goals to improve your Tier 1 classroom behavior support.

Professional Goals

1.

2.

3.

FIGURE 14.2. Components of a successful classroom self-assessment. From Hawken (2008). Reprinted by permission.

comparable team involved in developing and evaluating the behavior support systems in the school. At this meeting, the coach or trainer provides an overview of CICO, detailing its key features. Together, the team and coach/trainer make a plan to obtain full staff buy-in for the intervention. In some schools, a significant number of teachers may have heard of CICO and be eager to implement it. In other schools, the staff may be new to designing Tier 2 support in general and have no experience in implementing a system of support like CICO. Other schools may have tried similar interventions in the past, such as daily behavior report cards or behavior contracts, and have found them to be ineffective. For these schools, it will be critical to emphasize the importance of appreciating CICO as a systemic intervention and how it differs from other behaviorial interventions commonly implemented in schools. Based on these factors, the team should determine when and how to present information on CICO to the broader school audience.

After the schoolwide behavior support team meeting has taken place, it is time to meet with the entire school staff. An overview of the key features of CICO can be covered in 15–20 minutes in a staff meeting. A sample presentation that can be used to briefly explain CICO is provided with the supplementary materials on The Guilford Press website (see the box at the end of the table of contents). If more time is allocated (e.g., 25–30 minutes) for securing staff buy-in, we recommend showing the whole staff the CICO DVD (Hawken & Breen, 2017), which comprehensively outlines the intervention. The first 22 minutes of the video can be shown to the staff (the video should be paused before discussing the section on how to use data in decision making), followed by a short period in which any questions or concerns that school personnel have can be addressed. After all questions and concerns have been addressed, a vote can be taken to determine if the staff are willing to implement the intervention. If 80% or more of the school staff agree to implement the intervention, a time can be scheduled to meet with the schoolwide leadership team to develop CICO in a way that fits the school's culture. If less than 80% of the staff are convinced, more time should be spent on consensus building and gathering data to demonstrate a need for the intervention in the school.

GET SET: PREPARE FOR TRAINING DAYS

Once buy-in and consensus have been reached, the trainer should prepare for the CICO training by examining the HQPD checklist to determine what features need to be established to provide evidence-based professional development. To begin with, a minimum of 3 hours should be set aside to meet with the schoolwide leadership team to develop the intervention. The principal *must* be included in the training, and we recommend that the training occur offsite or during nonschool days (e.g., during inservice training or professional development time), so that members of the team are not distracted by daily teaching and administrative responsibilities. The trainer will use the CICO Development and Implementation Guide that was presented in Chapter 4 (and is also found in Appendix C.3) as a curriculum to follow during the training day. All eight questions on the CICO Development and Implementation Guide should be answered before the team pilots the intervention with students in the school.

Seasoned trainers can move through this guide in approximately 3 hours with the schoolwide leadership team. This estimate includes embedded team time throughout the training day for the team to answer the questions in the guide. For new trainers, we recommend scheduling at least 4 hours to cover all the material and include enough time for team breakouts. The CICO Development and Implementation Guide details how to design basic CICO. If a leadership team is interested in learning more about advanced applications of CICO and/or advanced problem solving when CICO is not working with individual students, a full day of training is recommended. In our experience, providing an initial training on basic CICO allows leadership teams to pilot the intervention in their school. Once schools have had some time to implement the basic intervention, a more advanced training can be offered for troubleshooting and addressing frequently asked questions.

A training session on CICO can include leadership teams from one or more schools. Regardless of the number of school teams involved, we recommend that each leadership team designate a facilitator to lead discussions during team time. We recommend that the facilitator be someone other than the administrator to help establish parity among team members. To provide for maximum collaboration, we recommend that teams sit at large tables with movable chairs or in some other arrangement that allows team members to communicate and work together, rather than in an auditorium or theater-style setting. More training logistics are included in Figure 14.3.

Before the training starts, the trainers should send participants (1) the training agenda, (2) the objectives to be covered in the session, and (3) prereading materials to be completed before the training day. The objectives for the basic CICO training are included in Figure 14.4. There are a couple of different prereading options that can be considered. Some schools choose to purchase this book for all team members and request they read certain pages or chapters prior to the training. Other schools include a copy of a CICO overview article, such as the one by Hawken (2006).

- Schedule one-half to full day (i.e., 3½–6 hours) with the schoolwide PBIS team (*must* include principal).
  - Participants must come in teams (can train multiple teams).
  - Each team should have a facilitator/leader (*not* the principal).
  - Each team should have a note taker.
- Secure training location that will allow for collaborative work.
  - An ideal workspace has large tables with movable chairs.
  - Theater-style training venues do not allow for collaborative work.
- Determine if you are working primarily with elementary schools, secondary schools, or combination of both.
  - Slides can be tailored to add additional secondary and/or elementary examples, depending on your audience.
- Prepare slides (see sample on The Guilford Press website; see the box at the end of the table of contents).
- Prepare handouts (see sample on The Guilford Press website; see the box at the end of the table of contents).
  - Teams need electronic copies to work from (provided typically on a flash or shared drive).
- Send teams the agenda, objectives, materials to bring (see below), and prereading for teams to prepare for training.
- Teams bring:
  - One or more laptops.
  - ODR data.
  - Current versions of DPRs (if any) or other types of behavioral trackers currently used.

FIGURE 14.3. Training logistics.

By the end of this training, participants will be able to . . .

1. Describe how CICO fits into the context of schoolwide PBIS.
2. List and describe the critical features of CICO.
3. Identify for which students CICO is appropriate.
4. Create a DPR to support your schoolwide PBIS Tier 1 system.
5. Design a reinforcement system for students receiving CICO.
6. Develop a referral system and identify a data system for monitoring the progress of students who receive CICO.
7. Determine the criteria for fading the intervention.
8. Determine who will train the students, faculty, and parents on CICO.

FIGURE 14.4. CICO workshop objectives.

GO: TRAINING DAY

On the day of training, it is important to review the objectives for the day. As specified in the sample agenda (see Figure 14.5), the first 10 minutes of training should consist of a welcome and introduction. It is helpful to determine what groups are represented in the workshop to get a sense of participants' backgrounds and experiences that might be relevant to designing and implementing CICO. If the training includes one leadership team, each member can individually say what they do in the school building or district. If multiple leadership teams are involved, it is easier to have people raise their hands to identify themselves in different school roles, such as general education teacher, special education teacher, counselor/school psychologist, and administrator. Ideally, each leadership team attending the training should consist of a representative group from each school along with the administrator. The inclusion of school personnel in different roles helps to ensure that CICO is designed in a way that maximizes contextual fit, which can also boost the buy-in of all school personnel. When participants introduce themselves, it is also helpful to gather information about whether they have past experience in implementing CICO. If this is the case, they may have materials (e.g., sample DPRs) to work with and use during this training. During the introduction, also confirm that participants have copies of and electronic access to the PowerPoint presentations and handouts (both of which are included in the supplementary materials on The Guilford Press website; see the box at the end of the table of contents). Hard copies of these materials can be printed, but are preferably provided in an electronic format (e.g., a shared drive before the training), so that teams can manipulate the electronic files and leave the training with materials that will help in implementing the intervention.

One of the key points to emphasize at the beginning of the training is that CICO is a Tier 2 intervention and that basic CICO should be implemented similarly with all students. Participants need to have a clear understanding up-front that individualizing CICO should not occur at the basic level. If leadership teams have not viewed the CICO DVD, we recommend that the first 22 minutes of the video be shown at the beginning of the training. In addition to ensuring that everyone has the same background information about CICO implementation, the DVD covers the first two objectives of the training. On most teams, only one or two individuals will likely have seen the DVD, so it is important to share this information again for consistency.

After showing the CICO DVD, the coach/trainer should walk the teams through the CICO Development and Implementation Guide (see Figure 4.4) and answer questions that arise throughout the workshop. The sample training agenda in Figure 14.5 provides typical stopping points for teamwork and answering questions. Note that this agenda is just a sample of timing, and it may need to be adjusted, depending on the size of the group. During the workshop, the coach/trainer walks around and guides the teams. If a large group is being trained, it is helpful to have multiple coaches or trainers who can answer questions during team time. As detailed in the agenda, the coach/trainer should explain each section, provide the teams with collaborative time, and then bring the teams back together as a full group to share ideas and ask questions. This process should be followed for each set of questions in the guide, so that participants gradually become more familiar with what the CICO intervention will look like when they implement it in their school. To get through all the material, the trainer will need to limit the number of questions that can be asked during whole-group time and provide additional guidance during the individual team time. This format also allows the coach/trainer to differentiate the level and type of support provided, based on each team's specific needs.

At the end of the training, the trainer describes the big picture of where and how CICO fits into the overall system of behavior support in schools. We recommend that the teams pilot with three to five students initially before fully implementing CICO to work out any glitches related to check-in, teacher feedback, and check-out. The coach/trainer ends the day with ways of accessing additional information and research related to implementing CICO. The list of references, included at the end of this book, can be provided to the audience.

CROSS THE FINISH LINE: POSTTRAINING

When teams are ready to implement CICO in their schools, we recommend that a coach or someone familiar with CICO observe the check-in and check-out routine ideally for the first week (or at a minimum of the first 3 days) to provide feedback on implementation. If issues arise during this phase, school teams can be directed to Chapter 15 of this book, which covers frequently asked questions, to find helpful solutions and tips for common questions or issues encountered during implementation.

After 1 month of implementation, a coach should gather data to determine the extent to which CICO is being implemented with fidelity. The CICO Fidelity of Implementation Measure featured in Chapter 7 should be completed at least monthly during the first phases of implementation. Although not included in the fidelity measure, we recommend that multiple teachers be observed directly to determine if DPR feedback is occurring at the prespecified intervals. Also, student outcome data on the intervention should be examined. As stated in Chapter 7, if 70% of the students are not making progress on CICO, the system features of the intervention need to be examined. Chapter 15 provides troubleshooting guidance when schools are not experiencing high success rates with students on CICO.

8:30–8:40—Welcome and introductions

8:40–9:15—Provide an overview and show CICO DVD (first 22 minutes)

Objectives Covered

- Describe how CICO fits into the context of schoolwide PBIS.
- List and describe the critical features of CICO.

9:15–9:30—Screening and DPR development

Objectives Covered

- Identify for which students CICO is appropriate.
- Create a DPR to support your schoolwide PBIS Tier 1 system.

9:30–9:55—Team time

- Teams work to answer questions 1 and 2 of the CICO Development and Implementation Guide.

9:55–10:00—Whole-group share-out and questions

- Allow participants to share ideas and ask questions.

10:00–10:10—Break

10:10–10:20—Reinforcement system development

Objectives Covered

- Design a reinforcement system for students receiving CICO.

10:20–10:35—Team time

- Teams work to answer question 3 of the CICO Development and Implementation Guide.

10:35–10:45—Whole-group share-out and questions

- Allow participants to share ideas and ask questions.

10:45–10:55—Set-up referral and data system.

Objectives Covered

- Develop a referral system and identify a data system for monitoring the progress of students who receive CICO.

10:55–11:05—Team time

- Teams work to answer questions 4 and 5 of the CICO Development and Implementation Guide.

11:05–11:10—Whole-group share-out and questions

- Allow participants to share ideas and ask questions.

11:10–11:15—Determine intervention success and fading.

Objectives Covered

- Determine the criteria for fading the intervention.

11:15–11:25—Team time

- Teams work to answer question 6 of the CICO Development and Implementation Guide.

11:25–11:30—Whole-group share-out and questions

- Allow participants to share ideas and ask questions.

11:30–11:40—Training considerations

Objectives Covered

- Determine who will train the students, faculty, and parents on CICO.

11:40–11:50—Team time

- Teams work to answer questions 7 and 8 of the CICO Development and Implementation Guide.

11:50–12:00—Whole-group share-out and questions

- Allow participants to share ideas and ask questions.
- Final wrap-up.
- Provide additional information for coaching and follow-up.

FIGURE 14.5. Sample CICO workshop agenda.

Providing a systematic training for CICO development and consistent coaching during implementation can increase the likelihood that schools implement CICO with fidelity. If schools are considering making adjustments to the CICO intervention, or developing adapted versions (see Chapter 8), we recommend that a coach/trainer facilitate an abbreviated, but similar training and coaching process as the one presented in this chapter to ensure that all versions of CICO are implemented as intended.

CHAPTER 15

Frequently Asked Questions and Troubleshooting CICO Implementation

Implementing CICO is relatively straightforward and takes a minimum amount of staff time. There are, however, common issues that have come up in schools that have implemented this intervention. The purpose of this chapter is to address frequently asked questions regarding establishing a CICO intervention.

WHAT IF A STUDENT DOES NOT CHECK IN IN THE MORNING?

One of the first questions we are asked is what to do if students are not checking in on a regular basis. Part of the duties of the CICO coordinator or facilitator are to determine if students on CICO are absent or have merely forgotten to check in in the morning. If a student has simply forgotten to check in, the CICO coordinator delivers the DPR to the student and prompts them to try to remember to check in the next day. Although the CICO coordinator should not make a habit of delivering DPRs to students, students who forget to get the form should not miss out on opportunities for feedback and for meeting their daily point goal. After all, this is a system for increasing positive feedback and the success of students at risk for severe problem behavior.

Other suggestions for students who do not check in include reteaching the check-in process (e.g., where to check in, what time to check in) and/or pairing the student with a "check-in buddy" who will help them remember to check in.

WHAT IF A STUDENT
DOES NOT CHECK OUT IN THE AFTERNOON?

To begin with, the student receives a "0" if they do not check out. Recording multiple zeros into the database allows team members to identify when check-out is a problem. If students are allowed to bring their DPRs back the next school day and receive points without having checked out the previous day, it will be unclear to the behavior team which students are checking out on a regular basis versus which students who are not.

In terms of troubleshooting check-out, one of the first steps should be to ask the student why they are not checking out. Sometimes it is because they forgot, and at other times it is because there are bus or transportation issues. Many of these issues can be simply resolved by reminding the student that check-out is a necessary part of participation. Teachers can also play a role in reminding students to check out by prompting them toward the end of the school day (e.g., "Kiran, remember to check out when the bell rings"). This prompting from teachers should be faded over time, so that students can become independent in participating in the program. For younger students, the prompting may need to occur for a longer period of time. We have found that placing sticky notes on the student's desk is another good way to prompt check-out.

HOW DO STUDENTS CHECK OUT
AND STILL GET TO THE BUS ON TIME?

In some schools, we have found that check-out is not possible after school due to busing or other transportation issues (e.g., transport to after-school care). In these instances, when designing CICO to fit your school, the last 10–15 minutes of the school day must be available to CICO students for check-out. You will need to get agreement from the whole staff for this type of scheduling change. In addition, we have found that the staff are concerned about students with behavior problems roaming the halls just before the school day ends. Students on CICO can be given passes to leave class that are easily recognizable (e.g., a brightly colored, laminated pass that can be reused each day) by other staff members, who may encounter them in the hallways. Some elementary school settings have extended check-out to two short time periods at the end of the school day. The upper elementary (e.g., grades 3–6) students check out from 3:10 P.M. to 3:20 P.M., while the lower elementary (e.g., grades K–2) students check out from 3:20 P.M. to 3:30 P.M. This schedule has led to fewer students roaming the halls before school ends.

WHAT IF A STUDENT
IS *CONSISTENTLY* NOT CHECKING IN OR CHECKING OUT?

The CICO coordinator should sit down with the student and determine what barriers are preventing them from checking in or out. For example, one student we worked with was not checking out after school because they would miss the bus if they did. To resolve this issue, the CICO coordinator spoke with their sixth-period teacher, who agreed that the student could leave 5 minutes early from class to check out at the end of the day.

Some students may say, "I forgot to check in or check out." If a student forgets, there are several solutions that can be tried. Enlist the help of the student's friends or siblings to remind them to check in and check out. Simple statements, such as "Hey, can you do me a favor? Can you help your buddy Sean remember to check in in the mornings?" by the CICO coordinator, often work. It is a good idea to reinforce the buddy you have enlisted for helping the student on CICO. Another suggestion is to go to the student's last class and escort them to check-out for several days a week to help the student practice this behavior. Remember, some of the students are on CICO due to poor organization skills and may need extra practice in learning a new routine.

Some students may not check out because they have had a bad day and have not met their daily point goal. In these cases, there should be an incentive for checking out, even if the point goal has not been met. For example, the raffle system mentioned earlier, in which students receive a CICO raffle ticket just for checking in or checking out, is effective. The raffle can be held once a week only for students on CICO. The more times a student checks in and checks out, the more tickets they have, and thus the more chances to win. Raffle prizes can be small and inexpensive, consisting mainly of small treats, pencils, or small toys.

When troubleshooting why students are not consistently checking in and out, it is advisable to determine whether the student has "bought in" to the intervention and is voluntarily participating. There have been times when a parent wants the student on CICO, but the student resists by not following through with the program requirements. Remember that CICO is a voluntary positive support system. Efforts should be made to find reinforcers that are meaningful for students who have not bought into the intervention. One student we worked with was having difficulty meeting the requirements of CICO, but was interested in earning a baseball hat rather than receiving daily rewards. An individual contract was developed for this student, so that after a certain number of weeks of meeting their goal they would be able to earn the hat. There will be students who refuse to participate no matter what adaptations are made; for these students more individualized, intensive assessment and intervention are likely necessary.

The location of where students check in and check out is critical. It needs to be a place that students can access easily, as well as one that is separated from the loud disruption of common areas, such as hallways and cafeterias. In some schools where we have seen inconsistency in students checking in and out, either the location was inconvenient (i.e., not centrally located) or there had not been a permanent place set up for the process. For example, one of the schools we worked in chose the library as a check-in/check-out location. This location usually worked well, but was not available at times when parent groups met in the library after school, which disrupted the check-out process.

Although the check-in/check-out location needs to be in a quiet place, it does help if it is located near a common area so that the CICO coordinator can scan the area to look for students who are supposed to check in and out. Although encouraging students to become independent is part of the process of participating in CICO, it also helps to prompt students who may need reminders. In middle and high schools, in particular, students are heavily invested in peer interaction. It may take some prompting to help break them away from their peers to check in and out.

WHAT IF *SEVERAL* STUDENTS
ARE NOT CHECKING IN AND CHECKING OUT?

If several students are not checking in and out, the implementation of the whole intervention needs to be examined. One question that should be answered is *Has the school given CICO a high profile?* Elsewhere in this book we describe how to give CICO a high profile and ensure that it is a positive intervention. Without that boost, CICO may be seen as just another educational innovation that will pass with time. In one of the schools in which we worked, the staff were not well trained on how to implement the intervention. There was disagreement about which students should be placed on CICO, and issues were raised about existing interventions that interfered or overlapped with CICO. In that school, some of the staff were "sabotaging" the intervention. That is, since the staff members were not in agreement about how CICO should be implemented and with whom, they did not put much effort into the intervention and were not providing students with regular feedback. From this experience, we have learned that schools should complete the CICO Implementation Readiness Questionnaire. Staff commitment prior to implementation is critical in achieving success with this system of support.

Another question to consider is *Is the CICO coordinator or facilitator a person whom students like and with whom they look forward to interacting?* In some of the schools in which we have worked, the CICO coordinator is chosen based on time availability, rather than on whether their personality "fits" with the students. Although educators often go into the business of working in schools in part because they enjoy working with children, there are usually certain teachers or paraprofessionals with whom the students really resonate and enjoy being around, and for whom they will work hard. In our experience with one middle school, the CICO coordinator had an art of joking with students to improve their moods or reduce tension. These students could not wait to interact with this coordinator on a daily basis, and they were often sought out for problem solving with other staff members around student issues.

In another school we worked in, the CICO coordinator was a paraprofessional who was placed in the position by default because she was the person who was available before and after school. Although she was very effective in supporting teachers, she did not really want the CICO coordinator job, and her attitude came through in her interactions with students. She was often curt with them, more negative than positive, and had a hard time managing the number of students who were checking in and out daily. She would complain in students' presence that she did not like CICO. It is easy to see why, over time, students would not want to engage in the CICO intervention with this person.

WHAT IF STUDENTS WHO DO NOT NEED CICO
WANT TO BE ON IT IN ORDER TO EARN
REINFORCERS AND RECEIVE ADULT ATTENTION?

We have been asked this question in schools across the country. We see this trend in elementary schools more often than in middle or high school settings. Younger students tend to seek out adult attention more than older students; as kids get older, peer attention becomes more important.

In terms of solving this issue, several adjustments can be made during the setup of CICO to reduce the likelihood that it will become a problem. We often hear from students and staff that it is not "fair" for students with behavior problems to receive extra attention and reinforcement. First, staff members need to understand and believe that being "fair" does not mean treating each student the same way, but rather giving each student what each one needs to be successful.

Oftentimes, staff members have a harder time accepting the extra attention received by CICO students than do non-CICO students. Students are used to seeing fellow students pulled out for services (e.g., special education, speech and language therapy, counseling) and getting additional attention and/or instruction for their identified needs. CICO is similar to these supplementary services in that we are providing services to students who need them, rather than providing a supplementary intervention to all students.

It is also necessary to assess whether or not your schoolwide Tier 1 reinforcement system (e.g., schoolwide token system for following behavioral expectations) is working well, and if students who are engaging in appropriate behavior most of the time are getting acknowledged consistently for their behavior. Some of the schools we work in keep track of the number of positives (i.e., tokens or tickets) that are given out by school personnel as a way to ensure that all students in the school are receiving reinforcement.

The next step is to ensure that check-in and check-out occurs in a nonpublic location, so that the extra attention and reinforcement are not as salient to students not on the intervention. We have found that if other students, particularly younger ones, see the check-in and check-out process they are more likely to want to be involved. Students who are on CICO should be taught not to flaunt and antagonize other children with the reinforcers that they have earned. For example, when they earn a tangible reinforcer (e.g., small toy), they should be taught to put it in their backpacks and not take it out until they are away from the other students in the school.

Another way to reduce the desire for students to be on the intervention is to limit the distribution of tangible reinforcers, such as candy, food, and toys. The goal of the intervention is for students to receive more feedback and reinforcement for appropriate behavior. This reinforcement does not need to be in the form of something tangible. Having students earn activities and time with preferred adults or other peers will also help reduce the desire by their peers to be on the intervention. In some of our schools, students who are on CICO can earn reinforcers for their whole class or can include four to five peers who are not on the intervention. Finally, if certain students are heavily invested in being on CICO, perhaps they can serve as helpers during check-in and check-out. That way, they can receive the extra adult attention but also not have to engage in the full intervention.

SINCE CICO IS AN INTERVENTION FOR STUDENTS AT RISK, SHOULD STUDENTS ALREADY IDENTIFIED AS HAVING A DISABILITY BE INCLUDED IN THE INTERVENTION?

Yes, if they are also appropriate candidates for CICO. CICO is designed to support students who are at risk but are not currently engaging in severe problem behavior. Many students who have learning or communication disabilities may just be beginning to engage in problem behavior. These students are perfect candidates for CICO, as the goal is to prevent students from entering a higher-risk group. The main issue when assessing whether students with disabilities qualify for CICO is to determine that the student is not acting out to escape schoolwork. Many students with learning disabilities may be acting out because academic work is too difficult, so it is important to determine if the material is being taught at the student's instructional level.

Students with emotional and behavior disabilities have individualized IEP goals for behavior and likely require more intensive intervention than basic CICO can provide. Since CICO is administered similarly to students across the board, it does not support the individualized requirements of the IEP. Students with more severe disabilities (e.g., serious cognitive delays) can benefit from the program, but may need additional support to successfully participate on CICO. For more information about adapting CICO for students with severe disabilities, see Hawken and O'Neill (2006).

HOW MANY STUDENTS CAN ONE CICO COORDINATOR SUPPORT?

Our experience tells us that for elementary school students, one CICO coordinator can support 15–20 students at a time. For middle and high school settings, up to 30 students can be supported by one CICO coordinator. The number of students who can be supported depends *greatly* on the skills of the CICO coordinator in managing groups of students. Some CICO coordinators become frazzled with too many students in a room, whereas others are comfortable with checking in multiple students at a time. What has happened frequently in our schools is that students need to be taught the check-in/check-out process as well as what to do when they are waiting to check in and out. One school we worked in had a line of tape on the floor to indicate where students were supposed to stand while waiting to check in or out.

An additional factor in determining how many students can be supported depends on whether check-in and check-out can occur at staggered times. For example, if the school allows check-in 20–30 minutes prior to the start of school, this time frame allows students to stagger the check-in process. If check-in can only occur 10 minutes before school starts, it will be more difficult to have as many students on the program.

We are often asked *What if we have more than 30 students who need CICO?* There are several answers to this question. First of all, CICO should be only one type of Tier 2 intervention that is implemented in your school. There should be a menu of other Tier 2 interventions to help students who are at risk. If, however, the staff feel that more students can benefit from the intervention, it would be wise to have one CICO coordinator who oversees the intervention with one or more CICO facilitators who help with the check-in and check-out process, as outlined in Chapter 6. We have also seen the need for more than one CICO facilitator if a school building is rather large or houses multiple floors. Some schools will have a CICO facilitator for each wing of the school or for each floor.

We have also been asked whether one person can handle check-in and a second person can lead check-out. As long as the assigned person is consistent on a daily basis (e.g., students check in with the Ms. Singh every morning and check out with Mr. Myer every afternoon), this arrangement tends to work fine. Also, it is critical that these two individuals communicate regularly about how the students are doing, and predetermine who will be the CICO coordinator in charge of data entry and graphing, versus who will be the CICO facilitator. What doesn't work is if different people lead check-in/check-out every day; for example, if on Monday, one staff member handles the process and on Tuesday, a different person does so, and so on. One goal of CICO is to foster a positive connection with an adult, which is difficult to do if there is a different adult in charge from day to day.

WHAT IF STUDENTS LOSE THEIR DPRS?

One of the responsibilities for the student on CICO includes carrying the DPR from class to class, and from teacher to teacher, or, in the case of elementary school students, from setting to setting. We recommend that students be taught to get another DPR as soon as they realize they have lost it. That way, although they may have lost some points toward their goal by losing their DPRs, they have not lost their points for the entire day. They can receive feedback on their new DPRs and continue to receive positive feedback throughout the day. For younger students, some may need their DPRs to be placed on a clipboard so that they are less likely to get lost during transitions. In some schools we have worked in, classroom teachers keep extra copies of the DPRs, in case a student loses one.

Students may also "lose" DPRs if they find that being on CICO is not helpful or rewarding. For such students, we suggest that you troubleshoot ways to improve the intervention, which often involves asking the student what types of rewards they are interested in working for. Some students may "lose" their DPRs if they have had a bad day and are afraid to bring the forms home to their parents. As sad as it may be, there are parents who punish students severely for having a "bad day" at school. In these situations, we have either encouraged the parents to use the program positively, or we have had students not take their cards home as part of the intervention. We cannot overemphasize that CICO needs to be a positive intervention that students enjoy participating in. If students get into even more trouble by being on CICO, they are going to be unlikely to participate.

WHAT HAPPENS WHEN A STUDENT GETS AN ODR IN AN UNSTRUCTURED SETTING, AND IT IS NOT REFLECTED ON THE DPR?

CICO targets student behavior in the classroom throughout the day. Often, however, students on CICO receive a referral on the playground, in the hallway, or in the lunchroom, and the referral is not reflected on the DPR. On a few occasions, students get into a fight at recess, but do well enough in the classroom to earn enough points to get a reward at the end of the day. In such situations, teachers become upset. They feel that the student did not deserve to earn a reward because of the major infraction. Schools we have worked with have chosen different ways to address this issue. Some schools will deduct an automatic 20 points from the DPR for any ODR. This means that unless the student has had an otherwise perfect day, they are not likely to meet the daily point goal. Other schools do not want to institute a response cost (i.e., removal of points) for ODRs. Instead, these schools do not allow students to earn a reward on a day an ODR is obtained or to exchange points for a larger reward. Whatever system of consequences is put into place, there must be good communication between the school staff and CICO coordinators when students receive ODRs, so that this situation is always handled consistently.

HOW DO CHECK-IN AND CHECK-OUT OCCUR WITH MULTIPLE STUDENTS? HOW DOES EACH STUDENT GET ONE-ON-ONE ATTENTION?

The purpose of check-in and check-out is to provide a positive link to an adult other than the student's teacher. Check-in and check-out are not counseling sessions, but rather quick, positive, and brief interactions that provide students with prompts about things to work on. If a student is having a difficult time (e.g., just got into a fight or is crying), the CICO coordinator can ask the student to have a seat and spend more time with them after the check-in process is finished for the rest of the students. In some circumstances, it is more appropriate to ask for help from the counselor, school psychologist, or principal if the student is seriously distressed.

How well multiple students are handled at a time depends greatly on the skills of the CICO coordinator. All of the materials for the students and for the check-in and check-out process should be well organized and easily accessible to the CICO coordinator. In addition, many elements of check-in can be completed by the student. For example, students can write their own names on their DPRs each morning. During check-out, students can calculate their own percentage of points. Students on CICO receive brief, one-on-one adult attention, not only in the morning and afternoon, but from their classroom teacher(s) throughout the day. Also, the CICO coordinator is typically a member of the school staff and therefore sees the students throughout the day to provide additional attention. For example, in some of our schools the CICO coordinator also supervises the lunchroom and chats with the students on CICO at that time as well.

WHAT IF THE STAFF ARE NOT IMPLEMENTING CICO CORRECTLY?

The entire staff should receive inservice training on the purpose of CICO, the positive nature of the intervention, and how to provide feedback to students. At times, teachers will write negative comments on the DPR. Some teachers may misuse it as a tool to punish students by writing down all of the inappropriate behaviors in which students engaged. Other teachers may need individual training and follow-up to reemphasize the positive nature of the intervention and to offer prompts for positive feedback. Many schools we have worked with have a line for teacher feedback on the DPR that prompts them to write positive rather than negative comments. More detail about positive feedback is presented in Chapter 6.

One way to keep the system positive and to keep teachers invested in it is to make sure that they are receiving feedback, at least quarterly, on how students on CICO are doing. One problem that occurs frequently in schools is that teachers help in the data-collection process (e.g., filling out ODR forms for students engaging in severe or dangerous behavior or completing the DPR), but never see a data summary or how the data are used to make decisions in schools. Staff members should be updated about how many students are served on CICO, about how many are meeting their goals on a regular basis, and about other outcome data associated with CICO improvements (e.g., student improvements in grades and test scores).

As mentioned in Chapter 6, to keep the system positive, a school may also want to reward staff members on a frequent basis for their participation in CICO. For example, staff members are required to initial DPRs for students participating in CICO and are asked to write positive comments when appropriate. Teachers' names could be randomly selected from the student DPRs at monthly staff meetings to earn small prizes. Alternatively, prizes could be given for the most creative or encouraging comments written on student DPRs. Students on CICO could also nominate staff members whom they felt helped them be successful on CICO. These individuals could be recognized at a faculty meeting or assembly or in the school newsletter.

HOW DO WE KNOW IF TEACHERS ARE GIVING POSITIVE AND CONSTRUCTIVE FEEDBACK THROUGHOUT THE DAY (ELEMENTARY SCHOOL) OR DURING PERIODS (SECONDARY SCHOOL)?

The only way to know if teachers are giving feedback throughout the day in elementary school or during periods in middle and high school settings is to observe them in their classrooms. In many schools we work in, the principals observe instruction on a regular basis and examine the teacher's ability to manage behavior as they observe a class. Often called "principal walk-through" observations, they provide a time during which principals can give feedback to teachers on how CICO is being implemented. In other schools we work in, instructional coaches observe teachers in classrooms and provide them with feedback on Tier 1 classroom instruction. The instructional coaches we work with observe teachers and track the extent to which they are delivering a 5:1 positive-to-negative ratio of feedback to students. These same instructional coaches also observe the extent to which CICO is being implemented with fidelity with a particular student or students who are in the class. Some of the questions that can be added to the CICO fidelity of implementation measure if direct observation of teachers is possible include:

1. The teacher provides specific positive and corrective feedback throughout   **Y**   **N** the observation.
2. The feedback ratio is 5:1 in a 20-minute observation.   **Y**   **N**

Positives	Negatives

3. The teacher initiates feedback at the end of the instructional block.   **Y**   **N**
4. The teacher rates the student's behavior on the DPR (i.e., circles the   **Y**   **N** numeric rating and initials the form).

This type of observation is robust and provides a true assessment of the active ingredient of the CICO intervention. Often teachers will only give students feedback during the marking periods, but not give students any indication of how they are performing throughout the rest of the 50- to 90-minute block of time in which they are rated. Or teachers provide neutral or positive feedback during the marking periods, but throughout the rest of the time block communicate negative feedback (e.g., "Stop it"; "Don't do that"; "Knock it off") to the student. We recommend that teachers who struggle to provide high rates of positive to negative feedback use a signaling device, such as a MotivAider or a phone app, to remind them to catch the student(s) "being good." The goal of CICO is to increase contingent teacher feedback and praise, and direct observation is the only way to assess that this positive feedback is occurring. Since this type of observation is less likely to happen on a regular basis due to the time and costs associated with it, there are other ways to check the constructiveness of teacher feedback.

One important sign is that the teacher is circling each individual number on the DPR at each period, rather than circling all the numbers at the end of the day. When we examine DPRs, it is easy to spot which teachers have waited until the end of the day to score the student. Alternatively, you can directly ask the students how often they are receiving feedback. In some of our schools, the CICO coordinator is a paraprofessional who works with students in multiple school settings. This person can do spot-check observations of how the intervention is being implemented. In fact, some schools have developed a system that involves having a staff member observe the teacher during the first few days of the CICO implementation to double check that feedback is occurring at regular intervals. This task is difficult for a paraprofessional to do, but often a counselor or school psychologist can fill this role.

WHAT IF PARENTS/CAREGIVERS ARE NOT FOLLOWING THROUGH OR USE CICO AS A PUNITIVE SYSTEM?

One of the strengths of CICO is the increased connection between home and school. Parents and caregivers are given daily reports on how their child is performing in school. In some cases, we have had difficulty in getting parents to follow through with reviewing the DPR nightly and providing positive feedback to the student. In these cases, we may call or meet with the parents to emphasize the importance of their participation. Many of the schools that we work with have the parents, school staff, and students sign a "CICO Contract," in which they agree to the responsibilities of participating in CICO. This contact gives parents clear expectations for the intervention and can be referred to as a reminder to parents of their responsibilities.

Some schools we have worked in have decided that daily caregiver/parental signing of the DPR is not necessary and opt for DPRs to be sent home once a week for signing and review. Weekly parental contact will decrease the load on parents and also on the school staff, while keeping with the critical elements of the CICO intervention.

An interesting finding from our research is that the parent element of CICO tends to be the weakest link when examining the fidelity of CICO implementation. Results from Hawken and Horner (2003) indicate that four of the critical features of CICO (i.e., students checking in, regular teacher feedback, students checking out, and daily DPR data used for decision making) were implemented with an average of 87% fidelity across students. Parental feedback (i.e., a signature on the DPR) was provided during only 67% of the fidelity implementation checks. It should be noted, however, that many of the students were successful on CICO and were meeting daily point goals despite the lack of parental participation. This finding has been replicated across several studies (e.g., Hawken, 2006; Hawken et al., 2007). Parental feedback is encouraged, but not necessary for student success on CICO. There are many students who could benefit from CICO who live in chaotic home environments. These students should be given an equal opportunity to benefit from CICO even if their parents are unable to participate. (Note: Parents should always still give permission for the student to participate in CICO.)

There are unfortunate circumstances that we have encountered in schools, in which students participating in CICO are punished for having "bad days." A bad day may mean that the student has not met their goal for that day. Some parents have implemented harsh punishments (e.g., spanking, hitting, yelling, extreme limitation of activities) when they reviewed the DPR and found that their child had not done as well as expected. The school staff typically hears about the parents' negative reaction from the student, or the student stops wanting to participate in CICO. In these instance, schools have arranged to have "surrogate parents" at the school who serve as an additional person who provides feedback, praise, and comments on the DPR. The surrogate parent could be a teacher (other than the student's regular teacher), custodian, paraprofessional, or volunteer who is in the school daily, or some other adult, who can commit 5 minutes each day to reviewing the student's DPR and providing positive feedback. The issue of harsh punishment will need to be addressed with the parent and would probably be best handled by having either the school counselor, principal, or vice principal meet with the parent.

WHAT IF STUDENTS ARE CONSISTENTLY PARTICIPATING IN CICO, AND THEIR BEHAVIOR GETS WORSE?

It is expected that within about 2 weeks, students' behavior should improve on CICO. For students who are receiving support to improve academic outcomes, it may take longer to notice changes in grades, but there should be increased organization skills, homework completion, and the like. Students whose behavior gets worse may need a modified version of basic CICO, as detailed in Chapter 9.

WHAT IF TEACHERS COMPLAIN THAT THEY CANNOT GIVE FEEDBACK TO THE SEVEN STUDENTS ON CICO IN THEIR CLASS DURING EACH MARKING PERIOD?

At most, teachers should have no more than 3 students in their classes who are receiving the basic CICO intervention. As stated previously, CICO is only one type of Tier 2 intervention that should be available for students at risk in your school. If a teacher is referring lots of students to CICO, it's likely to be a Tier 1 classroom-behavior management problem. We highly recommend that schools evaluate the extent to which Tier 1 classroom procedures have been put into practice prior to referring additional students to CICO. What we've seen in some of our schools it that the most competent teachers are given the students who are behavioral challenges. If this is the case, the schools should examine their at-risk students and try to distribute them equally across the grade. Caution should also be taken with middle and high school teachers, so that they are not giving feedback to seven or eight students each period; rather, having teachers work with two or three students each period is more feasible.

IS THERE A CONCERN WITH HAVING A CICO COORDINATOR/ FACILITATOR CHECKING ONLY ONE STUDENT IN AND OUT?

Yes! The main concern about having the CICO coordinator/facilitator checking only one student in and out is that the nature of the intervention changes and becomes more of a mentoring or counseling session. The goal is to provide a quick greeting and check-in rather than a counseling session. The paraprofessionals or teachers who agree to serve as CICO facilitators are not trained in counseling, nor should they be serving in a counselor's role. We suggest at a minimum that a CICO facilitator have at least three to five students to prevent the intervention from becoming a one-on-one encounter. In addition, we recommend that CICO coordinators/facilitators be trained on the types of conversations to have with students and when to refer issues to the school psychologist or counselor.

FINAL COMMENTS ON CICO IMPLEMENTATION

CICO is an effective, evidence-based intervention, but it requires a deep commitment from the school staff and a focus on prevention. In our experience, several factors indicate that schools will have a difficult time with implementing CICO. Schools will struggle with putting CICO into practice if:

- The administrator is not a member of the team that *develops* CICO and *examines data* for decision making.
- CICO is used as punishment, rather than as a preventative intervention.
  - For example: "You have six ODRs, and your punishment is CICO."
  - The DPR is used as a means for teachers to vent their frustrations about challenging students.
- The CICO coordinator or facilitator lacks the skills to implement the intervention.
  - *Note:* Skills related to behavior intervention, managing multiple students, and data entry/using computers are needed.
  - *Note:* Refer to the training needed for the CICO coordinator/facilitator in Chapter 5.
- Schools expect CICO to solve all behavior problems.
  - *Note:* Schools need several interventions at the Tier 2 level to support students at risk.
  - *Note:* Schools need good academic supports and the ability to identify escape-maintained behavior.
  - *Note:* Schools need intensive interventions for students who are not successful with basic CICO.
- The evaluation of CICO data is not embedded into existing teams, with a focus on alterable variables versus unalterable ones (e.g., poor parenting practices).

Appendices

List of Abbreviations and Definitions

BSP. Behavior Support Plan. An individualized plan to address a student's behavioral goals and objectives. The BSP should describe the intervention strategies to be used, the person responsible for implementation, a timeline for implementation, and the means by which the outcomes of the BSP will be evaluated.

CICO. Check-In, Check-Out intervention. The CICO intervention is a daily check-in/check-out system that provides the student with immediate feedback on their behavior (via teacher rating on a Daily Progress Report) and increased positive adult attention.

DPR. Daily Progress Report. The DPR is the form used in the Check-In, Check-Out intervention to track a student's daily progress toward meeting their behavioral goals. Samples of several DPRs are provided in the Appendices.

EL. English learner. An EL student is a student whose native language is not English. EL students are often provided with language support and instruction through placement in EL classrooms or programs.

FBA. Functional behavioral assessment. An assessment of a person's behavior that is based on determining the function that the behavior serves for that person. The assessment typically consists of interviews with teachers, the student, and parents, as well as observations of the student's behavior in the problematic setting. The information gained from the FBA is used to develop a hypothesis regarding the purpose of the student's behavior and the circumstances under which the behavior occurs. The assessment information is used to build an individualized behavior support plan for that student.

IEP. Individualized education plan. An IEP describes the educational program that has been designed to meet the needs of any student who receives special education and related services. Each IEP should be a truly individualized document. The document identifies the student's needs, goals, and objectives, and the strategies that will be implemented in the school to meet those objectives. The frequency and duration of the strategies should be included as well.

ODR. Office discipline referral. A system used in many schools in which a student is sent to the main office to receive consequences following a behavioral infraction in the classroom or other social setting. The ODR refers to the documentation of that incident.

Working Smarter, Not Harder Matrix

Committee, project, or initiative	Purpose	Outcome	Target group	Staff involved

Reprinted with permission from George Sugai.

From *Responding to Problem Behavior in Schools, Third Edition*, by Leanne S. Hawken, Deanne A. Crone, Kaitlin Bundock, and Robert H. Horner. Copyright © 2021 The Guilford Press. Permission to photocopy this material is granted to purchasers of this book for personal use or use with students (see copyright page for details). Purchasers can download additional copies of this material (see the box at the end of the table of contents).

Request for Assistance Form

Date: _____   Teacher/Team: _____

Student name: _____   Grade: _____   IEP: Yes   No   (Circle)

1. Check the area(s) of concern:

Problem behavior	Academic problems	What is your primary concern?
___ Aggressive ___ Noncompliant ___ Disruptive ___ Withdrawn ___ Tardy ___ Lack of social skills ___ Other (specify) ___ _____ ___ _____	___ Reading ___ Math ___ Spelling ___ Writing ___ Study skills ___ Organization	

2. Check the strategies you have tried so far:

General review	Modify environment or teaching	Teach expected behaviors	Consequences tried
___ Review cumulative file ___ Talk with parents ___ Talk with previous teacher ___ Seek peer help ___ Classroom assessment ___ Other (specify) ___ _____ ___ _____	___ Change seating arrangement ___ Provide quiet space ___ Encourage work breaks ___ Change schedule of activities ___ Modify assignments ___ Arrange tutoring to improve student's academic skills ___ Other (specify) ___ _____ ___ _____	___ Give reminders about expected behavior when problem behavior is likely ___ Self-management program ___ Clarify rules and expected behavior for whole class ___ Practice expected behaviors in class ___ Contract with students ___ Other (specify) ___ _____ ___ _____	___ Increase rewards for expected behavior ___ Phone call to parents ___ Office referral ___ Time-out ___ Reprimand ___ Lunch detention ___ Loss of privileges ___ Meeting with parents ___ Other (specify) ___ _____ ___ _____

(continued)

3. Why do you believe the student is engaging in problem behavior?

___ Adult attention   ___ Peer attention   ___ Escape from difficult work/tasks

___ Escape from peers   ___ Escape from adults

___ Gain access to preferred activity/item (computers, games, toys, etc.)

Teacher gathers:

- *Academic performance data*—Acadience Learning Assessments/CBM, percent of in-class/homework completion, documentation of grade-level performance
- *Behavior data*—behavior logs, documentation of in-class consequences, interclass time-outs

Front office gathers:

SWIS _____   Attendance _____   Tardies _____

    (# of ODRs)   (# of absences)   (# of tardies)

Parental Permission Form

Permission for Check-In, Check-Out (CICO)

Date: _____

Student: _____ Grade: _____

Teacher: _____

Parent/Guardian: _____

I would like to include your child in our CICO intervention. A report will be filled out daily by the teacher(s) and checked at the end of the day by our CICO coordinator, _____. Students will need to pick up their report every morning between _____ and _____ A.M. and then return to _____ between _____ and _____ P.M. The student will be able to earn incentives and rewards for appropriate behavior. As parents, you are responsible for making sure your child arrives on time each day for check-in and that you review and sign the daily progress report. Together, we can make this a positive experience for your child.

_____ I **do** give consent for my student to participate.
_____ I **do not** give consent for my student to participate.

_____ Date: _____
              (Parent/Guardian)

For further information, please call:

_____ at: _____
              (Coordinator)

or call: _____ .

Daily Progress Report—Middle School, Example 1

A- Day   B-Day

Name: _____   Date: _____

Teachers: Please indicate Yes (2), So-So (1), or No (0) regarding the student's achievement for the following goals.

Goals	1/5			2/6			3/7			HR			4/8		
Be respectful	2	1	0	2	1	0	2	1	0	2	1	0	2	1	0
Be responsible	2	1	0	2	1	0	2	1	0	2	1	0	2	1	0
Keep hands and feet to self	2	1	0	2	1	0	2	1	0	2	1	0	2	1	0
Follow directions	2	1	0	2	1	0	2	1	0	2	1	0	2	1	0
Be there— be ready	2	1	0	2	1	0	2	1	0	2	1	0	2	1	0
TOTAL POINTS															
TEACHER INITIALS															

CICO Daily Goal   / 50   CICO Daily Score   / 50

In training _____   CICO Member ____   _____
                                            Student signature

Teacher comments: Please state briefly any specific behaviors or achievements that demonstrate the student's progress. (If additional space is required, please attach a note and indicate so below.)

Period 1/5 _____

Period 2/6 _____

Period 3/7 _____

Homeroom _____

Period 4/8 _____

Parent/Caregiver Signature: _____

Parent/Caregiver Comments: _____

Daily Progress Report—Middle School, Example 2

Name: _____

Materials to Class	Worked and Let Others Work	Follow Directions the First Time			Teacher	Parent
2 1 No	2 1 No	2 1 No	Assignments:			
			Wow,			
2 1 No	2 1 No	2 1 No	Assignments:			
			Wow,			
2 1 No	2 1 No	2 1 No	Assignments:			
			Wow,			
2 1 No	2 1 No	2 1 No	Assignments:			
			Wow,			
2 1 No	2 1 No	2 1 No	Assignments:			
			Wow,			

Thumbs-Up! Ticket

THUMBS-UP! TICKET

Student name: _____

Issued by: _____

Date: _____

WAY TO GO!

Daily Progress Report—Elementary School, Example 1

Name: _____   Date: _____

| 2 = Wow! |
| 1 = OK |
| 0 = Tough time |

GOALS		8:15–Recess	Recess–Lunch	Lunch–Recess	Recess–2:50
Be Safe	• Walk in building • Keep hands and feet to self	2 1 0	2 1 0	2 1 0	2 1 0
Be Respectful	• Follow directions	2 1 0	2 1 0	2 1 0	2 1 0
	• Use kind words and actions	2 1 0	2 1 0	2 1 0	2 1 0
Be Responsible	• Take care of myself and my belongings • Be in the right place and be ready	2 1 0	2 1 0	2 1 0	2 1 0
	Teacher Initials _____				
Total Points = _____	Points Possible = _____		Today _____ % Goal _____ %		

Way to Be: _____

Parent Signature: _____

Daily Progress Report—Elementary School, Example 2

Date: _____

Teacher: _____   Student: _____

0 = No	1 = Good	2 = Excellent

	Be Safe	Be Respectful	Be Your Personal Best		
	Keep hands, feet, and objects to self	Use kind words and actions	Follow directions	Work in class	Teacher initials
9:00–A.M. Recess	2 1 0	2 1 0	2 1 0	2 1 0	
A.M. Recess– Lunch	2 1 0	2 1 0	2 1 0	2 1 0	
Lunch–P.M. Recess	2 1 0	2 1 0	2 1 0	2 1 0	
P.M. Recess–3:40	2 1 0	2 1 0	2 1 0	2 1 0	
Total Points = Points Possible = 32	Today _____%		Goal _____%		

Parent Signature: _____

WOW: _____

CICO Implementation Readiness Questionnaire

Is your school ready to implement the CICO intervention? Prior to the implementation of CICO, it is recommended that the following features be in place. Please circle the answer that best describes your school at this time.

Yes   No   1. Our school has a schoolwide positive behavioral interventions and supports system in place. In essence, we have decided on three to five rules and have explicitly taught the rules to all students. We provide rewards to students for following the rules and mild consequences for rule infractions.

Yes   No   2. Our teachers are implementing Tier 1 classroom management strategies, including explicitly teaching what schoolwide expectations look like in the classroom, teaching classroom routines (e.g., how to ask for help, where to turn in homework, appropriate noise levels), having a high positive-to-negative ratio of praise to negative feedback, and engaging students with multiple opportunities to respond.

Yes   No   3. We have secured staff commitment for the implementation of CICO. The majority of the staff agree that this intervention is needed to support students at risk for serious problem behavior, and they are willing to actively participate in the intervention.

Yes   No   4. There is administrative support for the implementation of the CICO intervention. The administrative staff are committed to implementing and maintaining CICO in our school. Administrators have allocated the necessary financial and staff resources to support implementation of the program.

Yes   No   5. There have been no major recent changes in the school system that could hinder a successful implementation of the CICO intervention. Major changes include developments, such as teacher strikes, high teacher or administrative turnover, or a major increase or decrease in funding.

Yes   No   6. We have made implementation of the CICO intervention one of the school's top three priorities for this school year.

Voting Form for Implementing the CICO Intervention

☐ **YES**, I would be willing to participate in the Check-In, Check-Out intervention if it were implemented in our school as part of our schoolwide positive behavioral interventions and supports program.

☐ **NO**, I would *not* be willing to participate in the Check-In, Check-Out intervention if it were implemented in our school as part of our schoolwide positive behavioral interventions and supports program.

Questions, comments, or concerns: _____

_____

_____

_____

_____

_____

_____

CICO Development and Implementation Guide

1. Determine personnel needs and logistics.
   - Who will be the CICO coordinator? Will there be one CICO coordinator OR one CICO coordinator with multiple CICO facilitators?

   - Who will supervise the CICO coordinator?

   - Who will check students in and out when the coordinator is absent? (Name **at least two** people who can substitute for the coordinator.)

   - Where will check-in and check-out occur?

   - What is the maximum number of students that can be served on CICO at one time?

   - What is the name of CICO at your school, and what will the Daily Progress Report (DPR) be called?

2. Develop a DPR.
   - What will the behavioral expectations be?

     o Consistent with schoolwide expectations?

   - Are the expectations positively stated?

   - Is the DPR teacher friendly? How often are teachers asked to rate the student's behavior?

   - Is the DPR age appropriate, and does it include a range of scores?

   - Are the data easy to summarize?

(continued)

3. Develop a reinforcement system for students on the CICO intervention.
   - What will the students' daily point goal be?

   - What reinforcers will students receive for checking in (e.g., praise and lottery ticket)?

   - What reinforcers will students receive for checking out **AND** meeting their daily point goal?

   - How will you ensure students do not become bored with the reinforcers?

   - What are the consequences for students who receive major and minor referrals?

4. Develop a referral system.
   - How will students be referred to CICO? What are the criteria for placing students on CICO?

   - What does the parental consent form look like for students participating in CICO?

   - What is the process for screening students who transfer into the school?

   - What is the process for determining whether students will begin the next school year on CICO?

5. Develop a system for managing the daily data.
   - Which computer program will be used to summarize data?

   - Which team in the school will examine the daily CICO data, and how frequently will the data be examined? (Note: Data should be examined at least twice monthly.)

   - Who is responsible for summarizing and bringing the data to team meetings?

(continued)

- How frequently will data be shared with the whole staff?

- How frequently will data be shared with parents?

6. Plan to fade students off the intervention.
   - What are the criteria for fading students off the CICO intervention?

   - How will CICO be faded, and who will be in charge of helping students fade off CICO?

   - How will graduation from the CICO intervention be celebrated?

   - What incentives and supports will be put in place for students who graduate from the program?

7. Plan for staff training.
   - Who will train staff on the CICO intervention?

   - Who will provide teachers with individual coaching if the CICO intervention is not being implemented as planned?

   - Who will provide yearly booster sessions about the purpose of CICO and key features in implementing the CICO intervention?

8. Plan for student and parent training.
   - Who will meet with students to train them on the intervention?

   - How will parents be trained on the intervention?

CICO Check-In/Check-Out Form—Elementary School

Student	Check-out (% of points earned)	Goal	Check-in	Delivered contract	Signed parent copy of DPR

CICO Check-In/Check-Out Form—Middle/High School

Date: _____   CICO coordinator: _____

| | Check-in | | | | Check-out |
Student name	Paper	Pencil	Notebook	CICO parent copy	% of points earned

Reinforcer Checklist

(To be completed by the student)

Please circle YES or NO if the item or activity is something you would like to earn.

Activity Reinforcers

Video game	YES	NO	Basketball	YES	NO
Swimming	YES	NO	Magazine	YES	NO
Watching video/DVD	YES	NO	Drawing	YES	NO
Walking	YES	NO	Field trips	YES	NO
Comic books	YES	NO	Puzzles	YES	NO
Play-Doh	YES	NO	Board game	YES	NO
Craft activities	YES	NO	Card game	YES	NO

Please list any other favorite activities you would like to earn.

_____

_____

_____

Material Reinforcers

Stickers	YES	NO	Erasers	YES	NO
Special pencils	YES	NO	Bubbles	YES	NO
Lotions	YES	NO	Play-Doh	YES	NO
Colored pencils/crayons	YES	NO	Rings	YES	NO
Free tardy pass	YES	NO	Puzzles	YES	NO
Bookmarks	YES	NO	Trading cards	YES	NO
Action figures	YES	NO	Small toys	YES	NO
Free assignment pass	YES	NO	Necklaces	YES	NO

Please list any other favorite items you would like to earn.

_____

_____

_____

(continued)

Edible Reinforcers

Small one-bite candies	YES	NO	Cereal	YES	NO
Larger candy	YES	NO	Fruit	YES	NO
Vending machine drink	YES	NO	Pretzels	YES	NO
Juice/punch	YES	NO	Potato chips	YES	NO
Vegetables and dip	YES	NO	Corn chips	YES	NO
Crackers	YES	NO	Cookies	YES	NO
Donuts	YES	NO	Bagels	YES	NO
Candy bars	YES	NO	Cheese	YES	NO

Please list any other favorite name brands or snacks you would like to earn.

_____

_____

_____

Social Reinforcers

Pat on the back	YES	NO	Verbal praise	YES	NO
Extra P.E./gym time	YES	NO	Free time	YES	NO
Games with teacher	YES	NO	Field trips	YES	NO
Games with friends	YES	NO	Special seat	YES	NO
Lunch with friends	YES	NO	High five	YES	NO
Visit with friends	YES	NO	Awards	YES	NO

Please list any other favorites you would like to earn.

_____

_____

_____

CICO Fidelity of Implementation Measure (CICO-FIM)

Scoring Guide

School: _____ Date: _____ Pre: _____ Post: _____

District: _____ State: _____ Data collector: _____

Evaluation Question	Data Source (P = permanent product; I = interview; O = observation)		Score (0–2)
1. Does the school employ a CICO coordinator whose job is to manage the CICO with 10–15 hours per week allocated? (0 = no CICO coordinator, 1 = CICO coordinator but less than 10 hours per week allocated, 2 = CICO coordinator, 10–15 hours per week allocated)	Interviews with administrator and CICO coordinator	I	
2. Does the school budget contain an allocated amount of money to maintain the CICO intervention (money for reinforcers, DPR forms, etc.)? (0 = no, 2 = yes)	CICO budget Interviews	P/I	
3. Do students who are referred to the CICO intervention receive support within a week of the referral? (0 = more than 2 weeks between referral and CICO support, 1 = within 2 weeks, 2 = within a week)	Interviews CICO referrals and CICO start dates	P/I	
4. Does the administrator serve on the behavior support team or review CICO data on a regular basis? (0 = no, 1 = yes, but not consistently, 2 = yes)	Interviews	I	
5. Do 90% of CICO team members state that the CICO intervention system has been taught/reviewed on an annual basis? (0 = 0–50%, 1 = 51–89%, 2 = 90–100%)	Interviews	I	
6. Do 90% of the students on the CICO intervention check in daily (randomly sample 3 days for recording)? (0 = 0–50%, 1 = 51–89%, 2 = 90–100%)	CICO Check-In, Check-Out Form	P	
7. Do 90% of students on the CICO intervention check out daily (randomly sample 3 days for recording)? (0 = 0–50%, 1 = 51–89%, 2 = 90–100%)	CICO Check-In, Check-Out Form	P	
8. Do 90% of students on the CICO report that they receive reinforcement (e.g., verbal, tangible) for meeting daily goals? (0 = 0–50%, 1 = 51–89%, 2 = 90–100%)	Interviews with students on CICO	I	

(continued)

Evaluation Question	Data Source (P = permanent product; I = interview; O = observation)		Score (0–2)
9. Do 90% of students on the CICO intervention receive regular feedback from teachers (randomly sample 50% of student DPRs across 3 days)? (0 = 0–50%, 1 = 51–89%, 2 = 90–100%)	CICO Daily Progress Reports	P	
10. Do 90% of students on the CICO intervention receive feedback from their parents? (0 = 0–50%, 1 = 51–89%, 2 = 90–100%)	CICO Daily Progress Reports	P	
11. Does the CICO coordinator enter DPR data at least once a week? (0 = no, 1 = every other week, 2 = once a week)	Interviews	I	
12. Do 90% of behavior support team members indicate that the daily CICO data are used for decision making? (0 = 0–50%, 1 = 51–89%, 2 = 90–100%)	Interviews	I	

Total = _____ / _____ = _____%

Functional Assessment Checklist for Teachers and Staff (FACTS)

FACTS—Part A

Step 1

Student/Grade: _____ Date: _____

Interviewer: _____ Respondent(s): _____

Step 2 **Student Profile: Please identify at least three strengths or contributions the student brings to school.**

_____

_____

Step 3 **Problem Behavior(s): Identify problem behaviors:**

___ Tardy	___ Inappropriate language	___ Disruptive	___ Theft
___ Unresponsive	___ Fight/physical aggression	___ Insubordination	___ Vandalism
___ Withdrawn	___ Verbal harassment	___ Work not done	___ Other _____

Describe problem behavior: _____

Step 4 **Identifying Routines: Where, when, and with whom are problem behaviors are most likely?**

Schedule (Times)	Activity	With Whom Does the Problem Behavior Occur?	Likelihood of Problem Behavior	Specific Problem Behavior
			Low High 1 2 3 4 5 6	
			1 2 3 4 5 6	
			1 2 3 4 5 6	
			1 2 3 4 5 6	
			1 2 3 4 5 6	
			1 2 3 4 5 6	
			1 2 3 4 5 6	

Step 5 **Select one to three routines for further assessment. Select routines based on (1) similarity of activities (conditions) with ratings of 4, 5, or 6 and (2) similarity of problem behavior(s). Complete the FACTS—Part B for each routine identified.**

(continued)

Adapted with permission from March et al. (2000).

FACTS—Part B

<u>Step 1</u> Student/Grade: _____ Date: _____

Interviewer: _____ Respondent(s): _____

<u>Step 2</u> **Routine/Activities/Context: Which routine (only one) from the FACTS—Part A is assessed?**

Routine/Activities/Context	Problem Behavior

<u>Step 3</u> **Provide more detail about the problem behavior(s):**

What does the problem behavior(s) look like?
How often does the problem behavior(s) occur?
How long does the problem behavior(s) last when it does occur?
What is the intensity/level of danger of the problem behavior(s)?

<u>Step 4</u> **What are the events that predict when the problem behavior(s) will occur?**

Related Issues (Setting Events)		Environmental Features	
___ illness	Other: _____	___ reprimand/correction	___ structured activity
___ drug use	_____	___ physical demands	___ unstructured time
___ negative social	_____	___ socially isolated	___ tasks too boring
___ conflict at home	_____	___ with peers	___ activity too long
___ academic failure	_____	___ other	___ tasks too difficult

<u>Step 5</u> **What consequences are most likely to maintain the problem behavior(s)?**

Things That Are Obtained		Things Avoided or Escaped From	
___ adult attention	Other: _____	___ hard tasks	Other: _____
___ peer attention	_____	___ reprimands	_____
___ preferred activity	_____	___ peer negatives	_____
___ money/things	_____	___ physical effort	_____

<u>Step 6</u> **What current efforts have been used to control the problem behavior?**

Strategies for Preventing Problem Behavior		Consequences for Problem Behavior	
___ schedule change	Other: _____	___ reprimand	Other: _____
___ seating change	_____	___ office referral	_____
___ curriculum change	_____	___ detention	_____

SUMMARY OF BEHAVIOR

<u>Step 7</u> **Identify the summary that will be used to build a plan of behavior support.**

Setting Events and Predictors	Problem Behavior(s)	Maintaining Consequence(s)

How confident are you that the Summary of Behavior is accurate?

Not very confident					Very confident
1	2	3	4	5	6

(continued)

Instructions

The FACTS is a two-page interview used by school personnel who are building behavior support plans. The FACTS is intended to be an efficient strategy for initial functional behavioral assessment. The FACTS is completed by people (teachers, family, clinicians) who know the student best, and is used to either build behavior support plans or to guide more complete functional assessment efforts. The FACTS can be completed in a short period of time (5–15 minutes). Efficiency and effectiveness in completing the forms increases with practice.

How to Complete the FACTS—Part A

Step 1: Complete Demographic Information

Indicate the name and grade of the student, the date the assessment data were collected, the name of the person completing the form (the interviewer), and the name(s) of the people providing information (respondents).

Step 2: Complete Student Profile

Begin each assessment with a review of the positive and contributing characteristics the student brings to school. Identify at least three strengths or contributions the student offers.

Step 3: Identify Problem Behaviors

Identify the specific student behaviors that are barriers to effective education, disrupt the education of others, interfere with social development, or compromise safety at school. Provide a brief description of exactly how the student engages in these behaviors. What makes their way of engaging in these behaviors unique? Identify the most problematic behaviors, but also identify any problem behaviors that occur regularly.

Step 4: Identify Where, When, and with Whom the Problem Behaviors Are Most Likely

A: List the times that define the student's daily schedule. Include the times between classes, lunch, and before school, and adapt for complex schedule features (e.g., odd/even days) if appropriate.

B: For each time listed, indicate the activity typically engaged in during that time (e.g., small-group instruction, math, independent art, transition).

C: Where appropriate, indicate the people (adults and peers) with whom the student is interacting during each activity, and especially list the people the student interacts with when they engage in problem behavior.

D: Use the 1-to-6 scale to indicate (in general) which times/activities are most and least likely to be associated with problem behaviors. A "1" indicates a low likelihood of problems, and a "6" indicates a high likelihood of problem behaviors.

E: Indicate which problem behavior is *most likely* in any time/activity that is given a rating of 4, 5, or 6.

Step 5: Select Routines for Further Assessment

Examine each time/activity listed as 4, 5, or 6 in the table from Step 4. If activities are similar (e.g., activities that are unstructured; activities that involve high academic demands; activities with teacher reprimands; activities with peer taunting) and have similar problem behaviors, treat them as "routines for further analysis."

(continued)

Select between one and three routines for further analysis. Write the name of the routine and the most common problem behavior(s). Within each routine identify the problem behavior(s) that are most likely or most problematic.

For *each* routine identified in Step 5 complete a FACTS—Part B.

How to Complete the FACTS—Part B

Step 1: Complete Demographic Information

Identify the name and grade of the student, the date that the FACTS—Part B was completed, who completed the form, and who provided information for completing the form.

Step 2: Identify the Target Routine

List the targeted routine and problem behavior from the bottom of the FACTS—Part A. The FACTS—Part B provides information about *one* routine. Use multiple Part B forms if multiple routines are identified.

Step 3: Provide Specifics about the Problem Behavior(s)

Provide more detail about the features of the problem behavior(s). Focus specifically on the unique and distinguishing features and the way the behavior(s) is disruptive or dangerous.

Step 4: Identify Events That Predict Occurrence of the Problem Behavior(s)

Within each routine what (1) setting events and (2) immediate preceding events predict when the problem behavior(s) will occur? What would you do to make the problem behavior(s) happen in this routine?

Step 5: Identify the Consequences That May Maintain the Problem Behavior

What consequences appear to reward the problem behavior? Consider that the student may get/obtain something they want, or that they may escape/avoid something they may find unpleasant.

Identify the *most powerful* maintaining consequence with a "1" and other possible consequences with a "2" or "3." Do not check more than three options. The focus here is on the consequence that has the greatest impact.

When problems involve minor events that escalate into very difficult events, separate the consequences that maintain the minor problem behavior from the events that may maintain problem behavior later in the escalation.

Step 6: Define What Has Been Done to Date to Prevent/Control the Problem Behavior

In most cases, school personnel will have tried some strategies already. List events that have been tried and organize them by (1) those things that have been done to prevent the problem from getting started and (2) those things that were delivered as consequences to control or punish the problem behavior (or reward alternative behavior).

Step 7: Build a Summary Statement

The summary statement indicates the setting events, immediate predictors, problem behaviors, and maintaining consequences. The summary statement is the foundation for building an effective behavior support plan. Build the summary statement from the information in the FACTS—Part A and the FACTS—Part B (especially the information in Steps 3, 4, and 5 of the FACTS—Part B). If you are confident that the summary statement is accurate enough to design a plan, begin plan development. If you are less confident, then continue the functional assessment by conducting direct observation.

References

Acadience Learning, Inc. (2019). Assessments. Retrieved from *https://acadiencelearning.org/resources/assessments*.

Alberto, P., & Troutman, A. (2017). *Applied behavior analysis for teachers* (9th ed.). New York: Pearson.

Algozzine, B., Barrett, S., Eber, L., George, H., Horner, R., Lewis, T., et al. (2014). *School-wide PBIS Tiered Fidelity Inventory*. Washington, DC: OSEP Technical Assistance Center on Positive Behavioral Interventions and Supports.

Algozzine, B., Putnam, R., & Horner, R. (2010). What we know about the relationship between achievement and behavior. In B. Algozzine, A. P. Daunic, & S. W. Smith (Eds.), *Preventing problem behaviors* (2nd ed., pp. 223–226). Thousand Oaks, CA: Corwin.

Allensworth, E. M., & Easton, J. Q. (2005). *The on-track indicator as a predictor of high school graduation*. Chicago: Consortium on School Research. Retrieved from *https://consortium.uchicago.edu/publications/track-indicator-predictor-high-school-graduation*.

American Psychiatric Association. (2013). *Diagnostic and statistical manual of mental disorders* (5th ed.). Arlington, VA: Author.

Anderson, C. M., & Borgmeier, C. (2010). Tier II interventions within the framework of school-wide positive behavior support: Essential features for design, implementation, and maintenance. *Behavior Analysis in Practice, 3*(1), 33–45.

Bandura, A. (1963). *Social learning and personality development*. New York: Holt, Rinehart & Winston.

Benazzi, L., Horner, R. H., & Good, R. H. (2006). Effects of behavior support team composition on the technical adequacy and contextual fit of behavior support plans. *Journal of Special Education, 40*(3), 160–170.

Benner, G., Nelson, J. R., Sanders, E., & Ralston, N. (2012). Behavior intervention for students with externalizing behavior problems: Primary-level standard protocol. *Exceptional Children, 78*(2), 181–198.

Bohanon, H., Fenning, P., Borgmeier, C., Flannery, K. B., & Malloy, J. (2009). Finding a direction for high school positive behavior support. In W. Sailor, G. Dunlap, G. Sugai, & R. Horner (Eds.), *Handbook of positive behavior support* (pp. 581–602). New York: Springer.

Borgmeier, C., & Homer, R. H. (2006). An evaluation of the predictive validity of confidence ratings in identifying functional behavioral assessment hypothesis statements. *Journal of Positive Behavior Interventions, 8*(2), 100–105.

Bottiani, J. H., Larson, K. E., & Debnam, K. J. (2017). Promoting educators' use of culturally responsive practices: A systematic review of inservice interventions. *Journal of Teacher Education, 69*(4), 367–385.

Bradshaw, C. P., Koth, C. W., Thornton, L. A., & Leaf, P. J. (2009). Altering school climate through school-wide Positive Behavioral Interventions and Supports: Findings from a group-randomized effectiveness trial. *Prevention Science, 10*(2), 100–115.

Bradshaw, C. P., Mitchell, M. M., & Leaf, P. J. (2010). Examining the effects of schoolwide positive behavioral interventions and supports on student outcomes: Results from a randomized controlled effectiveness trial in elementary schools. *Journal of Positive Behavior Interventions, 12*(3), 133–148.

Bradshaw, C. P., Pas, E. T., Bottiani, J. H., Debnam, K. J., Reinke, W. M., Herman, K. C., et al. (2018). Promoting cultural responsivity and student engagement through Double Check coaching of classroom teachers: An efficacy study. *School Psychology Review, 47,* 118–134.

Bradshaw, C. P., Waasdorp, T. E., & Leaf, P. J. (2012). Effects of school-wide positive behavioral interventions and supports on child behavior problems. *Pediatrics, 130*(5), e1136–e1145.

Breen, K. (2016). *Progress monitoring function-based behavior support plans.* Workshop presented to Buffalo Public Schools, NY.

Breen, K. (2017). *Check-In, Check-Out: A Tier 2 intervention for youth at-risk.* Workshop presented to Kern County Superintendent of Schools, Kern County, CA.

Bronfenbrenner, U. (1979). *The ecology of human development: Experiments by nature and design.* Cambridge, MA: Harvard University Press.

Bruhn, A. L., Lane, K. L., & Hirsch, S. E. (2014). A review of Tier 2 interventions conducted within multitiered models of behavioral prevention. *Journal of Emotional and Behavioral Disorders, 22*(3), 171–189.

Bundock, K., Hawken, L. S., Kladis, K., & Breen, K. (2020). Innovating the Check-In, Check-Out Intervention: A process for creating adaptations. *Intervention in School and Clinic, 55*(3), 169–177.

Campbell, A., & Anderson, C. M. (2008). Enhancing effects of Check-In/Check-Out with function-based support. *Behavioral Disorders, 33,* 233–245.

Carter, D. R., Carter, G. M., Johnson, E. S., & Pool, J. L. (2012). Systematic implementation of a Tier 2 behavior intervention. *Intervention in School and Clinic, 48*(4), 223–231.

Carver, P. R., Lewis, L., & Tice, P. (2010). *Alternative schools and programs for public school students at risk of educational failure: 2007–08* (NCES 2010-026). Washington, DC: U.S. Government-Printing Office.

Carver-Thomas, D., & Darling-Hammond, L. (2017). *Teacher turnover: Why it matters and what we can do about it.* Palo Alto, CA: Learning Policy Institute.

Chafouleas, S. M., Christ, T. J., Riley-Tillman, T. C., Briesch, A. M., & Chanese, J. A. M. (2007). Generalizability and dependability of direct behavior ratings to assess social behavior of preschoolers. *School Psychology Review, 36*(1), 63–79.

Chafouleas, S. M., Riley-Tillman, T. C., Sassu, K. A., LaFrance, M. J., & Patwa, S. S. (2007). Daily behavior report cards: An investigation of the consistency of on-task data across raters and methods. *Journal of Positive Behavior Interventions, 9*(1), 30–37.

Cheney, D., Blum, C., & Walker, B. (2004). An analysis of leadership teams' perceptions of positive behavior support and the outcomes of typically developing and at-risk students in their schools. *Assessment for Effective Intervention, 30*(1), 7–24.

Cheney, D., Stage, S. A., Hawken, L. S., Lynass, L., Mielenz, C., & Waugh, M. (2009). A 2-year outcome study of the Check, Connect, And Expect Intervention for students at risk for severe behavior problems. *Journal of Emotional and Behavioral Disorders, 17,* 226–243.

Christenson, S. L., & Sheridan, S. M. (2001). *School and families: Creating essential connections for learning.* New York: Guilford Press.

Christenson, S. L., Sinclair, M. F., Lehr, M. F., & Hurley, C. M. (2000). Promoting successful school completion. In K. M. Minke & G. C. Bear (Eds.), *Preventing school problems, promoting school success: Strategies and programs that work* (pp. 211–257). Bethesda, MD: National Association of School Psychologists.

Christenson, S. L., Stout, K., & Pohl, A. (2012). *Check & Connect: A comprehensive student engagement intervention: Implementing with fidelity.* Minneapolis: University of Minnesota, Institute on Community Integration.

Colvin, G., Kame'enui, E. J., & Sugai, G. (1993). Reconceptualizing behavior management and school-wide discipline in general education. *Education and Treatment of Children, 16*(4), 361–381.

Committee for Children. (2011). *Second Step Learning Program.* Seattle, WA: Committee for Children.

Compton, S. N., Burns, B. J., Egger, H. L., & Robertson, E. (2002). Review of the evidence base for treatment of childhood psychopathology: Internalizing disorders. *Journal of Consulting and Clinical Psychology, 70,* 1240–1266.

Cook, B. G., & Cook, S. C. (2013). Unraveling evidence-based practices in special education. *Journal of Special Education, 47,* 71–82.

Cook, C., Rasetshwane, K. B., Truelson, E., Grant, S., Dart, E. H., Collins, T. A., et al. (2011). Development and validation of the Student Internalizing Behavior Screening: Examination of reliability, validity, and classification accuracy. *Assessment for Effective Intervention, 36,* 71–79.

Costello, E. J., He, J., Sampson, N. A., Kessler, R. C., & Merikangas, K. R. (2014). Services for adolescents with psychiatric disorders: 12-month data from the National Comorbidity Survey–Adolescent. *Psychiatric Services, 65,* 359–366.

Crone, D. A., Hawken, L. S., & Bergstrom, M. K. (2007). A demonstration of training, implementing, and using functional behavioral assessment in 10 elementary and middle school settings. *Journal of Positive Behavior Interventions, 9*(1), 15–29.

Crone, D. A., Hawken, L. S., & Horner, R. H. (2010). *Responding to problem behavior in schools: The Behavior Education Program* (2nd ed.). New York: Guilford Press.

Crone, D. A., Hawken, L. S., & Horner, R. H. (2015). *Building positive behavior support systems in schools: Functional behavioral assessment* (2nd ed.). New York: Guilford Press.

Cruz, R. A., & Rodl, J. E. (2018). An integrative synthesis of literature on disproportionality in special education. *Journal of Special Education, 52,* 50–63.

Dart, E., Furlow, C., Collins, T., Brewer, E., Gresham, F., & Chenier, K. (2014). Peer-mediated Check-In/Check-Out for students at-risk for internalizing disorders. *School Psychology Quarterly, 30*(2), 229–243.

Davies, D. E., & McLaughlin, T. F. (1989). Effects of a Daily Report Card on disruptive behaviour in primary students. *BC Journal of Special Education, 13*(2), 173–181.

DeGeorge, K. (2015). *FBA/BIP implementation.* Workshop presented to Buffalo Public Schools, NY.

Dougherty, E. H., & Dougherty, A. (1977). The daily report card: A simplified and flexible package for classroom behavior management. *Psychology in the Schools, 14*(2), 191–195.

Drevon, D. D., Hixson, M. D., Wyse, R. D., & Rigney, A. M. (2018). A meta-analytic review of the evidence for check-in check-out. *Psychology in the Schools, 56*(3), 393–412.

Drummond, T. (1994). *The Student Risk Screening Scale* (SRSS). Grants Pass, OR: Josephine County Mental Health Program.

Duchesne, S., Vitaro, F., Larose, S., & Tremblay, R. E. (2008). Trajectories of anxiety during elementary-school years and the prediction of high school noncompletion. *Journal of Youth and Adolescence, 37,* 1134–1146.

Eber, L., Sugai, C., Smith, C. R., & Scott, T. M. (2002). Wraparound and positive behavioral interventions and supports in the schools. *Journal of Emotional and Behavioral Disorders, 10*(3), 171–180.

Eber, L., Swain-Bradway, J., Breen, K., & Phillips, D. (2013). Building tier 2/tier 3 capacity within a PBIS system of support: Model development and lessons learned. *National PBIS Center Website: Newsletter/TA brief.* Available online at *https://drive.google.com/file/d/1y7YcXdzrwI9TUNFggfHtFm9PppC HeOSp/view?usp=sharing.*

Ennis, R. P., Jolivette, K., Swoszowski, N. C., & Johnson, M. L. (2012). Secondary prevention efforts at a residential facility for students with emotional and behavioral disorders: Function-based check-in, check-out. *Residential Treatment for Children and Youth, 29*(2), 79–102.

Fairbanks, S., Sugai, G., Guardino, D., & Lathrop, M. (2007). Response to Intervention: Examining classroom behavior support in second grade. *Exceptional Children, 73*(3), 288–310.

Fallon, L. M., & Feinberg, A. B. (2017). Implementing a Tier 2 behavioral intervention in a therapeutic alternative high school program. *Preventing School Failure: Alternative Education for Children and Youth, 61*(3), 189–197.

Fergusson, D. M., Woodward, L. J., & Horwood, L. J. (2000). Risk factors and life processes associated with the onset of suicidal behaviour during adolescence and early adulthood. *Psychological Medicine, 30,* 23–39.

Filter, K. J., McKenna, M. K., Benedict, E. A., Horner, R. H., Todd, A. W., & Watson, J. (2007). Check in/ Check out: A post-hoc evaluation of an efficient, secondary-level targeted intervention for reducing problem behaviors in schools. *Education and Treatment of Children, 30*(1), 69–84.

Fixsen, D. L., Blase, K., Metz, A., & Van Dyke, M. (2013). Statewide implementation of evidenced-based programs. *Exceptional Children, 79,* 213–230.

Fixsen, D. L., Naoom, S. F., Blase, K. A., Friedman, R. M., & Wallace, F. (2005). *Implementation research: A synthesis of the literature* (FMHI Publication No. 231). Retrieved from *http://ctndisseminationlibrary.org/PDF/nirnmonograph.pdf.*

Flannery, K. B., & Kato, M. M. (2017). Implementation of SWPBIS in high school: Why is it different? *Preventing School Failure: Alternative Education for Children and Youth, 61*(1), 69–79.

Foley, R. M., & Pang, L. (2006). Alternative education programs: Program and student characteristics. *High School Journal, 89,* 10–21.

Gage, N. A., Whitford, D. K., & Katsiyannis, A. (2018). A review of schoolwide positive behavior interventions and supports as a framework for reducing disciplinary exclusions. *Journal of Special Education, 52*(3), 142–151.

Gay, G. (2000). *Culturally responsive teaching: Theory, research, and practice.* New York: Teachers College Press.

Good, R. H., & Kaminski, R. A. (Eds.). (2002). *Dynamic Indicators of Basic Early Literacy Skills* (6th ed.). Eugene, OR: Institute for the Development of Educational Achievement.

Gorney, D. J., & Ysseldyke, J. E. (1993). Students with disabilities use of various options to access alternative schools and area learning centers. *Special Services in the Schools, 7,* 135–143.

Gresham, F. M. (1989). Assessment of treatment integrity in school consultation and prereferral intervention. *School Psychology Review, 18*(1), 37–50.

Gresham, F. M., & Elliott, S. N. (1990). *Social Skills Rating System (SSRS).* Circle Pines, MN: American Guidance Service.

Grossman, J. B., & Bulle, M. J. (2006). Review of what youth programs do to increase the connectedness of youth with adults. *Journal of Adolescent Health, 39,* 788–799.

Handler, M. W., Rey, J., Connell, J., Thier, K., Feinberg, A., & Putnam, R. (2007). Practical considerations in creating school-wide positive behavior support in public schools. *Psychology in the Schools, 44*(1), 29–39.

Hanlon, T. E., Simon, B. D., O'Grady, K. E., Carswell, S. B., & Callaman, J. M. (2013). The effectiveness of an after-school program targeting urban African American youth. *Education and Urban Society, 42,* 96–118.

Hattie, J. (2008). *Visible learning: A synthesis of over 800 meta-analyses relating to achievement.* New York: Routledge.

Hawken, L. S. (2006). School psychologists as leaders in the implementation of a targeted intervention: The Behavior Education Program. *School Psychology Quarterly, 21*(1), 91–111.

Hawken, L. (2008). *Thinking functionally about problem behavior.* Paper presented at the Norway Positive Behavior Support Conference, Oslo, Norway.

Hawken, L. S., Adolphson, S. L., MacLeod, K. S., & Schumann, J. (2009). Secondary-tier interventions and supports. In W. Sailor, G. Dunlop, G. Sugai, & R. H. Horner (Eds.), *Handbook of positive behavior support.* (pp. 395–420). New York: Springer.

Hawken, L., & Breen, K. (2016). *Supporting students at-risk: Check-In, Check-Out (CICO), families and diversity.* Paper presented at the Behavior Education Technology Conference, Phoenix, AZ.

Hawken, L. S., & Breen, K. (2017). *Check-In, Check-Out (CICO): A Tier 2 intervention for students at risk* (2nd ed.). [DVD]. New York: Guilford Press.

Hawken, L. S., Bundock, K., Barrett, C. A., Eber, L., Breen, K., & Phillips, D. (2015). Large-scale implementation of Check-In, Check-Out: A descriptive study. *Canadian Journal of School Psychology, 30*(4), 304–319.

Hawken, L. S., Bundock, K., Kladis, K., O'Keeffe, B., & Barrett, C. (2014). Systematic review of the Check-In, Check-Out Intervention for students at risk for emotional and behavioral disorders. *Education and Treatment of Children, 37*(4), 632–655.

Hawken, L. S., & Horner, R. H. (2003). Evaluation of a targeted intervention within a schoolwide system of behavior support. *Journal of Behavioral Education, 12*(3), 225–240.

Hawken, L. S., MacLeod, K. S., & Rawlings, L. (2007). Effects of the Behavior Education Program (BEP) on problem behavior with elementary school students. *Journal of Positive Behavior Interventions, 9*(2), 94–101.

Hawken, L. S., & O'Neill, R. E. (2006). Including students with severe disabilities at all levels of schoolwide positive behavioral support. *Research and Practice for Persons with Severe Disabilities, 31,* 46–53.

Hawken, L. S., O'Neill, R. E., & MacLeod, K. S. (2011). An investigation of the impact of function of problem behavior on effectiveness of the Behavior Education Program (BEP). *Education and Treatment of Children, 34*(4), 551–574.

Horner, R. H., Newton, J. S., Todd, A. W., Algozzine, B., Algozzine, K., Cusumano, K., et al. (2018). A randomized waitlist controlled analysis of team-initiated problem solving professional development and use. *Behavior Disorders, 43*(4), 444–456.

Horner, R. H., & Sugai, G. (2015). School-wide PBIS: An example of applied behavior analysis implemented at a scale of social importance. *Behavior Analysis Practice, 8,* 80–85.

Hughes, A. A., Lourea-Waddell, B., & Kendall, P. C. (2008). Somatic complaints in children with anxiety disorders and their unique prediction of poorer academic performance. *Child Psychiatry and Human Development, 39,* 211–220.

Hunter, K. K., Chenier, J. S., & Gresham, F. M. (2014). Evaluation of Check In/Check Out for students with internalizing behavior problems. *Journal of Emotional and Behavioral Disorders, 22*(3), 135–148.

Individuals with Disabilities Education Act Amendments of 1997 [IDEA]. (1997). Retrieved from *www.congress.gov/105/plaws/publ17/PLAW-105publ17.pdf.*

Individuals with Disabilities Education Act Amendments of 2004, 20 U.S.C. section 1400 *et seq.*

Jeynes, W. H. (2007). The relationship between parental involvement and urban academic achievement: A meta-analysis. *Urban Education, 42,* 82–110.

Jeynes, W. H. (2012). A meta-analysis of the efficacy of different types of parental involvement programs for urban students. *Urban Education, 47,* 706–742.

Jolivette, K. (2016). *Multi-tiered systems of support in residential juvenile facilities.* Washington, DC: National Technical Assistance Center for the Education of Neglected or Delinquent Children and Youth (NDTAC).

Jolivette, K., Kimball, K. A., Boden, L. J., & Sprague, J. R. (2016). The utility of a multi-tiered behavioral system in juvenile corrections: The positive behavior interventions and supports (PBIS) framework. *Corrections Today, 78,* 42–47.

Jolivette, K., McDaniel, S. C., Sprague, J. R., Swain-Bradway, J., & Ennis, R. (2012). Embedding the Positive Behavioral Interventions and Supports framework into the complex array of practices within alternative education settings: A decision-making process. *Assessment for Effective Intervention, 38,* 15–29.

Jolivette, K., Sprague, J. R., & Doyle, C. (2018, October). *Feasibility of facility-wide PBIS in secure juvenile facilities across the years.* Paper presented at the PBIS Forum, Chicago, IL.

Jolivette, K., Swoszowski, N. C., McDaniel, S. C., & Duchaine, E. L. (2016). Using positive behavioral interventions and supports to assist in the transition of youth from juvenile justice facilities back to their neighborhood school: An illustrative example. *Journal of Correctional Education, 67,* 9–24.

Kalberg, J. R., Lane, K. L., & Menzies, H. M. (2010). Using systematic screening procedures to identify students who are nonresponsive to primary prevention efforts: Integrating academic and behavioral measures. *Education and Treatment of Children, 33*(4), 561–584.

Kato, M. M., Flannery, B., Triplett, D., & Saeturn, S. (2018). Investing in freshmen: Providing preventative support to 9th graders. In K. B. Flannery, P. Hershfeldt, & J. Freeman (Eds.), *Lessons learned on implementation of PBIS in high schools: Current trends and future directions* (pp. 54–69). Eugene: University of Oregon Press.

Kendall, P. C., Safford, S., Flannery-Schroeder, E., & Webb, A. (2004). Child anxiety treatment: Outcomes in adolescence and impact on substance use and depression at 7.4-year follow-up. *Journal of Consulting and Clinical Psychology, 72,* 276–287.

Killu, K. (2008). Developing effective behavior intervention plans: Suggestions for school personnel. *Intervention in School and Clinic, 43,* 140–149.

Kim, J., McIntosh, K., Mercer, S. H., & Nese, R. N. (2018). Longitudinal associations between SWPBIS fidelity of implementation and behavior and academic outcomes. *Behavioral Disorders, 43*(3), 357–369.

Kittelman, A., Monzalve, M., Flannery, K. B., & Hershfeldt, P. A. (2018). Adaptations of Check-In/Check-Out to meet the needs of high school students. *High School Journal, 102*(1), 4–17.

Kladis, K., Hawken, L. S., & O'Neill, R. E. (2018). Addressing attendance and tardiness through adaptation of the Check-In, Check-Out Intervention. *Educational Applications Review, 3,* 1–5.

Kladis, K., Hawken, L. S., O'Neill, R. E., Fischer, A. J., Stokes, K., O'Keeffe, B. V., et al. (2020). *Effects of Check-In, Check-Out on engagement with students experiencing internalizing behaviors in an elementary school setting.* Manuscript submitted for publication.

Klingbeil, D. A., Dart, E. H., & Schramm, A. L. (2019). A systematic review of function-modified check-in/check-out. *Journal of Positive Behavior Interventions, 21*(2), 77–92.

Kovacs, M., & Devlin, B. (1998). Internalizing disorders in childhood. *Journal of Child Psychology and Psychiatry, 39,* 47–63.

Kuchle, L. B., & Riley-Tillman, T. C. (2019). Integrating behavior and academics in intervention planning. In R. Zumeta Edmunds, A. G. Gandhi, & L. Danielson (Eds.), *Essentials of intensive intervention* (pp. 51–70). New York: Guilford Press.

Lane, K. L., Capizzi, A., Fisher, M., & Ennis, R. (2012). Secondary prevention efforts at the middle school level: An application of the Behavior Education Program. *Education and Treatment of Children, 35*(1), 51–90.

Lane, K. L., Menzies, H. M., Oakes, W. P., & Kalberg, J. R. (2012). *Systematic screenings of behavior to support instruction: From preschool to high school.* New York: Guilford Press.

Lane, K. L., Oakes, W. P., Harris, P. J., Menzies, H. M., Cox, M. L., & Lambert, W. (2012). Initial evidence for the reliability and validity of the Student Risk Screening Scale for internalizing and externalizing behaviors at the elementary level. *Behavioral Disorders, 37,* 99–122.

Lane, K. L., Oakes, W. P., Swogger, E. D., Schatschneider, C., Menzies, H., M., & Sanchez, J. (2015). Student Risk Screening Scale for internalizing and externalizing behaviors: Preliminary cut scores to support data-informed decision making. *Behavioral Disorders, 40,* 159–170.

Lane, K. L., Wehby, J. H., Menzies, H. M., Doukas, G. L., Munton, S. M., & Gregg, R. M. (2003). Social skills instruction for students at risk for antisocial behavior: The effects of small-group instruction. *Behavioral Disorders, 28*(3), 229–248.

Lane, K. L., Wehby, J. H., Robertson, E. J., & Rogers, L. A. (2007). How do different types of high school students respond to schoolwide positive behavior support programs?: Characteristics and responsiveness of teacher-identified students. *Journal of Emotional and Behavioral Disorders, 15,* 3–20.

Leach, D. J., & Byrne, M. K. (1986). Some "spill-over" effects of a home-based reinforcement programme in a secondary school. *Educational Psychology, 6*(3), 265–276.

Lee, V. E., Bryk, A. S., & Smith, J. B. (1993). The organization of effective secondary schools. *Review of Research in Education, 19,* 171–267.

Lehr, C. A., Tan, C. S., & Ysseldyke, J. (2009). Alternative schools: A synthesis of state-level policy and research. *Remedial and Special Education, 30,* 19–32.

Leone, P., & Fink, C. (2017). *Raising the bar: Creating and sustaining quality education services in juvenile detention.* Washington, DC: National Technical Assistance Center for the Education of Neglected or Delinquent Children and Youth.

Leone, P., & Weinberg, P. (2010). *Addressing the unmet educational needs of children and youth in the juvenile justice and child welfare systems.* Washington, DC: Center for Juvenile Justice Reform, Georgetown University.

Lewis, T. J., & Sugai, G. (1999). Effective behavior support: A systems approach to proactive school-wide management. *Focus on Exceptional Children, 31*(6), 1–24.

Lewis-Palmer, T., Sugai, G., & Larson, S. (1999). Using data to guide decisions about program implementation and effectiveness. *Effective School Practices, 17*(4), 47–53.

Mace, F. C., Hock, M. L., Lalli, J. S., West, B. J., Belfiore, P., Pinter, E., et al. (1988). Behavioral momentum in the treatment of noncompliance. *Journal of Applied Behavior Analysis, 21*(2), 123–141.

MacLeod, K. S., Hawken, L. S., O'Neill, R. E., & Bundock, K. (2016). Combining Tier 2 and Tier 3 supports for students with disabilities in general education settings. *Journal of Educational Issues, 2*(2), 331–351.

Maggin, D. M., Zurheide, J., Pickett, K. C., & Baillie, S. J. (2015). A systematic evidence review of the Check-In/Check-Out program for reducing student challenging behaviors. *Journal of Positive Behavior Interventions, 17*(4), 197–208.

March, R. E., & Horner, R. H. (2002). Feasibility and contributions of functional behavioral assessment in schools. *Journal of Emotional and Behavioral Disorders, 10*(3), 158–170.

March, R. E., Horner, R. H., Lewis-Palmer, T., Brown, D., Crone, D., Todd, A. W., et al. (2000). *Functional Assessment Checklist: Teachers and Staff (FACTS).* Eugene, OR: Educational and Community Supports.

Marchant, M., Brown, M., Caldarella, P., & Young, E. (2010). Effects of Strong Kids curriculum on students with internalizing behaviors: A pilot study. *Journal of Evidence-Based Practices for Schools, 11,* 123–143.

May, S., Ard, W., Todd, A., Horner, R., Glasgow, A., Sugai, G., et al. (2018). *School-wide Information System 6.5.5b32.* Eugene: University of Oregon.

McGinnis, E. (2011). *Skillstreaming the elementary school child: A guide for teaching prosocial skills* (3rd ed.). Champaign, IL: Research Press.

McGinnis, E., Sprafkin, R. P., Gershaw, N. J., & Klein, P. (2011). *Skillstreaming the adolescent: A guide for teaching prosocial skills* (3rd ed.). Champaign, IL: Research Press.

McIntosh, K., Campbell, A. L., Carter, D. R., & Dickey, C. R. (2009). Differential effects of a tier two behavior intervention based on function of problem behavior. *Journal of Positive Behavior Interventions, 11*(2), 82–93.

McIntosh, K., Campbell, A. L., Carter, D. R., & Zumbo, B. D. (2009). Concurrent validity of office discipline referrals and cut points used in schoolwide positive behavior support. *Behavioral Disorders, 34,* 100–113.

McIntosh, K., Frank, J. L., & Spaulding, S. A. (2010). Establishing research-based trajectories of office discipline referrals for individual students. *School Psychology Review, 39,* 380–394.

McIntosh, K., Girvan, E. J., Horner, R. H., Smokowski, K., & Sugai, G. (2014). *Recommendations for addressing discipline disproportionality in education.* Washington, DC: OSEP Technical Assistance Center on Positive Behavioral Interventions and Supports. Retrieved from *www.pbis.org/ Common/Cms/files/pbisresources/A%205-Point%20Intervention%20%20Approach%20for%20Enhancing%20%20Equity%20in%20School%20Discipline.pdf.*

McIntosh, K., & Goodman, S. (2016). *Integrated multi-tiered systems of support: Blending RTI and PBIS.* New York: Guilford Press.

McIntosh, K., Massar, M. M., Algozzine, R. F., George, H. P., Horner, R. H., Lewis, T. J., et al. (2017). Technical adequacy of the SWPBIS Tiered Fidelity Inventory. *Journal of Positive Behavior Interventions, 19*, 3–13.

McIntosh, K., Reinke, W. M., & Herman, K. C. (2009). Schoolwide analysis of data for social behavior problems: Assessing outcomes, selecting targets for intervention, and identifying need for support. In G. Gimpel Peacock, R. A. Ervin, E. J. Daly, & K. W. Merrell (Eds.), *The practical handbook of school psychology: Effective practices for the 21st century* (pp. 135–156). New York: Guilford Press.

McIntosh, K., Ty, S. V., & Miller, L. D. (2014). Effects of school-wide positive behavioral interventions and supports on internalizing problems: Current evidence and future directions. *Journal of Positive Behavior Interventions, 16*(4) 209–218.

Melius, P., Swoszowski, N. C., & Siders, J. (2015). Peer-led check-in/check-out: A secondary tier intervention in an alternative educational setting. *Residential Treatment for Children and Youth, 32*, 58–79.

Mitchell, B. S. (2012). *Investigating use of the behavior education program for students with internalizing behavioral concerns* (Doctoral dissertation). Retrieved from ProQuest Dissertations & Theses Global.

Mitchell, B. S., Adamson, R., & McKenna, J. W. (2017). Curbing our enthusiasm: An analysis of the Check-In/Check-Out literature using the Council for Exceptional Children's evidence-based practice standards. *Behavior Modification, 41*(3), 343–367.

Mitchell, B. S., Stormont, M., & Gage, N. A. (2011). Tier two interventions implemented within the context of a tiered prevention framework. *Behavioral Disorders, 36*(4), 241–261.

Muscott, H. S., Mann, E. L., & LeBrun, M. R. (2008). Positive behavioral interventions and support in New Hampshire: Effects of a large-scale implementation of schoolwide positive behavior support on student discipline and academic achievement. *Journal of Positive Behavior Interventions, 10*, 190–205.

National Juvenile Justice Network. (2009, August). *National Juvenile Justice network policy platform: Conditions of confinement.* Washington, DC: Author.

National Research Council & Institute of Medicine. (2009). *Preventing mental, emotional, and behavioral disorders among young people: Progress and possibilities.* Washington, DC: National Academies Press.

Neal, J. W., & Neal, Z. P. (2013). Nested or networked?: Future directions for ecological systems theory. *Social Development, 22*(4), 722–737.

Noonan, P., Gaumer Erickson, A., Brussow, J., & Langham, A. (2015). *Observation checklist for high-quality professional development in education* [Updated version]. Lawrence: University of Kansas, Center for Research on Learning.

Oakes, W. P., Lane, K. L., & Ennis, R. P. (2016). Systematic screening at the elementary level: Considerations for exploring and installing universal behavior screening. *Journal of Applied School Psychology, 32*(3), 214–233.

Office of Juvenile Justice and Delinquency Prevention. (2011). Statistical briefing book. Retrieved from *www.ojjdp.gov/ojstatbb/corrections/qa08201.asp?qaDate=2010.*

O'Neil, K. A., Conner, B. T., & Kendall, P. C. (2011). Internalizing disorders and substance use disorders in youth: Comorbidity, risk, temporal order, and implications for intervention. *Clinical Psychology Review, 31*, 104–112.

O'Neill, R. E., Albin, R. W., Storey, K., Horner, R. H., & Sprague, J. R. (2014). *Functional assessment and program development for problem behavior: A practical handbook* (3rd ed.). Stamford, CT: Cengage Learning.

OSEP Technical Assistance Center on Positive Behavioral Interventions and Supports. (2017). Positive behavioral interventions and supports. Washington, DC: Author. Retrieved from *www.pbis.org.*

Osher, D., Dwyer, K. P., & Jackson, S. (2004). *Safe, supportive and successful schools step by step.* Longmont, CO: Sopris West Educational Services.

Paris, S. G., & Paris, A. H. (2001). Classroom applications of research on self-regulated learning. *Educational Psychologist, 36*(2), 89–101.

Pianta, R. C., & Walsh, D. (1996). *High-risk children in the schools: Creating sustaining relationships.* New York: Routledge.

Pool, J. L., Carter, D. R., & Johnson, E. S. (2013). Tier 2 team processes and decision-making in a comprehensive three-tiered model. *Intervention in School and Clinic, 48*(4), 232–239.

Powers, K., Hagans, K., & Linn, M. (2017). A mixed-method efficacy and fidelity study of Check and Connect. *Psychology in the Schools, 54*(9), 1019–1033.

Powers, L. J. (2003). *Examining effects of targeted group social skills intervention in schools with and without school wide systems of positive behavior support* (Doctoral dissertation, University of Missouri, Columbia). Retrieved from ProQuest Dissertations & Theses Global.

Quinn, M. M., Rutherford, R. B., Leone, P. E., Osher, D. M., & Poirer, J. M. (2005). Students with disabilities in detention and correctional settings. *Exceptional Children, 71*(3), 339–345.

Rapport, M. D., Denney, C. B., Chung, K., & Hustace, K. (2001). Internalizing behavior problems and scholastic achievement in children: Cognitive and behavioral pathways as mediators of outcome. *Journal of Clinical Child Psychology, 30,* 536–551.

Reynolds, C. R., & Kamphaus, R. W. (2004). *BASC-2: Behavior Assessment System for Children.* Circle Pines, MN: American Guidance Service.

Rodriguez, B. J., Loman, S. L., & Borgmeier, C. (2016). Tier 2 interventions in positive behavior support: A survey of school implementation. *Preventing School Failure: Alternative Education for Children and Youth, 60*(2), 94–105.

Ross, S. W., & Sabey, C. V. (2014). Check-In Check-Out + social skills: Enhancing the effects of check-in check-out for students with social skill deficits. *Remedial and Special Education, 36*(4), 246–257.

Sailor, W., Dunlap, G., Sugai, G., & Horner, R. H. (Eds.). (2009). *Handbook of positive behavior support.* New York: Springer.

Schiller, K. S. (1999). Effects of feeder patterns on students' transition to high school. *Sociology of Education, 72,* 216–233.

Sedlak, A. J., & Bruce, C. (2010, December). Youth's characteristics and backgrounds: Findings from the survey of youth in residential placement. *Juvenile Justice Bulletin,* pp. 1–11. Retrieved from *www.ncjrs.gov/pdffiles1/ojjdp/227730.pdf.*

Sheffield, K., & Waller, R. J. (2010). A review of single-case studies utilizing self-monitoring interventions to reduce problem classroom behaviors. *Beyond Behavior, 19,* 7–13.

Sheridan, S. M. (2014). *The tough kid: Teachers and parents as partners.* Eugene, OR: Pacific Northwest.

Sheridan, S. M., Clarke, B. L., Marti, D. C., Burt, J. D., & Rohlk, A. M. (2005). *Conjoint behavioral consultation: A model to facilitate meaningful partnerships for families and schools.* Cambridge, MA: Harvard Family Research Project. Retrieved from *www.researchgate.net/publication/242234891_Conjoint_Behavioral_Consultation_A_Model_to_Facilitate_Meaningful_Partnerships_for_Families_and_Schools.*

Shinn, M. R. (1989). *Curriculum-based measurement: Assessing special children.* New York: Guilford Press.

Shore, B. A., Iwata, B. A., DeLeon, I. G., Kahng, S. W., & Smith, R. G. (1997). An analysis of reinforcer substitutability using object manipulation and self-injury as competing responses. *Journal of Applied Behavior Analysis, 30,* 21–41.

Simonsen, B., Freeman, J., Goodman, S., Mitchell, B., Swain-Bradway, J., Flannery, B., et al. (2015). *Supporting and responding to behavior: Evidence-based classroom strategies for teachers.* Washington, DC: OSEP Technical Assistance Center.

Simonsen, B., Jeffrey-Pearsall, J., Sugai, G., & McCurdy, B. (2011). Alternative setting-wide positive behavior support. *Behavioral Disorders, 36,* 213–224.

Simonsen, B., Myers, D., & Briere, D. E. (2011). Comparing a behavioral Check-In/Check-Out (CICO) Intervention to standard practice in an urban middle school setting using an experimental group design. *Journal of Positive Behavior Interventions, 13*(3), 31–48.

Simonsen, B., & Sugai, G. (2013). PBIS in alternative education settings: Positive Behavior Support for youth with high-risk behavior. *Education and Treatment of Children, 36,* 3–14.

Simonsen, B., Sugai, G., & Negron, M. (2008). Schoolwide positive behavior supports: Primary systems and practices. *Teaching Exceptional Children, 40*(6), 32–40.

Sinclair, M. F., Christenson, S. L., Elevo, D. L., & Hurley, C. M. (1998). Dropout prevention for youth with disabilities: Efficacy of a sustained school engagement procedure. *Exceptional Children, 65*(1), 7–21.

Skedgell, K., & Kearney, C. A. (2018). Predictors of school absenteeism severity at multiple levels: A classification and regression tree analysis. *Children and Youth Services Review, 86*, 236–245.

Skowyra, K., & Cocozza, J. (2007). *Blueprint for change: A comprehensive model for the identification and treatment of youth with mental health needs in contact with the juvenile justice system.* Delmar, NY: Policy Research Associates, Inc., National Center for Mental Health and Juvenile Justice.

Smith, H. M., Evans-McCleon, M. T. N., Urbanski, B., & Justice, C. (2015). Check-In/Check-Out Intervention with peer monitoring for a student with emotional-behavioral difficulties. *Journal of Counseling and Development, 93*(4), 451–459.

Sugai, G., & Horner, R. H. (1999). Discipline and behavioral support: Preferred processes and practices. *Effective School Practices, 17*(4), 10–22.

Sugai, G., & Horner, R. H. (2002). The evolution of discipline practices: School-wide positive behavior intervention and support. *Child and Family Behavior Therapy, 24*, 23–50.

Sugai, G., & Horner, R. H. (2008). What we know and need to know about preventing problem behavior in schools. *Exceptionality, 16*(2), 67–77.

Sugai, G., & Horner, R. H. (2009a). Responsiveness-to-Intervention and school-wide positive behavior supports: Integration of multi-tiered system approaches. *Exceptionality, 17*(4), 223–237.

Sugai, G., & Horner, R. H. (2009b). Defining and describing schoolwide positive behavior support. In W. Sailor, G. Dunlap, G. Sugai, & R. H. Horner (Eds.), *Handbook of positive behavior support* (pp. 307–326). New York: Springer.

Sugai, G., Horner, R. H., Dunlap, G., Hieneman, G., Lewis, T. J., Nelson, C. M., et al. (2000). Applying positive behavior support and functional behavioral assessment in schools. *Journal of Positive Behavior Interventions, 2*(3), 131–143.

Sugai, G., Lewis-Palmer, T., Todd, A., & Horner, R. H. (2005). *School-wide evaluation tool.* Eugene: University of Oregon.

Sugai, G., Sprague, J. R., Horner, R. H., & Walker, H. M. (2000). Preventing school violence: The use of office discipline referrals to assess and monitor school-wide discipline interventions. *Journal of Emotional and Behavioral Disorders, 8*, 94–101.

Swain-Bradway, J. L. (2009). *An analysis of a secondary level intervention for high school students at risk of school failure: The high school behavior education program* (Doctoral dissertation, University of Oregon). Retrieved from *https://core.ac.uk/download/pdf/36685104.pdf.*

Swain-Bradway, J., Pinkney, C., & Flannery, K. B. (2015). Implementing SWPBIS in high schools: Contextual factors and stages of implementation. *Teaching Exceptional Children, 47*(5), 245–255.

Swoszowski, N. C. (2014). Adapting a tier 2 behavioral intervention, Check-In/Check-Out, to meet students' needs. *Intervention in School and Clinic, 49*, 211–218.

Swoszowski, N. C., Evanovich, L. L., Ennis, R. P., & Jolivette, K. (2017). Implementers view of CICO: Facilitators and barriers to successful implementation in residential settings. *Residential Treatment for Children and Youth, 34*, 107–121.

Swoszowski, N. C., Jolivette, K., & Fredrick, L. D. (2013). Addressing the social and academic behavior of a student with emotional and behavioral disorders in an alternative setting. *Journal of Classroom Interaction, 48*, 28–36.

Swoszowski, N. C., Jolivette, K., Fredrick, L. D., & Heflin, L. J. (2012). Check In/Check Out: Effects on students with emotional and behavioral disorders with attention- or escape-maintained behavior in a residential facility. *Exceptionality, 20*, 163–178.

Swoszowski, N. C., McDaniel, S. C., Jolivette, K., & Melius, P. (2013). The effect of Check In/Check Out including adaptation for non-responders on the off-task behavior of students with E/BD. *Education and Treatment of Children, 36*, 63–79.

Swoszowski, N. C., Patterson, D. P., & Crosby, S. (2011). Implementing Check In/Check out for students with emotional and behavioral disorders in residential and juvenile justice settings. *Beyond Behavior, 20*, 32–36.

Tanner, N., Eklund, K., Kilgus, S. P., & Johnson, A. H. (2018). Generalizability of universal screening measures for behavioral and emotional risk. *School Psychology Review, 47*(1), 3–17.

Taylor-Greene, S., Brown, D., Nelson, L., Longton, J., Gassman, T., Cohen, J., et al. (1997). School-wide behavioral support: Starting the year off right. *Journal of Behavioral Education, 7*(1), 99–112.

Todd, A. W., Campbell, A. L., Meyer, G. G., & Horner, R. H. (2008). The effects of a targeted intervention to reduce problem behaviors: Elementary school implementation of Check In-Check Out. *Journal of Positive Behavior Interventions, 10*(1), 46–55.

Todd, A. W., Horner, R. H., Berry, D., Sanders, C., Bugni, M., Currier, A., et al. (2012). A case study of team-initiated problem solving addressing student behavior in one elementary school. *Journal of Special Education Leadership, 25*, 81–89.

Todd, A. W., Horner, R. H., Sugai, G., & Sprague, J. R. (1999). Effective behavior support: Strengthening school-wide systems through a team-based approach. *Effective School Practices, 17*(4), 23–37.

Turtura, J. E., Anderson, C. M., & Boyd, J. R. (2014). Addressing task avoidance in middle school students: Academic behavior Check-In/Check-Out. *Journal of Positive Behavior Interventions, 16*(3), 159–167.

Tyack, D. (2001). Introduction. In S. Mondale & S. Patton (Eds.), *School: The story of American public education* (pp. 1–10). Boston: Beacon Press.

U.S. Department of Education. (2010). College- and career-ready standards and assessments. Retrieved from *www2.ed.gov/policy/elsec/leg/blueprint/faq/college-career.pdf*.

Van Acker, R. (2007). Antisocial, aggressive, and violent behavior in children and adolescents within alternative education settings: Prevention and intervention. *Preventing School Failure, 51*, 5–12.

Vincent, C., Tobin, T., Hawken, L. & Frank, J. (2012). Discipline referrals and access to targeted support in elementary and middle schools: Patterns across African-American, Hispanic-American, and White students. *Education and Treatment of Children, 35*, 431–458.

Walker, H. M., Horner, R. H., Sugai, G., Bullis, M., Sprague, J. R., Bricker, D., et al. (1996). Integrated approaches to preventing antisocial behavior patterns among school–age children and youth. *Journal of Emotional and Behavioral Disorders, 4*(4), 194–209.

Walker, H. M., Kavanagh, K., Stiller, B., Golly, A., Severson, H. H., & Feil, E. G. (1998). First step to success: An early intervention approach for preventing school antisocial behavior. *Journal of Emotional and Behavioral Disorders, 6*(2), 66–80.

Walker, H. M., Seeley, J. R., Small, J., Severson, H. H., Graham, B. A., Feil, E. G., et al. (2009). A randomized controlled trial of the first step to success early intervention: Demonstration of program efficacy outcomes in a diverse, urban school district. *Journal of Emotional and Behavioral Disorders, 17*(4), 197–212.

Walker, H. M., Severson, H. H., & Feil, E. G. (1994). *The Early Screening Project: A proven child-find process.* Longmont, CO: Sopris West.

Walker, H. M., Severson, H. H., & Feil, E. G. (2014). *Systematic Screening for Behavior Disorders (SSBD) technical manual: Universal screening for PreK–9* (2nd ed.). Eugene, OR: Pacific Northwest.

Warberg, A., George, N., Brown, D., Chauran, K., & Taylor-Greene, S. (1995). *Behavior Education Plan handbook.* Elmira, OR: Fern Ridge Middle School.

Whitford, D. K., Katsiyannis, A., & Counts, J. (2016). Discriminatory discipline: Trends and issues. *NASSP Bulletin, 100*(2), 117–135.

Williams, D. D. (2015). *Effects of the Strong Kids curriculum as a targeted intervention for students at-risk for developing depressive disorders* (Doctoral dissertation). Retrieved from ProQuest Dissertations & Theses Global.

Wolfe, K., Pyle, D., Charlton, C. T., Sabey, C. V., Lund, E. M., & Ross, S. W. (2016). A systematic review of the empirical support for Check-In Check-Out. *Journal of Positive Behavior Interventions, 18*(2), 74–88.

Wright, J. A., & Dusek, J. B. (1998). Compiling school base-rates for disruptive behavior from student disciplinary referral data. *School Psychology Review, 27,* 138–147.

Wu, P., Hoven, C. W., Bird, H. R., Moore, R. E., Cohen, P., Alegria, M., et al. (1999). Depressive and disruptive disorders and mental health service utilization in children and adolescents. *Journal of the American Academy of Child and Adolescent Psychiatry, 38,* 1081–1089.

Zhou, L., Goff, G. A., & Iwata, B. A. (2000). Effects of increased response effort on self-injury and object manipulation as competing responses. *Journal of Applied Behavior Analysis, 33,* 29–40.

Index

Note. *f* or *t* following a page number indicates a figure or a table.